CHURCH AND STATE IN MEXICO
1822-1857

CHURCH AND STATE
IN MEXICO

1822-1857

BY

WILFRID HARDY CALLCOTT

1 9 6 5

OCTAGON BOOKS, INC.

NEW YORK

Copyright 1926, by Duke University Press

Reprinted 1965
by special arrangement with Duke University Press

OCTAGON BOOKS, INC.
175 FIFTH AVENUE
NEW YORK, N. Y. 10010

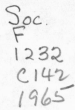
LIBRARY OF CONGRESS CATALOG CARD NUMBER: 65-16767

Printed in U.S.A. by
NOBLE OFFSET PRINTERS, INC.
NEW YORK 3, N. Y.

TO

My Parents

ACKNOWLEDGMENT

This study was begun at the suggestion of Professor William R. Shepherd of Columbia University, whose friendly suggestions and valuable assistance have contributed in no small degree to the final form in which the material is here presented. Grateful acknowledgment is also made to the staff of the Library of the University of Texas for many courtesies extended, and particularly to Mrs. Lota Spell, Librarian of the García Collection, for the use of her valuable checklists and for other aid. Much material was secured from the Wagner Collection of Yale University, the New York Public Library, the libraries of the Hispanic Society of New York, Columbia Univercity, the University of South Carolina, and the Library of Congress. Officials and workers in all of these institutions were ever helpful and courteous, enabling the author to use the books and documents in their charge. The editors of the Duke University Press, Dr. William T. Laprade and Dr. Paul N. Garber, have read the manuscript and made valuable suggestions. Of their assistance the author is most appreciative.

W. H. C.

CONTENTS

CHURCH AND STATE IN MEXICO
1822-1857

PREFACE

In discussing those contests between church and state in Mexico which culminated in the Constitution of 1857 and the reforms connected therewith, it is well first to consider briefly the chief factors involved. At the present day most people look upon freedom of speech and of the press as a kind of natural right. Such has not always been the case in Mexico. There the fight was long and stern, with popular desires now repressed and now triumphant, as ultra-conservative or ultra-radical gained control.

People of English origin are proud of a judicial system developed since the time of the Norman kings of England. With them it has become a foregone conclusion that, when a case is to be tried, justice will be done regardless of the status of the man concerned, be he rich or poor, old or young, clergyman or layman. In Mexico, on the contrary, the *fuero* system was of long standing. By it various classes of persons were given special exemption or privileges. Based on established precedent and backed by the influential elements in the community, it had skilled support. Opposition to it was widely scattered and disorganized. Most of the people were dominated by a great but vague discontent, which was largely inarticulate. They knew something was wrong, but they did not know what it was. They were easily led by plausible or eloquent arguments, that ended in the sacrifice of their best friends, the men who were trying to lead them to higher things and greater liberties.

Ever since the Spanish conquest, and indeed before that time, the Mexican people had been accustomed to the domination of the masses by the classes. Absolutely unable to use all the privileges or to exercise all the duties of full, civil and political citizenship when granted, they nevertheless held liberty as an ideal to be striven for. With blundering steps and many backsets, they advanced to secure the prize. It is this series of struggles that the present study seeks to trace, bearing in mind that, while a handful of leaders will naturally be most prominent in the picture, it was really the mass of the Mexican people that was striving to secure freedom.

In the contest, the most important factor was the Roman Catholic Church.[1] As will be seen, its enormous economic interests and its control of education, to say nothing of its spiritual hold upon the people, made it dominant in the political and social life of the country. It naturally became associated with the upper classes. When the *fueros* were attacked, the protection of its own privileges caused it to plunge at once into the strife. For the same reason, the army was often ranged by its side. Thus the struggle took on a more ominous aspect. Joined with these two groups were the great private landholders. Conservatives by instinct, they wished to see perpetuated the régime under which they were flourishing. The Church had acquired its property in accordance with both the laws and customs of the time. Hence, when the clergy saw the radicals attempting

[1] Hereafter when the term "the Church" is used it will refer to the Roman Catholic organization.

to overturn the existing system and to appropriate ecclesiastical property for so-called public uses, they protested vigorously and fought with all the power of their well-organized machinery of control. This system, aided by the army and most of the men prominent in civil affairs, engaged in a life and death struggle with the great masses of the Mexican people. The latter were championed by a group of skilful leaders, who rose, some from the ranks and some from the upper classes, as a result of a conversion to the principles of French philosophy and of the democracy of the United States.

The following monograph has been prepared with the hope that it may shed some light on these conditions and struggles during the period from 1822 to 1857. In the latter year the constitution which remained the official foundation of the Mexican government till 1917 was adopted. Much information on the subject is not yet available even to Mexican readers. Those of English speech know still less about it.

CHAPTER I

HISTORIC BACKGROUND OF THE STRUGGLE

Mexico, roughly speaking, extends from the sixteenth to the thirty-second parallel of north latitude. Before the treaty of Guadalupe Hidalgo, it claimed an area of about 1,725,000 square miles, but, after that treaty and the Gadsden Purchase, it was reduced to the above parallels and to about 767,000 square miles.[1]

In this region there awaited the Spaniard of the sixteenth century untold wealth, a climate that, apart from the sea coast, was healthy and pleasant,[2] and natives who were docile and accustomed to servitude. For a long period the king of Spain was the supreme political and, in a measure, even religious ruler there as in other large areas of the New World. Pope Alexander VI had granted to the Spanish sovereigns of his time ecclesiastical oversight and control so complete that no papal bull, brief, or order emanating from the Holy See could be published or carried out without first being submitted to and passed upon by the Council of the Indies. The king nominated the higher dignitaries of the Church, and the religious orders paid him tithes.[3]

[1] Antonio García y Cubas, *Noticias Geográficas y Estadísticas de la República Mexicana*, p. 5.

[2] G. McC. McBride, *The Land Systems of Mexico*, p. 6.

[3] The generally accepted facts of the narrative portion of this work may be verified by reference to H. H. Bancroft, *History of Mexico*, hereafter cited as Bancroft; Niceto de Zamacois, *Historia de Méjico*, hereafter cited as Zamacois; or any other standard historical work on that country.

This direct influence of the king in religious matters accounts, in part, for the constant aid given the clergy during the period of the conquest. In fact, even a cursory reading of the story of the Spanish acquisition of Mexico shows that the priests were one of the most important factors in the process. The statement that Spanish colonization was based upon "gospel, glory and gold" does not contain the slightest reflection on the first word from the second and third. The Spaniard was intensely religious, and, when that sentiment was aroused, might become a fanatic on the subject. On occasion during the expedition of Cortés, policy might have advised a different sort of conduct from that actually adopted, but, when his zeal was once kindled, the Spaniard ignored consequences and was ready and willing to die for his faith. A modern critic may be tempted to say that the representatives of the Church gravely compromised themselves from time to time and that the following statement indicates the real order of Spanish interests: "It was useless to demand gold, for there was little or none here. So they proceeded at once to expound the doctrines of their faith, . . ."[4] Whatever the validity of such an assertion, there was undoubtedly an enormous missionary program adopted at once. In the period 1524-1539, the Franciscans alone reported baptisms as follows: City of Mexico and neighboring villages, over a million; Michoacán and other provinces, three millions; and the District of Tezcuco, one million.[5]

[4] Bancroft, I. 92; H. C. Lea, *The Inquisition in the Spanish Dependencies,* p. 191.

[5] Bancroft, II. 408.

This conversion(?) of the natives to Christianity naturally resulted in many explorations with the monks as leaders. In fact, many new lands were opened up in this fashion. An unarmed ecclesiastic would be opposed in few communities, since a majority of the Indians were friendly. To the regular clergy in particular a tribute of appreciation is due for the inspiring examples they gave of Christian devotion and service. If this service was later turned to political account by those who made it possible, the failing was not peculiar to Spaniards.

It was also quite natural that, in a large number of cases, priests should exercise undue influence, not because of their sacred calling alone, but because of their education and training. Laymen who could read and write were, indeed, few and far between. Hence secretarial work fell to the priests; reports were made out by them—and colored accordingly. When diplomacy was needful, they were the obvious representatives to be employed, since they were close to their leaders and had the requisite education as well. As time went on, after serving this splendid apprenticeship, they had their abilities recognized and were appointed to office. To attempt to list the names of ecclesiastics who held high positions in the civil government would be quite a task. During the colonial period they held many posts, ranging from that of viceroy down.[6]

[6] Some examples of bishops and archbishops called upon to act as viceroys are:

García Guerra, archbishop, viceroy in 1611, Bancroft, III. 20-21.
Palafox, bishop, viceroy in 1642, Bancroft, III. 108.
Torres y Rueda, bishop, viceroy in 1647, Bancroft, III. 127.

With the clergy scattered throughout the country
and controlled by their thoroughly centralized organization, the growth of their power is not surprising.
As in the case of the Spaniards, so the Indians were
held in line through the collection of fees, the maintenance of schools and charitable institutions, and the
use of the confessional. The last named agency was
especially effective in dealing with the ignorant and
the illiterate. When it did not elicit the information
desired from the aborigines themselves, there were a
large number of *mestizos,* or half breeds, who aspired
to recognition, and many of them were only too glad
to provide what was wanted. When the gentle means
of moral suasion were not sufficient to effect a given
result, sterner measures were applied, such as flogging,
imprisonment, and clipping the hair of the offenders.
However, the priests did not control the Indians entirely in this fashion. They were real friends of the
natives and did all in their power to assist them and
to protect them from oppression. One of the best
examples of this is the "New Laws", published in 1543.
These laws were largely the fruit of the work of the
famous Las Casas, the "Apostle of the Indies", and
were designed to protect the Indians from the evils
of what, in practice, was a species of slavery. It is
true that these laws were not adequately enforced in
Mexico, but they exerted a very considerable influence,
and beyond doubt they bound the Indians more thor-

Osorio, archbishop, viceroy in 1664, Bancroft, III. 167.
Rivera, archbishop, viceroy in 1680, Bancroft, III. 186.
Montáñez, bishop, viceroy in 1696, Bancroft, III. 256.
Haro y Peralta, archbishop, viceroy in 1737, Bancroft, III. 456.
Javier y Lizana, archbishop, viceroy in 1809, Bancroft, IV. 76.

oughly to the Church. Together with the work of Bishop Zumárraga, they helped to create a condition which first secured the emancipation of the children of Indian slaves and then gradually restricted slavery as such to the Negro race.[7]

To control the Spaniard was a more difficult matter. However, the Spanish priest was equal to his task. The strain of religious enthusiasm could be evoked when necessary by almost any skilful ecclesiastic. Also the fact that every good Catholic attended the confessional once a year, and frequently oftener, gave to the priest the whip hand in many a difficult situation. Then, as already noted, the clergy had friends at the Spanish court and were usually sure of getting justice—and even a little more than justice—in any situation that might arise. With the active support of the home government, moreover, the Church was able to keep the colonies practically uncontaminated by Jews and all other non-Catholics. "Moors and Jews, and the descendants of those who had been stamped by the Inquisition, were expelled so that their presence might not profane the increasing number of converts."[8] If any of the slaves brought from Africa were found to be Mohammedans, they had to be sent at once to Spain, in order that the Christian faith, newly planted, might not become defiled.[9] The private lives of the *encomenderos,* or grantees of land and Indian

---

[7] Bancroft, II. 331.

[8] *Ibid.,* II. 333.

[9] J. F. Pacheco and F. de Cárdenas, *Colección de Documentos Inéditos Relativos al Descubrimiento, Conquista y Colonización de las Posesiones Españolas en América y Oceanía,* XVIII. 9-12. Hereafter this work will be cited simply as *Doc. Inéd.* with the volume and page reference.

labor, were also subject to regulation, when the priests saw fit. An order addressed to Peru, but equally applicable to Mexico, is an example of how matters were handled. Due to reports of misconduct on the part of unmarried *encomenderos,* the order was issued that all such persons must take a wife within three years, unless after an examination by the archbishop or bishops they were exempted. Any who neglected this examination were to lose their right to the Indian labor so profitable to them.[10]

Another, and in fact one of the strongest, of the holds that the clergy had over the Spaniard was that secured during childhood. The whole educational system of the country was under their control. Ideas planted at such a time were apt to be lasting. This did not mean that the clergy were absolute dictators in their communities. For instance, their attempt to prohibit the use or sale in Mexico City of *pulque,* a drink made from the fermented juice of the century plant (*Agave Americana*), and thus to prevent the habitual intoxication by it of the natives, was ignored. The law was passed in 1692, partially enforced for a time, and then officially revoked.

The accumulation of Church property on a huge scale was inevitable under the circumstances. The tithes soon amounted to a very large sum. For instance, according to official records, the gross amount collected in all dioceses in the decade 1769-79 was 13,357,157 *pesos,* while that collected for the next ten years was 18,353,821 *pesos.*[11] "The friars spoke and

[10] *Doc. Inéd.,* XVIII. 16-18.

[11] Alexander von Humboldt, *Political Essay on the Kingdom of New Spain,* III. 96-97.

worked in the name of the past, and the large amounts of property of which they became possessed represented the reward for immense services to the cause of civilization."[12]

Large estates, or portions of them, were frequently bestowed upon the Church. Sometimes these came as the result of a spirit of philanthropy, or out of appreciation of the excellent work done by various individuals or groups of the clergy. At other times, bequests were made on the understanding that a certain number of masses would be said by the ecclesiastical recipients on behalf of the soul of the former owner.[13]

Among the fees for ceremonies performed and other minor sources of income were those derived from papal bulls, both for the living (*bulas de vivos*) and for the dead (*bulas de difuntos*). The latter were purchased by friends and relatives of the deceased in order to relieve his soul from purgatory. The *bulas de vivos* were subject to abuses, certainly in cases where robbers secured them as a means of legitimizing their ownership of stolen goods, and members of the clergy, to enable them to enjoy gastronomic indulgences during Lent. The proceeds from the various bulls dur-

[12] M. Moheno, *Partidos Políticos* . . . *en la República Mexicana*, p. 79.

[13] A typical example of the growth of Church estates is given in the following extract from a letter written about 1640 by the Bishop of Puebla, Juan de Palafox y Mendoza, to Father Horacio Carochi, and quoted by A. Molina Enríquez in *La Reforma y Juárez*, p. 29:

"In this place . . . the fathers began with a very moderate and small estate fifty years ago, and now they have fourteen very large ones. Furthermore, the estates of these kingdoms [in the New World] are not like those of Spain, of thirty-five to seventy acres (*de cuatro, seis y ocho fanegas*) of land, because here they are of thirty to sixty square miles (*cuatro, seis y catorce leguas*) or more."

ing 1798 alone amounted to the not inconsiderable sum of 340,897 *pesos*.[14]

All this would not have been such a serious matter, perhaps, had it not been for the right of mortmain held by the Church. According to the Church law and custom, property acquired could never be alienated. Hence, as the Church grew in power, wealth, and prestige, its landed estate increased proportionately. The greater became the Church holdings, and they were usually of the best land in a given community, the less land was left for the laity to own, and the fewer were the chances that the very small incipient middle class would get a foothold.

At this point something should be said of the work of the regular clergy as contrasted with the secular. The former were especially active in educational and missionary undertakings. After the Jesuits, possibly the most important of the regular orders were the Franciscans and Dominicans. How vast was the influence of the Franciscan provincials in Mexico is shown by the fact that on several occasions the king requested them to support viceroys in their administrations. Indeed, such was the royal appreciation of the order that the authorities of New Spain were instructed not to interfere in its internal concerns.[15]

Even a very frank critic of the Roman Catholic Church has this to say of the regular clergy:

The Franciscans by zealous missionary work among the natives, gained a powerful influence over their converts, which they used judiciously to strengthen the position obtained for the

[14] Bancroft, III. 664-666; B. M. in *Southern Quarterly Review*, XII. 347-348 (October, 1847).
[15] Bancroft, III. 714.

Spaniards through conquest, and maintained by force of arms. The Jesuits, who arrived in the year 1572, true to the purpose of their order, tried to foster learning in the new land, though [for a while] with but limited success. . . .

The Dominicans were not slow in establishing the detestable Inquisition; but it was for the express and very plausible purpose of keeping the colonists and foreigners in order, and advancing the spiritual interests of the Church. The Indians were, by specific command, exempted from its operations. Of all the orders, the Dominicans exerted the most powerful influence in political affairs.[16]

During the colonial period, more trouble arose from relations of the civil government with the Jesuits than from any other single religious issue. Because of their successful work of conversion and education, their power increased very rapidly. In the New World as in the Old, they saw fit to take a hand in temporal affairs; so much so, in fact, that friction soon broke out, which, by 1647, had become quite serious. Finally, due to the spirit of the age as well as for other reasons, it was decided that the Jesuits constituted a real menace to the prosperity of the Spanish empire; hence, in 1767, the drastic order for their expulsion was issued. In the case of Mexico it read:

I invest you with my whole authority and royal power that you shall forthwith repair with an armed force—á mano armada—to the houses of the Jesuits. You will seize the persons of all of them, and despatch them within twenty-four hours as prisoners to the port of Vera Cruz, where they will be embarked on vessels provided for that purpose. At the very moment of such arrest you will cause to be sealed the records of said houses, and the papers of such persons, without allowing them to remove anything but their prayer-books, and such garments as are absolutely necessary for the journey. If after

[16] A. H. Noll, From Empire to Republic, pp. 9-11.

the embarkation there should be found in that district a single Jesuit, even if ill or dying, you shall suffer the penalty of death.

The ruthless execution of this order added greatly to the furor created by its contents. It may well have been a cause of the first persistent plots that gradually spread and increased until they culminated in the revolution.[17]

One other institution of the Church remains to be mentioned here, the Inquisition. While the one most denounced, it is possibly the least understood of any of them. It was introduced into Mexico about 1570 and immediately found work to do. The papacy itself, however, appears to have used no pressure to extend the institution to Mexico, or indeed to the New World at all.[18] The first great *auto da fé* is stated to have taken place February 28, 1574. At this time seventy-four persons suffered various penalties.[19] As already observed, the Indians were specifically exempted from the jurisdiction of the inquisitors. In fact, Philip II secured from Pope Gregory XIII a brief granting full faculties to the bishops to absolve the Indians from the sin of heresy and all other reserved cases. This was based popularly on the ground that the Indians were not "rational" enough to be responsible.[20]

The relations between the viceregal government and the Inquisition were an odd mixture of politics, policy, and coöperation *versus* religious quarrels and

---

[17] Bancroft, III. 438-439. Zamacois, XV. 283, note, gives the value of the Jesuit property confiscated at 9,423,389.37 *pesos*. (See appendix B).

[18] Lea, *op. cit.*, p. 199.

[19] *Ibid.*, pp. 200-205.

[20] *Ibid.*, pp. 210-211.

opposition. The grand climax of the career of the Inquisition is said to have been the *auto da fé* of 1649, which furnished it with funds to the extent of some three million *pesos*. Here arose a petty quarrel. The crown had been furnishing about ten thousand *pesos* annually for the support of the tribunal. It did not think this appropriation should last indefinitely, especially with the Inquisition receiving such an income as the above *auto* would indicate, and a good deal of agitation and discussion followed. Finally, about 1677, the royal subvention was stopped.[21] Much later an outstanding example of the power of the Inquisition appeared in 1806, when King Charles IV wanted a report on the boundary of the Louisiana Purchase and ordered Fray Melchor de Talamantes to make it. The latter found that he needed the works of Robertson and Raynal. These were on the Index, so he applied to the Inquisition through the viceroy for permission to use them. The request was refused, but two "qualifiers" (*calificadores*), Fray José Paredo and Fray José Pichardo, were commissioned to read the works and report to Talamantes such material on the subject as they might find.[22] Still later the viceregal government used the Inquisition as a means of disposing of the patriot leaders, Hidalgo and Morelos.[23]

The activities of the Holy Office aroused hatred for the religious authorities of the country. This hatred was easily and naturally transferred to the political government that enforced and supported the religious system.[24] Another source of popular dis-

[21] *Ibid.*, pp. 216-220.
[22] *Ibid.*, p. 274.
[23] *Ibid.*, pp. 284, 292-296.
[24] Noll, *op. cit.*, p. 11.

content with the clergy probably arose from the constant quarrels among the monastic orders. A further source of trouble seems to have been the tithes. Payment of these was frequently resisted on the ground of the privileges and exemptions known as *fueros*.[25] Even nuns showed a contentious spirit in the matter. In fact, the nunnery of Santa Clara quarreled so vigorously with the vice-commissary of the Franciscans that the civil authorities had to intervene. Further trouble arose over the question of supervision of the nuns by the local prelates. The king instructed Viceroy Mancera not to intervene and to prevent the civil authorities from doing so. This "relieved the government of much annoyance."[26] All of these dissensions stopped at once, however, when the privileges and immunities (*fueros*) of a particular body were menaced by an outsider.

Many a time there was a battle royal between the religious orders, or the Church as a whole and the secular officials. So long as the Church did not offend the crown it was fairly safe, provided it played its part skilfully and retained its hold on the people. The bishops always had that terrible weapon, excommunication, which could be launched with such drastic effect as a last resort. More than one civil authority found this out to his sorrow. Even a viceroy would feel safe from the menace of a *visitador*, or official inspector of administration, so long as he had the support of the Church. After about 1540, certainly, the

[25] For an accurate but brief description of the *fuero* system see the article by B. M. in *Southern Quarterly Review*, XII. 242-243 (October, 1847).

[26] Bancroft, III. 710-711.

Church was powerful enough to be sought after and catered to. When disagreements could not be settled in America, they were frequently sent back to Spain, and it was left to the sovereign to render a decision in the matter. In the seventeenth century, disputes between the two powers, ecclesiastical and secular, also seem to have arisen frequently as a result of the custom of assigning to an archbishop an *ad interim* appointment as viceroy, when vacancies occurred in that office.[27]

As early as the middle of the sixteenth century, on the other hand, the king gave instructions to Viceroy Velasco to the effect that "churchmen must not interfere with matters foreign to their calling." Again, orders were issued to send back to Spain all friars and clergymen who had come to the New World without the requisite royal permission. Also friars were not supposed to hold grants of land and Indian labor, (*encomiendas*), though this regulation was usually ignored by mutual consent of officials and clergy, while the bishops, on their part, were forbidden to collect personal tithes. A final most effective check that the crown had over the Church lay in the power of patronage, which could be used to expand royal control to indefinite limits.[28]

A source of more serious dispute was the extent of the jurisdictions of the courts. The ecclesiastical tribunals, if left to themselves, under a broad interpretation of the *fueros* concerned, would have tried all cases in any way connected with the clergy or Church property. This could not be countenanced; for the

[27] H. I. Priestley, *The Mexican Nation,* pp. 139-140.
[28] *Doc. Inéd.,* XVIII. 150-151.

Church courts would not allow a right of appeal to secular courts, since this would imply inferiority. Nevertheless, for more than two centuries the secular clergy enjoyed great privileges, though these were in later times gradually reduced. By a royal decree of October 25, 1795, the common courts were allowed to take jurisdiction over crimes committed by ecclesiastics. The *sala del crimen,* or criminal court, now proceeded to act with rigor against priests, especially curates. Questions of jurisdiction in these cases were to be settled by the viceroy.

In these respects as in others, there were plenty of restrictive laws passed. The Spanish colonial system was so paternalistic that it saw fit to regulate the most minute details of everyday life; hence its officials were literally swamped with laws and instructions and could not carry out the important ones because of the multitude of petty affairs to be cared for.[29] Later, it is true, the situation became somewhat improved, consonant with the more enlightened and progressive policy adopted by Spain in the latter part of the eighteenth century.

[29] No lower official in the class of administrators, such as a *gobernador, corregidor,* or *alcalde mayor,* could marry in any part of their districts during their term of office without express royal permission. In case of violation of this order, the penalty was loss of office as well as prohibition of all future office-holding in the Spanish colonies. *Doc. Inéd.,* XVIII. 148-150.

A decree illustrating the minuteness of Spanish oversight sets forth the fact that the length of swords and knives was causing many inconveniences, deaths, and wounds. The length of the weapons was reported to be from six to nine *palmos* (a *palmo* was equal to 8.64 inches). Fifteen days after the publication of the decree no person of any station was to wear a sword of more than one and one-fourth *varas* in length (a *vara* was equal to 2.78 feet). The first offense was to be punished by a fine of ten ducats, ten days in prison, and the loss of the weapon; the second with a fine of twenty ducats, one year banishment from the colony, and loss of the weapon. Royal decree of April 20, 1565. *Doc. Inéd.,* XVIII. 50-53.

An institution so wealthy as the Church required necessarily a considerable amount of supervision. Very early in the colonial period, therefore, the Spanish courts entered upon a policy of restricting ecclesiastical ownership of land. It has already been observed that friars were not to be allowed to act, at least lawfully, as *encomenderos*. In 1535 Mendoza was directed to dispose of public land, but, at the same time, to prevent its falling into mortmain.[30] These good intentions seem to have had little effect. Not only did huge quantities of land fall into mortmain, but, protected by the *fuero* of the Church, it did not have to pay taxes and so to contribute its share to the support of the viceroyalty. This was partially offset by occasional loans, scarcely voluntary, but something less than forced. These, of course, created friction and trouble for all concerned and frequently worked a real hardship upon the Church, due to the manner in which the levies were made and the times chosen for them. The government even went farther than this, when, as in 1767, it seized the property of the Jesuits and, in 1804, sequestrated other ecclesiastical property. By royal order of December 26 of this last year, all the real estate belonging to benevolent institutions, most of which were controlled by the clergy, was taken over. This confiscation also included the sums invested as loans on city and rural property. The measure caused severe distress and much uncertainty, even though less than three per cent. of the amount affected was secured by the end of the first year of collecting, after which the law seems to have been ignored.[31]

[30] Priestley, *Mexican Nation*, p. 56.
[31] Humboldt, *op. cit.*, III. 99-100.

This attack by the Spanish government on the institution of mortmain was not directed at the Church only, but also at the evil of huge landed estates in general. To the Spaniard of the day, land ownership was a badge of superiority and carried with it a kind of social standing.[32]   Hence many a person of the lower classes simply did not consider it as a part of his scheme of existence to own land. He had always lived on another man's property and expected to do so to the end. The natives, of course, had no conception of individual ownership of land until the Spaniards introduced it. Thus the number of actual land holders was comparatively small, and for this number there were all kinds of opportunities for a man of influence to amass enormous holdings on numberless pretexts. According to one writer:[33]

Up to the middle of the eighteenth century everything had favored the accumulation of land in a few hands. *Encomiendas* which could not be divided, *mayorazgos* [entail] which preserved intact the holdings of the aristocracy, the concentration of property in the hands of the clergy, all had contributed to the maintenance of large holdings. Now, however, the spirit of democracy that was sweeping over the western world seems to have affected, in some degree, even the institutions of Spain and her American colonies. From this time forward, for a full century, there was a slow but almost uninterrupted movement in Mexico toward the division of the land and the creation of small holdings.

In Spain itself the movement went on quite actively from 1787 to 1797. During this time the number of ecclesiastics decreased from 182,425 to 168,248, and

[32] McBride, *op. cit.*, p. 40.
[33] *Ibid.*, p. 61.

the nobles from 480,589 to 402,059.[34]   In Mexico,
however, the movement was particularly slow because
of red tape and distance.

The historic background of the army is soon disposed of. From the days of the conquest onward, aris-
tocrats and army officers were almost identical. Men
of aristocratic lineage and all who could be classed as
"caballeros", or "gentlemen", could only enter three
professions without losing caste: the law, the Church,
and the army; or, failing that, the honorable occupa-
tion of managing the home estate. The army was
needed in the colonies, and here was wealth and glory
to be had for the taking, as was also rapid advancement in the Church. The same sentiments dominated
both. Army officers and clergy were kindred spirits and
saw things with the same eyes. Advancement in the
army or in the Church, except for one of the chosen,
was very slow and next to impossible. As was to be expected, this "closed corporation" of officers handed
down their ideas and ideals as time passed. The men
in the ranks scarcely counted. They seldom knew
what they were fighting for, since they were forced
to serve their masters and simply obeyed orders. When
they got a chance, the regular soldiers often deserted,
and, if they could, went home. If desertion was im-
practicable, they fought as little as possible and hoped,
doubtless, that the war would soon be over so that
they could get away.[35]

In addition to the items mentioned, other elements,
primarily social in character, figure in the background.

[34] C. E. Chapman, *History of Spain*, p. 459. These facts may be
found also in R. Altamira, *Historia de España y la Civilización Española*, IV., but they are much scattered.

[35] Brantz Mayer, *Mexico, Aztec, Spanish, Republican*, II. 119; Waddy
Thompson, *Recollections of Mexico*, pp. 6-7.

The population of the country during the late colonial period is hard to determine. The census of Viceroy Revilla Gigedo, taken in 1793, gives a little less than four and a half millions of people, but this was in part an estimate. In his memorial on the population of the kingdom of New Spain, just after the turn of the century, Fernando Navarro y Noriega put the total at 6,122,354.[36] According to Porfirio Parra, there were, in 1799, 450,000 Spaniards, 2,700,000 Indians, and 1,350,000 mixed breeds, forming respectively about ten, sixty, and thirty per cent. of the total population of 4,500,000.[37] Humboldt, on the other hand, estimated the total population of the country at 5,837,000, though unfortunately there are serious discrepancies in his figures.[38] He considered it "extremely probable that the population in Mexico in 1808 exceeded 6,500,-000."[39]

Most authors seem to agree that the pure Indian population was about fifty to sixty per cent. of the total. The wide variation to be found in the estimates of whites and *mestizos* is explicable on the ground that every halfcaste who could possibly do so passed himself off for white. In this many seem to have been fairly successful, when the amount of Indian blood in their veins was slight. In fact, it was often the case that a *mestizo,* whose skin was not too definitely off-color, could secure a court decree to the effect that he was white. When there was considerable doubt about the matter, the court would simply declare "that such

[36] Bancroft, III. 734-737. For a tabulated report of the various estimates, see Mayer, *op. cit.,* II. 41-43.

[37] Porfirio Parra, *Estudio Histórico-Sociológico sobre La Reforma en México,* pp. 27-28.

[38] Humboldt, *op. cit.,* II. 309.

[39] *Ibid.,* I. 110.

and such individuals may consider themselves as
whites (*que se tengan por blancos*)."[40] On the basis of
a compromise, and resorting to round numbers, it may
be estimated that genuine whites constituted perhaps
fifteen per cent. and *mestizos* thirty-five per cent. of the
whole. Considering the length of the colonial period
and the comparative freedom of intermarriage, one is
inclined to think that this estimate is quite liberal to
the whites, if it errs on either side.

After the conquest, the Indian was allowed for a
time to secure office and preferment, but this soon
ceased, even in the Church. In other words, the fifteen per cent. referred to above were the rulers of
Mexico in every sense of the word. The fact of being
a pure-blooded Spaniard was in itself a sort of certificate of aristocracy. One split in the white group,
however, should be noted. The Spaniard born in the
home country was prone to look down upon the creole,
or Spaniard born in America. This caused a serious
situation, for the Spanish court kept alive the feud by
giving the former preference in bestowing the best
offices.[41]

At the other end of the social scale were the Indians, between three and four times as numerous as

[40] *Ibid.*, I. 246-247.

[41] Jaime Balmes, *Observaciones Sociales, Políticas y Económicas sobre
Bienes del Clero*, p. 34.

"Of the one hundred and seventy viceroys who have governed in
this country (the New World), *but four of them were Americans;* and
of six hundred and ten captains general and governors, *all but fourteen*
were natives of old Spain." *Southern Quarterly Review*, XII. 342-343
(October, 1847).

A letter showing an English view of conditions, is found in *The
Historical Magazine*, III. 101-102 (April, 1859):

Sir: Yr Excellency may be assured nothing is more ardently wished
for in Mexico, & all ye Spanish Possessions in America, than to be

the whites.   Their character, then as now, was not, as
a rule, warlike.   As a recent writer puts it:[42]

We should not think of the Mexican Indian as a Mohawk
or a Sioux.   He is a tiller, not hunter, and is by nature quiet,
serious and peaceful.   His servile past makes him dread to face
life alone, and so he brings his problems to his employer, look-
ing for sympathy and help.   He is as easily led as a child, and
the master who understands him and means right generally has
no difficulty in managing him.   But bad designing men can play
upon him and stir him up to atrocities which are quite out of
his character.

This seems to be an accurate description, and all
Mexican history bears it out.   According to an earlier

released from the Ignominious tyranny they at present labour under.
The Creole Spaniards to a Man, detest the Europe Bashaws & they are
but few Compared to ye Natives.   The Indians to a Man wd second
gladly any Invasion—on the landing but of a Handful of Men they wd
almost Immediately be Joined by the Major part of ye Country—
toleration of Religion & Freedom granted to them & ye whole Spanish
Possessions in both divis of the Continent, are your own—but if even
meeting with opposition (wch is Improbable) ten thousand bold fellows
wd make it yrs but on the least Hint of ye Design ten times that Number will Join the Standard.   Spain has no right to an Inch of ground
on ye whole Continent but by Conquest.   Yr. claim is as good—you
have Shipping more than Sufficient to transport them—or they cou'd
march thro' florida in spite of opposition, few Stores wd be necessary
—ye Country is rich & well Cultivated make ye Capital Mexico yrs &
all is yr own—the Wealth is Literally Immense—a landing effected abt
Vera Cruz, wd be most elegible—but if done it must be a sudden blow
like Lightning no delay or formal treaty's or demurs.   When I was
there there was nothing but for ye troops to land ye Country was their
own so much do ye people detest their present government.

Yr Excellency will excuse this from a friend as it is necessary you
shd be Informed of this I have sent a duplicate to yr Excely.   I have
the Honor to be Yr Excely's

"Most obedt,
"Humble Servt,
"J. Snowden.

"London, *July* 23d, 86,
   "His Excellency, Governor Bowdoin,
      "Boston, America."

[42] E. A. Ross, *The Social Revolution in Mexico,* p. 15.

observer,[43] "The pure Indians with whom the churches and the whole city is crowded, are as ugly as can be imagined; a gentle, dirty and much-enduring race."

Under Aztec rule, the great bulk of the Indians had shown little initiative. During the later colonial period, it was those having more or less Spanish blood and imbued with French ideas who helped to start the movement toward democracy. Although the Indian could not control himself when tempted with *pulque,* he usually took his pleasures rather soberly.[44] The religious festivals were his gala occasions. At such times he would literally pledge his all, even his future services, in return for loans to be spent on rockets, music, wax candles, and other means of diversion, which commonly included *pulque* and gambling. His recreation over, he would return to the quasi-servitude, in which he and his family were little better than slaves at the beck and call of a master, till the arrival of the next *fiesta.*[45] In so far as the genuine Indians held property at all, it was usually on the communal basis.[46] Their personal honesty was well recognized, and thefts among them were almost unknown.[47]

When the Indian lived in a town, he usually occupied the status of a *lépero* (belonging to the rabble). Here he would work, beg, or steal as the occasion offered.[48] He simply lived from hand to mouth and looked forward to no other existence. With his family, he occupied any kind of a hovel. If they were all

[43] Mme Calderón de la Barca, *Life in Mexico,* p. 105.
[44] Moheno, *op. cit.,* p. 74; *Mexico, the Country, History and People,* pp. 260-261.
[45] Thompson, *op. cit.,* pp. 6-7; Mayer, *op. cit.,* II. 31-32.
[46] Molina Enríquez, *op. cit.,* pp. 25-26; McBride, *op. cit.,* pp. 58, 134.
[47] J. R. Poinsett, *Notes on Mexico,* pp. 266-267.
[48] *Ibid.*

ejected, it was seldom a serious matter, for the climate was usually kind and food fairly plentiful.[49]   Such a class of individuals might form a real menace to any government.   They were excellent material for a mob. They could easily be excited and led into all kinds of excesses, especially during days of revolution, when blood was hot and feeling likely to take the place of the judgment of even the more level-headed.

Between these two extremes, the whites and the Indians, there was the *mestizo,* ranging all the way— chromatically, economically, and politically—from the near Indian to the near white.   His was the material out of which the middle class was beginning to make its appearance.   He was a man who felt that he was capable of better things, but did not know just how to go about attaining them.   Certainly he hated the Spaniards, both peninsular and creole, who, in turn, looked down on him.[50]   The *mestizos* should have had the places of action and the creoles those of administration.[51]   Some of the former had secured an education, more or less thorough.   Together with discontented creoles and with foreigners who were coming into the country and working as artisans and professional men, they formed an excellent group of potential leaders from whom much could be expected.[52]

In recent times, and it is logical to conclude that the same was the case in the early nineteenth century, illegitimacy has been lower in *mestizo* communities

[49] Mayer, *op. cit.,* II. 26-27.

[50] Molina Enríquez, *op. cit.,* p. 31.

[51] *Ibid.,* p. 61.

[52] F. L., *Études Historiques sur le Méxique,* pp. 79-80; Justo Sierra, ed., *Mexico,-su Evolución Social,* I. 270.

than among their neighbors.[53]   This would indicate
a higher moral standard and a better family life.[54]

The fact has already been mentioned that during
the later years of the eighteenth century the Bourbons
were trying to redeem the situation in which they
found themselves.   Financially and politically, their
circumstances were difficult.[55]   The extreme formality
of earlier reigns was giving place to more democratic
customs, even at court.   Attempts at religious toleration came to naught, since the people repudiated them;
but a reduction was nevertheless secured in the number of the clergy[56] and their estates.[57]   One phase of
the more liberal policy of Spain met with marked success; namely, the opening of the colonial ports to a
greater freedom of trade with the mother country.[58]
Few of these reforms directly affected the Church, but,
if carried to their logical conclusion, they could have
had but one result.   Consequently, in the struggle for
liberty in Spain, as in America, the clergy were allied
with the conservatives.   The effect in Mexico was ob-

---

[53] *Ibid.*, I. 722.

[54] No space is devoted to the Negro slave population as such.   There
were practically no slaves in Mexico proper.   Humboldt estimated that in
1808 there were not more than nine or ten thousand in the whole of
New Spain. *Op. cit.*, I. 236.

[55] Altamira, *op. cit.*, IV. 178.

[56] *Ibid.*, IV. 245-252.

[57] *Ibid.*, IV. 236 ff; Chapman, *op. cit.*, p. 416.

[58] The effect of this opening of ports to freedom of trade with the
mother country may be seen from the following figures taken from
Humboldt, *op. cit.*, IV. 102-103:

Gross produce of the public revenue of New Spain:

      1765-1777 ....131,135,286 *pesos*

      1778-1790 ....233,302,557 *pesos*

Value of precious metals shipped from Vera Cruz for the king:

      1776-1778 .... 15,027,072 *pesos*

      1779-1791 .... 29,581,982 *pesos*

See also pp. 98-106 and *Southern Quarterly Review,* XII. 344 (October,
1847).

viously to confirm each party in its own beliefs. In
the colony at the time, the Church held property variously estimated in value from forty to fifty million
pesos. Through direct ownership, trust funds, mort-
gages, and other financial agencies, it is said to have
held, directly or indirectly, from one half to two thirds
of all the real property in the country.[59] To administer
this huge domain, there were from thirteen to fourteen thousand of those "in religion".[60] This included
lay brothers, servitors, and nuns. The few forced
loans that were made[61] were easily met, without very
serious effort, especially when the government helped
to collect the tithes and also considered most ecclesiastical property tax-exempt.

Of the clergy there were three classes. The upper
clergy (*clero alto*) comprised the bishops and members
of chapters, most of them being Spaniards. The lower
clergy (*clero bajo*) included the priests, curates, vicars,
and other ecclesiastics of the sort. These were socially
of a class quite distinct from the first, and the training they had received did not and could not entirely
remove prejudices arising out of birth, station, or local
circumstances. The regular clergy (*clero regular*)
tended to become centered in the towns. As a rule, its
members were dominated by the upper clergy and were
sticklers for precedent and privilege. Those who went
out as missionaries and mixed with the people at large
were usually sympathetic with the lower clergy.[62]

[59] Bancroft, III. 697. G. L. Rives, *The United States and Mexico*,
I. 66; *El Telégrafo*, September 8, 1833.
[60] Humboldt, *op. cit.*, I. 229-232.
[61] F. de P. de Arrangoiz, *Méjico desde 1808 hasta 1867*, I. 34-35;
hereafter cited as Arrangoiz.
[62] Mariano Otero, *Ensayo sobre . . . la Cuestión Social y
Política*, pp. 44-45.

According to Humboldt, the relative incomes of the higher ecclesiastics were no small items in determining social differentiation. For example, the archbishop of Mexico received one hundred and thirty thousand *pesos;* the bishop of Puebla, one hundred and ten thousand; of Valladolid, one hundred thousand; of Guadalajara, ninety thousand; of Durango, thirty-five thousand; of Monterey, thirty thousand; of Yucatán, twenty thousand; of Oaxaca, eighteen thousand, and of Sonora, six thousand. Furthermore, the bishop of Sonora, the poorest of them all, drew no tithes. His income amounted only to the twentieth part of that of the bishops of Valladolid and Michoacán; and, what was truly distressing, in the diocese of an archbishop whose revenue amounted to the sum of one hundred and thirty thousand *pesos,* there were clergymen of Indian villages whose yearly income did not exceed one hundred to one hundred and twenty-five *pesos.*[63]

What might be described, therefore, as the liberal movement of the early nineteenth century in Mexico reduced itself essentially to a struggle of the masses of the people, led by a few men who had adopted the ideals of the United States or of the French Revolution, against the classes, composed of the hierarchy, the large individual landholders, and the army. These classes, it has been seen, had deep roots in the very soil of Mexico. They were the social, political, military, economic, and religious powers in the country and were the apex of a European civilization that had been growing up in the country since 1520, while the mass of the population was the base.

[63] Humboldt, *op. cit.,* I. 229-232.

CHAPTER II

DEMOCRACY IN THE REVOLUTION

Turning from this preliminary survey to the origins of the uprising against Spanish rule, it may be said at the outset that in its beginning the Mexican Revolution was really a class war, having as its basis social jealousies and exclusion from preferments.[1] On both sides of the struggle, strangely enough, leadership was assumed by the clergy. Of the lower and potential middle class, the best spokesmen were those who had been educated for the priesthood, but who were in the lower ranks, with little hope of advancement. Hidalgo, Morelos, and Torres are names dear to every Mexican heart for the gallant part their bearers played in the early days of the Revolution. Of course they were opposed by the machinery of the Church; and it was a hard matter for them to face excommunication and the denunciation of those whom they had been taught to obey. "The revolution, having been begun by an ecclesiastic, had from its incipiency many members of the clergy, both secular and regular, among its leaders; and it may be said that at this time [1812] the war was kept up almost wholly by them. *There was hardly a battle in which priests were not found as leading officers.*"[2] This is all the more remarkable in view of the fact that a papal encyclical had directed the clergy to oppose all attempts to separate

[1] Bancroft, IV. 14-15.
[2] *Ibid.*, IV. 423-424. The italics are mine.

Mexico from Spain.[3] The circumstance may be partially explained by the poor supervision that had been
exercised over many of the country priests by their
superiors; for instance, in 1802, many towns in the
district of the bishop of Puebla had no priest and "had
not been visited by the Bishop . . . for 47 years."[4]

Even though the clergy were divided on the question of independence, with only the poorer group in
favor of it, still the viceroy proceeded cautiously in
dealing with rebel priests because of the respect of the
common people for all members of this holy class. In
1811, when three Augustinian friars were arrested
with other conspirators, that officer did not see fit to
have them executed in Mexico, but sent them to
Havana for confinement instead.[5]

Both rebels and loyalists tried to introduce the religious issue by the use of sacred banners dedicated to
the Virgin. "Thus in the . . . battlefields during
the war for independence, opposing armies fought
under emblems of the same divine interceder for mercy
before the heavenly throne."[6] With an opposition organized by wealth, the higher clergy, the army, and the
official class, the wonder is that the rebels in the early
part of the revolution held out as long as they did. In
1812 matters seemed to be quieting down somewhat; so

[3] Noll, *op. cit.*, pp. 54-55.

[4] Bancroft, III. 210.

[5] *Ibid.*, IV. 333.

[6] *Ibid.*, IV. 187. Arrangoiz in his work would make it appear that the
rebels frequently and consistently injured the Church. I. 292, 310. Considering the Mexican character, this is hard to believe. Such an action
would, to say the least, have been very foolish. It is quite possible, however, that hatred of the Spaniards brought about isolated cases of injury,
such as that of the expulsion of the Carmelites from Tehuacán.

the viceroy declared that the press, hitherto shackled, should be free. The supreme court [*Audiencia*] in the capital city, the metropolitan chapter, the bishops, except the bishop of Oajaca, and many other personages, lay and clerical, thought that he was making a serious mistake.[7] Feeling ran so high during an election for members of the town council held just at this time that the Viceroy was inclined to agree with his critics when the editor of *El Pensador* (*The Thinker*) referred to him as "a miserable mortal, a man like all others, and a despicable spot on the face of the Almighty; [a man who] had erred through the necessity of listening to foreign dictation, since malice, ignorance or flattery often twist the sanest intentions".[8]

By royal order of September 16, 1815, the Jesuits were formally reëstablished in the land with great ceremony.[9] Also, the dreaded Inquisition, which had been abolished, was once more set up, and, on January 21, 1815, the inhabitants of the land received a circular ordering them "under penalty to appear and denounce themselves and others for utterances against religion and the holy office".[10]

Meanwhile, the complexion of affairs was changing in Spain. In 1820 the king was forced to accept the constitution of that year. The *Cortes,* or legislative body, then dominating affairs, proceeded to run matters with a high hand by seizing the tithes of the

[7] Arrangoiz, I. 190-191.

[8] *Ibid.,* I. 197.

[9] *Ibid.,* I. 309-310; Bancroft, IV. 649. In 1820 they were again driven out, when the military revolution in Spain forced the king to accept the Constitution of 1812.

[10] Bancroft, IV. 599.

Church, abolishing the Inquisition, and advocating a
free press, popular elections, nonhereditary town councils, and representative government in a modified form.
Forthwith, in Mexico, the endorsement of the clergy
shifted to the ranks of the rebels. That group, which
it had once denounced, it now supported with all its
energy. A law of January 4, 1813 had been revived.
It provided that *terrenos baldíos,* or unoccupied lands,
were to be distributed only on the distinct understanding that they were never to pass into *Manos Muertas*
(mortmain).[11] Such restrictions, as well as actual
losses of property, were so imminent that priests declared from their pulpits that the very existence of
Catholicism in America demanded that Mexico be
freed from Spain.[12] With a new government, which
they might help to establish, they would have good
chances of liberal treatment.[13] A Declaration of Independence which had been issued by the erstwhile rebels, November 6, 1813, now became a perfectly good
Catholic document, recognizing, as it did, Roman
Catholicism as the only lawful religion; hence the
Church seemed to find no difficulty in supporting it.[14]
"Bishop Pérez of Puebla conspired openly against
Spain. The Bishop of Guadalajara loaned money to
the rebels. The Bishop and *cabildo* [chapter] of
Chiapas declared for freedom",[15] and so it happened
all over the land. "That powerful body [the clergy]

[11] Francisco Zarco, *Historia del Congreso Constituyente,* I. 416; hereafter cited as Zarco.

[12] Poinsett, *op. cit.,* appendix, p. 39.

[13] Molina Enriquez, *op. cit.,* p. 35; Noll, *op. cit.,* pp. 75-76.

[14] Arrangoiz, I. 227-228.

[15] Carlos Navarro y Rodrigo, *Vida de Agustín de Iturbide,* p. 111.

preferred to sacrifice the allegiance they owed to the king, from whom they had received their preferments, rather than run the risk of losing their privileges."[16] Their attempt now was to compromise with leaders advocating complete independence and to secure control of the movement. To this end, Spaniards, creoles, and the more important *mestizos* were to be found meeting in the "Church of the Profesa" in Mexico City. By the agreement reached, the Church not only supported the idea of independence, but was forced to accept, in form at least, the idea of government by the people, freedom of the press, and other liberal principles. The agreement was satisfactory to Agustín de Iturbide,[17] the chosen leader, and endorsed by him.

This change of attitude on the part of the Church turned the scale.[18] Up to this time, the moderates had been inclined to the side of the mother country. Now they hastened into the ranks of the patriots.[19] The Viceroy took such steps as he could to meet the storm. He called the Spaniards to the capital, where they

[16] R. A. Wilson, *Mexico, its Peasants and its Priests*, p. 36.

[17] Noll, *op. cit.*, pp. 75-76.

[18] Bancroft, IV. 814.

[19] Another indication of the popularity of this movement is the fact that Chiapas "by the wish of its people" joined its fate with that of Mexico, and left the Captaincy General of Guatemala to which it had belonged up to this time. Juan Suárez y Navarro, *Historia de México*, II. 71-72. So far as known, there is only one copy of the second volume of this work in existence. It contains ninety-six pages. The last page ends with an uncompleted sentence. In manuscript there is written the following: "Hasta aquí suspendí la impression y publicacion de esta obra, reservándola para cuando tenga mas juicio y esperiencia. (At this point I suspended the printing and publication of this work, postponing it till I should have more judgment and experience)."

(signed)   J. S. Navarro.

would be ready for eventualities, abolished the freedom of the press, and prepared for the worst.[20]

Not the least of the factors that had to be considered was the development of Freemasonry and its meaning. The date of the establishment of the first Masonic lodge in Mexico is apparently a matter of some dispute, though the year 1806 is the most probable.[21]

No official document exists which is able to give an idea of the origin of this lodge, its procedure, or its period of existence; or whether it had any political purpose, although, certainly, we must believe that it was the centre from which the idea of winning the independence of Mexico originated, since the persons who formed it all took an active part in the promotion of independence when happenings in Spain provided an opportunity.[22]

Masons also entered the country with the Spanish expeditionary forces in 1811.[23] These were of the well-to-do class and hence could not be regarded as "democrats" (*demócratas*). However, the brotherhood of man, a fundamental principle of the Masonic order, provided a connecting link with the ideas of the masses and with republican notions. During this early period, the opposition of the Church to the Masons[24] was only another force that tended to throw them more and more into the arms of the rebels.

[20] Arrangoiz, II. 55.

[21] Rives, *op. cit.*, I. 163-164.

[22] J. M. Mateos, *Historia de la Masonería en México*, pp. 8-9.

[23] Rives, *op. cit.*, I. 163-164; Bancroft, IV. 698. Many of their principles, such as manhood suffrage, are to be found in the proposed constitution of Apatzingán, announced in 1814, which, though it never went into effect, helped to create sentiment for the liberal cause.

[24] Rives, *op. cit.*, I. 62.

In the meantime, the principles of democracy were being actively advocated in Spain, where the liberal movement was largely dominated by the Masons. As a recent writer puts it:

The storm broke when orders were given in 1819 for the assembling of an army at Cadiz for the extremely unpopular service of the wars in the Americas. Colonel Riego raised the standard of revolt on January 1, 1820, proclaiming the constitution of 1812. The government seemed paralyzed by the outbreak. Uncertain what to do, it waited. Then late in February the example set by Riego was followed in the larger cities of northern Spain. The king at once yielded, and caused an announcement to be made that he would summon a Cortes immediately and would swear his adhesion to the constitution of 1812.[25]

As has been seen, it would be entirely too much to say that the Masons furnished the immediate cause for the liberal movement in Mexico, still there can remain little doubt that they contributed to it in a very marked degree. The Viceroy was quite certain of their influence in the Spanish revolution and feared that they had the same thing in mind for Mexico. Contemporary attacks on them were nearly all made from the religious standpoint, but it is not difficult to see that the Masons were standing for and attempting to develop more liberal ideas.[26]

[25] Chapman, op. cit., pp. 495-496.

[26] A little pamphlet, with no date of publication, and entitled, Intento de la Masonería, thus summarizes the purposes of the Masons on p. 13: "We are agreed then that when the sectarians [Masons in this case] preach the secularization of the source of sovereignty, that of the family, through civil marriage, when they deny the necessity of Christian baptism, when they attempt to secure possession of education, when they separate Christians from the sacraments and religious practices, when they change the appearance of towns by destroying temples and

These facts being taken into consideration, it was perfectly natural that the "Plan of Iguala",[27] of February 24, 1821, should be fairly conservative. The framing of it, of course, was a revolutionary proceeding, but, as already noticed, the venture was now led by classes that were conservative at heart. Its first article guaranteed the Roman Catholic religion and denied toleration to any other, while its fourth took a clear-cut stand for the conservation of the rights and properties of the regular and secular clergy. This was the plan upon which was organized the army of the "Three Guarantees", *i.e.,* the preservation of the Roman Catholic religion and clerical privileges, independence, and equality of creoles and Europeans in the government.[28]

In spite of arrays of figures to the contrary,[29] there were probably few then willing to undertake a prolonged war in behalf of the mother country. The Masons lent their aid to the liberal movement,[30] and

monasteries, excloistering religious communities, silencing the bells, prohibiting religious and priestly garb, secularizing charity, profaning Christian festivals, introducing death without sacraments, civil burial and [control of] cemeteries, when they despoil the Church, weave restrictions against the Holy See, elaborate constitutions and laws, open lay schools, organize Masonic associations, etc., etc., in regard to all this we say: they do nothing less than fight without quarter against the reign of Christianity on earth."

[27] This was the new Plan of the rebels, after they had secured the support of the upper classes. It was announced February 24, 1821.

[28] Arrangoiz, II. 30-31.

[29] Arrangoiz claims that at the beginning of this year the royal army was composed of: 8448 troops sent from the home country between 1812 and 1817; 10,620 veterans already in the country; 21,968 provincial militia, beside 44,000 loyal men who could be called upon. This gave a grand total of 85,036, of whom 25,000 were cavalry. I. 400.

[30] Carlos de Gagern, *Apelación de los Mexicanos a la Europa,* p. 40, says: "But what we ought to admire is the coöperation of the Bourbon-Scottish Rite party in this liberal pronouncement,—a new proof of the

it was only a matter of a few months till the country was in the hands of the rebels.

The first serious consideration was the formation of the new government. A republic was not only contrary to the training and background of the Mexican people, but—what was far more serious—it was entirely foreign to the character and temperament of nine tenths of them. Iturbide was the dashing hero of the multitudes; he was the leader of the army and could rely upon the support of the clergy for any movement that would tend to centralize the government and so make it more easily controlled and less radical. The war being over, he was rapidly losing in popularity and needed some means of once more getting before the public eye. Nothing could be more natural than that, no foreign prince being immediately available for the throne, he should be asked to ascend it. As a matter of fact, there were three distinct parties in the congress which met in February, 1822: the "Bourbonists", who wished a constitutional monarchy under a Bourbon king; the "Iturbidists", who accepted the Plan of Iguala but who wished now to place their own leader in charge of affairs; and the "Republicans", who denied that the army had the right to carry out the plan of the Iturbidists and who wished for a republic.[31] The

truth which we have stated; that the spirit of the century knows how to use for the accomplishment of its purposes even those men with ideas directly opposed to their own; since when that faction seconded the plan of December 6, 1822, called [the Plan] of Casa Mata, it did so with the questionable idea of itself taking control of the destinies of the nation, and of again laying bare, if that were possible, our political relations with the metropolis."

[31] Bancroft, IV. 760.

support of the first two parties was rather easily secured, while the republicans were partially won over.

Some would say that the election of Iturbide as
emperor by sixty-seven out of eighty-two votes was
illegal, since there was a rule that one hundred delegates or more were necessary to form a quorum.[32]
However, the Mexican people appear to have been
satisfied, especially since it was Valentín Gómez Farías,
of Zacatecas, who introduced the measure. This man
was to bear such a distinguished part in the whole liberal movement that, if he were satisfied, almost all the
liberals would be also—for the time being at least.

In the absence of the Archbishop, the coronation
was performed, July 22, 1822, by the Bishops of Guadalajara, Puebla, Durango, and Oaxaca.[33] But, despite
the rise of reports of miracles connected with the life
of Iturbide,[34] opposition soon began to develop. In the
words of an American historian:

The cheated absolutists, disappointed borbonistas, cajoled
insurgents, distanced comrades, eclipsed leaders and unsuccess-
ful claimants, the patriots, indignant that a cruel royalist should

[32] There is great variation as to the figures in this election. Bancroft,
IV. 773, note; Arrangoiz, II. 115-116.

[33] Bancroft, IV. 778. The so-called "Spanish priests" held themselves
aloof in the main, for they wanted a Bourbon on the throne. Most of
them, however, seem gradually to have accommodated themselves to the
new régime. An interesting study can be made by comparing the report
of this situation by Arrangoiz, who is obviously biased, with that of
other writers. II. 121.

[34] The following is a typical example of the origin of the miracles
frequently encountered: "At the age of eleven months it appears that
the child saved his life as by a miracle. They say that a careless servant
girl having placed a light near the awning (*pabellón*) that covered the
cradle in which the child was sleeping, that (the awning) caught fire.
When some of the ropes that held the (swinging) cradle caught fire,
the child, with happy instinct, grasped vigorously the rope that remained
intact and saved his life." Navarro y Rodrigo, *op. cit.*, p. 14.

be the heir of the revolution, the republicans, few in number but increasingly influential, the friends of those he had massacred or plundered, and behind all the Scottish Rite Freemasons [the York Rite lodges were of later growth], who were liberals yet partisans of Spain—all these hated and dogged him.[35]

On the other hand, it should not be forgotten that there was a group who considered that the "Empire of 1822 must be regarded as a national protest of the *respectable* and *influential* classes against the institution of a Democratic Republic."[36]

Just at this time there comes into view a character destined to bear a prominent part through the next thirty-five years of his country's history—Antonio López de Santa Ana, or Santa Anna, as he is known in the United States. Trained in the army from boyhood, knowing the Mexican character and how to appeal to it, of a splendid personality, with money and the sense to use it, a man with noble impulses, especially in his early career, but with an inordinate ambition that drove him on, in a few years he became veritably mad for power, throwing all scruples to the wind, and was ruled by his passion for political domination. In 1823 he was only a young man of twenty-seven, nevertheless one to be reckoned with. To quote his own words:

At that time Don Agustín Iturbide did not know how to rise above temptation or the flattery of those who surrounded him. He wished to occupy the throne of Montezuma, to which he was not called, without foreseeing the consequences which quickly followed: his loss of prestige and anarchy. General

[35] J. H. Smith, *The War With Mexico*, I. 34.
[36] *London Quarterly Review*, CXV. 191 (April, 1864). The italics are mine.

opinion favored a regency, though the nation's representatives were actually disposing of its destiny. I shared this opinion.[37]

Santa Anna's opponents would say that this is simply an ingenuous explanation, written later to support his treachery. It is certain that to Iturbide his acts were at once suspicious. He was called to meet the Emperor to explain a "grave act of insubordination". Soon afterwards, he appeared at Vera Cruz, denounced the Emperor, and raised troops to oppose him.[38]

As Iturbide proved himself incapable of handling the difficult situation, the *"Escoceses"* (Scottish Rite Masons) grew in power and prestige. Their lodges were excellent centres for the distribution of propaganda. Even the old Bourbonists were inclined to join them, "because of the conviction they had that a monarchy with a dynasty of recent origin unites all the evils of a republic to all the inconveniences of a monarchy."[39] There seems to be little doubt that some of the methods used were decidedly questionable. Active intrigues also were being carried on with Iturbide's generals. The same leaders were making connections with the republicans while actually supporting those standing for the Plan of Iguala—two mutually contradictory groups. Spies of the Masons constantly followed Iturbide, "and, to their shame be it said, plotted his assassination."[40]

Meanwhile, a somewhat concerted movement developed against bigotry and in favor of religious as

[37] Antonio López de Santa Anna, *Mi Historia Militar y Política*, p. 10.
[38] *Mexico; the Country, History and People* (Anonymous), p. 176.
[39] Arrangoiz, II. 142-143.
[40] Bancroft, IV. 804.

well as political liberty. A pamphlet in circulation was entitled "A Hundred Questions for Today Concerning Priests and Ecclesiastical Incomes". This was really a Mexican edition, dated 1821, of "The Questioner of 1786" (*El Preguntador del año 1786*) from Spain itself. Nevertheless, it raised nearly all the issues that were later so bitterly contested. While at the time the clergy had great influence, it was one largely restricted to the upper and lower classes, since the majority of the nascent middle class were exempt from it, many of them having become skeptics and infidels.[41] Even monarchist and conservative opinion could not fail to note the rising opposition to the ecclesiastical *fuero*.[42] Part of this movement harked back, in spirit at least, to the decrees of the Spanish Cortes, if not also to the royal order for the sale of Jesuit property, which, beyond doubt, had caused serious trouble in such places as Puebla and in other ecclesiastical centres.[43] At first this trouble created many partisans for the cause of Iturbide. When he appeared in Puebla, he was given a splendid reception, it being thought that he would help to reëstablish the Jesuits in the land.[44]

[41] Poinsett, *op. cit.*, p. 164.

[42] Arrangoiz, II. 96-97.

[43] "In fact fifteen hundred persons had asked in 1820 in a petition to the Viceroy that he would not give effect to the decree of the Cortes suppressing the Company [of Jesus]; and this year the ecclesiastical chapters of the capital, Guadalupe, Puebla, Oajaca, Valladolid, Guadalajara, Durango, and Yucatán; the provincial delegation, the Supreme Court, the Town Council (*Ayuntamiento*), and the rector of the University of the Capital, the provincial delegations and the town councils of Puebla, Tehuacán, Oajaca, Comitán, Durango, Guadalajara, Querétaro, Orizaba, Jalapa, Tulancingo, Lagos, and Cholula; the landholders (*vecinos*) of most of the large and small towns; almost the whole country in fact, said the same to the Provisional Governing Council (*Junta*)." Arrangoiz, II. 107.

[44] *Ibid.*, II. 59.

Once independent, at all events, Mexico continued the work of reform. The first national congress decreed on July 4, 1822:

The property of the Philippine missions with all that belongs to it, likewise the funds *(capitales)* and property destined to religious work, [but] which does not have a vital part *(cumplimiento)* in the Mexican Empire, shall be confiscated by the government.[45]

This was followed, on May 16, 1823, by a law for the sale of the property of the Inquisition.

In spite of such provisions, and even while the Regency, formed just prior to the election of Iturbide as emperor, was still in power, the congress, at its wits' end for money, decreed a forced loan to fall chiefly on the ecclesiastical corporations of the cities of Mexico, Puebla, Guadalajara, and Vera Cruz. The amount of the loan was six hundred thousand *pesos,* to be repaid by a two per cent. tax on the "internal circulation of money". The same year, a forced loan of two million eight hundred thousand *pesos* was proposed, but it was not put into operation. The passage of time had made matters worse instead of better. The income of the government was twenty-one million *pesos* in 1820, sufficient to cover running expenses and to provide a neat surplus to apply on old debts.[46] From July 1, 1822, to March 31, 1823, the receipts amounted to 5,249,858 *pesos.* After deducting the expenditures of 3,830,878 *pesos,* there was a balance on hand of 1,418,980. This balance was composed

[45] Francisco Bulnes, *Juárez y las Revoluciones de Ayutla y de la Reforma,* p. 82.
[46] Arrangoiz, II. 24-25, 125.

of 1,410,459 *pesos* of paper money, 1719 of specie, and 6801 of ore and jewels. While it was bad enough to have so little "real" money on hand, there was an even more unpleasant side to the situation, when the origin of the receipts was taken into consideration: taxes yielded 371,656 *pesos;* a loan from the cathedrals, 366,174; a forced loan, ostensibly for 600,000 *pesos,* 286,460; and a specie train seized in Perote, 693,702. The balance was obtained by issuing paper money and by funds secured from the departments (states), much of which was to be repaid.[47]

Such financial conditions helped to draw the lines all the more closely, and the Church allied itself more and more with the Empire, because restrictions, forced loans, and confiscations seemed to be the firstfruits of republicanism. To the clergy, as to the classes with which they associated, the idea of a republic, in the broadest sense at least, was repulsive. Even ecclesiastics engaged in mission work, and frequently very sympathetic toward the masses, are said to have repudiated utterly the idea of conferring civil rights upon the Indians.[48] Unfortunately, the long period of turmoil had had a serious effect on the mission work of the Church. The priests felt that nearly everything they had was at stake, and so they did not pay any particular attention to the maintenance of missions that were not self-supporting. A report, furthermore, to the constituent congress, on November 8, 1823, stated that, besides the missions of California, "there are others in a lamentable state of ruin, particularly

---

[47] Arrangoiz, II. 133.
[48] Wilson, *op. cit.,* p. 148.

those of the province of Texas, which are completely deserted and abandoned."[49]

The financial stress was felt also by the common people of the towns in higher prices charged for products. The population of the four chief cities was Mexico City (in 1822), 155,000; Guadalajara (in 1825), 70,000; Puebla (in 1825), 60,000; and Guanajuato (in 1825), 32,000, as compared with about 155,000 in New York City in 1825.[50] According to an American contemporary, one out of every seven and a half of the inhabitants of the capital city was a *lépero,* living a hand-to-mouth and usually a vicious existence.[51] Yet there was an apparently successful opera season in full swing, with the boxes let by the year at prices ranging up to five hundred *pesos.*[52] In the country districts, to be sure, the rise in prices was much less noticeable, though even here there was oppo-

[49] Report read to Congress by Lúcas Alaman, Minister of Foreign Affairs and of the Home Department, November 8, 1823. Poinsett, *op. cit.,* appendix, p. 99.

[50] Rives, *op. cit.,* I. p. 53.

[51] Poinsett, *op. cit.,* p. 66-67.

Some typical prices given by Poinsett, (*Ibid.,* pp. 67-68) are:

Beef, 28 ozs.	12½c
Mutton and Veal, per lb.	12½c
Eggs, per doz.	25c
Fish from lakes, 9" to 12" long, per lb.	$1.00
Fowls, per pair	50c to 75c
Pigeons, per pair	25c
Turkeys, each	75c to $1.00
Peaches, per doz.	50c
Pears, per doz.	75c
Tuna (prickly pear), per doz.	25c
Alligator pears, per doz.	50c
Mameis (mammees), per doz.	33¾c
Grapes, per lb.	33¾c
Pineapples, each	12½c

[52] *Ibid.,* p. 109.

sition to the Iturbide government. The same American writer, commenting on the schoolmaster of the village of San Isidro between San Lina Potón and Tula, says:

He seemed perfectly unconscious of his uncouth appearance, but received me most courteously; dismissed his scholars immediately, and at once entered into conversation on the state of the country. He was not satisfied with the present order of things, and made some sarcastic observations on the change of masters which the people had undergone; contrasting the old colonial government with that of Iturbide, very much in favor of the former.[53]

Slavery, by this time, had virtually disappeared. A decree of 1808 for emancipation had not been enforced, but, during the struggle since that date, the slaves had at one time and another been drawn into the fighting. When it was over, they often failed to return to their old masters.[54] The best workers having gone, there was no object in keeping the financially dependent as slaves.

All of these conditions, taken together, provided an excellent opportunity for the growth in power of the army. Under the old Spanish régime, it had been carefully watched, so that it would not become too large. Since then, many would-be leaders had arisen. The nonenforcement of the laws also played into the hands of the army and made its continued existence explainable. As political questions were taken up by the military factions, the inevitable result was civil war.[55] This is seen in the revolt of Santa Anna against

[53] Poinsett, *op. cit.*, pp. 252-253.
[54] Arrangoiz, II. 92.
[55] Otero, *op. cit.*, pp. 71-73.

Iturbide. As emperor, Iturbide did not dare to reduce
his army so as to lessen expenses and relegate these
would-be leaders to private life. It was a case of
military men creating dissatisfaction and disorder and
running up bills. To put down disorder and collect the
taxes, more men were needed in the army. Thus the
vicious circle assumed an ever widening scope.[56]

As is quite obvious, the conditions were such that
it would have taken a genius to control affairs and ad-

[56] Poinsett, (op. cit., pp. 151-153) gives the following estimates of
troops in Mexico at different times:

1804:

Infantry:	Troops of the line	5,200
	Militia	11,000
Cavalry:	Troops of the line	4,700
	Militia	11,300
	Total	32,200

Just after the Plan of Iguala:

Infantry: Troops of the line	20,269
Artillery	1,449
Cavalry: Troops of the line	13,645
Troops with no exact count	3,000
	38,363
Militia	30,000
Total	68,363

1822:

Infantry	6,264
Cavalry	4,500
Troops of the line	10,764
Militia	30,000
Total	40,764

Alamán (Historia de Méjico, V. table facing p. 956) gives the following:

Troops in 1808	40,000
Troops in 1820	85,000
Troops in 1823	30,000
Troops in 1827	59,435

minister the Mexican government. This Iturbide was not. In a short time, the liberals had the upper hand and proceeded to drive him from the country. Then came the period from April 1, 1823, to October 10, 1824, with the government in the hands of a committee composed of N. Bravo, P. C. Negrete, M. Domínguez, G. Victoria, J. M. Michelena, and V. Guerrero.

At once the victors fell to quarreling over the spoils. They had united in ousting Iturbide, but a combination of the former Bourbonists with the full-fledged republicans to work together in the upbuilding of a new government proved impossible. The first two factions to claim attention were the Centralists and Federalists. In the former group were most of the Scottish-Rite Masons and the monarchists. They wanted a strong central government, which would dominate the provinces through a monarch. The Federalists, among whom were also to be found some of the old "Iturbidists" desirous of revenge, wanted a federal republic on the order of that of the United States.

The Masons themselves split into factions. The Scottish-Rite lodges had been leaders in the movement. However, they were not republican in the usual sense of the word, and so a York-Rite (*Yorkino*) lodge was organized. In this there were rapidly gathered together the leading spirits among the republicans. It was in this connection that the United States Minister, Joel R. Poinsett, figured. How far he was responsible for the formation of the new Masonic body, with the deliberate purpose of using it as a means by which to

spread republican doctrines, is difficult to determine.[57]
Guilty or innocent as he may have been, and, if guilty,
justified or unjustified as he may have been, the fact
is not altered that these lodges were established and
spread like wildfire among the more radical men of
the day.

Money again was badly needed to make the government effective. It was secured by all kinds of desperate
means. Tobacco in the official warehouses was sold
at greatly reduced prices so as to secure the needed
funds.[58] The ultimate effect upon the country seems
to have been ignored. Once more the temptation to
secularize ecclesiastical property was too great, and
further temporalities of the Jesuits, Hospitallers, and
the Inquisition were disposed of.[59]

In 1823 Mexican government bonds were sold in
London to the extent of £3,200,000 face value. They
were disposed of at a discount of fifty per cent. and so
really yielded ten per cent. interest instead of the apparent five per cent. which they called for. Of the
amount paid in by the purchasers, only £1,139,660
reached the government in actual money, since the

[57] Bancroft, V. 33-35.

[58] This had been a considerable source of income for the Spanish
government. Humboldt reported that in 1802 the government made a
net profit of 4,092,000 *pesos* from its tobacco business. *Op. cit.,* IV. 210.

[59] Bancroft, V. 4. Another act of the congress at the time was the
adoption of the national coat-of-arms and flag. The first shows an eagle
on a cactus plant growing from a rock jutting above the waters of
a lake or swamp. The eagle is tearing a snake with its beak, while
he grasps it with his right claw. The flag is of three horizontal
bars of green, white and red. These indicate the three guarantees of
the plan of Iguala: independence, the union of the Spaniards and native-
born in the government of Mexico and the purity of the Roman Catholic
religion.

balance was used in paying accrued interest and in effecting certain amortizations.[60] Poor as the national credit was, later in the same year a further loan was floated through the house of Barclay, Richardson and Co. of London. It also was for £3,200,000, but the interest rate was six per cent. Since confidence was being developed slowly, the issue sold at eighty-six and three-fourths per cent. and so produced £2,776,-000. A good part of this was used to repay the first loan and as interest, charges, and commissions, leaving a balance of £1,218,918 for the Mexican government. This sum was delivered "partly in money, and partly in armament, vessels and military clothing". The interest payments not being properly met, for the approximately £2,360,000 received from the two loans, in 1837 there was owing to the English bondholders the sum of £9,247,944.[61]

Turning anew to the political situation, it may be said that, by careful manipulations in the congress, the Federalists secured a declaration in favor of a federal republic in preference to a centralized government.[62] A call was at once issued for a convention to draw up a constitution.

When the constituent congress met on November 7, 1823, the Federalists had a majority under the leadership of a clergyman, Miguel Ramos Arispe. The Centralists were led by Father Mier. The Freemasons had lost the control they had had in the preceding

[60] Manuel Payno y Flores, *Mexico and Her Financial Questions,* pp. 5-6.

[61] *Ibid.,* pp. 7-9. Arrangoiz, II. 153-154.

[62] Priestley, *Mexican Nation,* p. 260.

body. The Federalists, carried away by the success
and prosperity of the United States as a federal republic, did not realize that in the northern neighbor's
territory the union of the thirteen States was one that
had arisen out of decentralization, whereas in Mexico
the reverse was true; decentralization was to follow
unity. A federal republic in Mexico would mean the
artificial division of a unit into a number of more or
less unrelated parts, with a consequent weakening, at
least for a time, of the whole.[63] Incidentally, the
weakening was also taking place at a time when the
Mexican people could ill afford it. The constitution of
1824 provided, nevertheless: "The nation adopts the
representative popular federal form for its government."[64] Moreover, as noted above, the leaders of
both groups were clergymen, hence one might expect
to find: "The religion of the Mexican nation is and
will be perpetually the apostolic Roman Catholic. The
nation will protect it by wise and just laws and will
prohibit the exercise of any other."[65] The Inquisition,
however, was abolished.

True, the idea of a federal republic was in itself
a step in the direction of liberalism, when compared
with the ideas of those who were in favor of a centralized government. But, outside of this, unless the
guarantee of the freedom of the press is considered
—a guarantee habitually violated—there were no particularly radical features in the new instrument. In

[63] Jesús Agras, *Reflecciones sobre la Naturaleza y Orígen de los
Males y Trastornos,* p. 16.
[64] Arrangoiz, II. 163.
[65] *Ibid.*

fact, a property qualification of eight thousand *pesos,* or an income of one thousand, was imposed for membership in the lower house. Possibly the chief gain for the democrats lay in the fact that the constitution recognized so freely that of the United States as an ideal to be striven for.[66]

[66] For details as to the remarkable similarity between this document and the Constitution of the United States see Priestley, *Mexican Nation,* p. 259 ff., for a brief account, and Bancroft, V. 18, note.

CHAPTER III

THE RISE OF THE CONSERVATIVES

In the presidential election, Guadalupe Victoria,[1] the candidate of the Federalists, secured a majority of the votes cast by the seventeen states.[2] Neither Nicolás Bravo nor Vicente Guerrero secured a majority of those cast for the vice-presidency, and the choice was left to the congress. This body elected Bravo, the candidate of the Centralists, thus giving the nation a president and vice-president of rival parties. The new officers were to have held office for four years, beginning April 1, 1825. However, according to the decree of the congress, their term of office dated from the preceding October 10.

On the whole, the new administration started off auspiciously. All districts recognized the executive and seemed to have confidence in him. In reality, this was the lull before a storm. One of the mistakes of Victoria was his attempt to act the part of a neutral

[1] Guadalupe Victoria was christened Juan Felix Fernández, but changed his name during the revolution, in honor of the virgin patroness of Mexico and to commemorate a victory over Spain. Bancroft says he was from Durango, "an honest, unassuming citizen, amiable and kindhearted, of undoubted courage, and a true lover of freedom." The fact that he was very irregular in regard to his meals, frequently going twenty-four or even thirty-six hours without food, gave his opponents a chance to characterize him as a wild beast that would gorge itself and then abstain for a time. Those who knew him always insisted that he ate little and was never a gourmand.

[2] In this connection it is interesting to note that the salary of the president was fixed at thirty-six thousand *pesos* and that of the vice-president at ten thousand. Bancroft, IV. 17.

between advisers of rival political parties.[3] Of these groups, perhaps the most prominent were the Scottish-Rite Masons, composed of conservatives and monarchists of various types, and the York-Rite Masons (*Yorkinos*), composed of liberals and democrats and including the chief creoles and *mestizos*.[4]

Thus the Masonic question was again launched into the arena, and this time with far more serious consequences. To appreciate the alignment of the two Masonic groups, a brief description of the origin of the York lodges in the country is in order:

In the year 1825 Don José María Alpuche é Infante, curate of a parish in the State of Tabasco, and at the time senator for the same State, conceived the idea of organizing the York Rite in Mexico, an idea which was aided by Don Ignacio Esteva, Minister of the Treasury, Don Miguel Ramos Arispe, canon of the cathedral of Puebla and first assistant (*Oficial Mayor*) of the Minister of Justice, Colonel José Antonio Mejía and other persons, the President of the Republic, General Guadalupe Victoria entering into the project. Five symbolical lodges were at once formed, and, after they were established, Mr. Poinsett, Minister Plenipotentiary of the United States in Mexico, was asked if they might secure through his friends the regulatory letters or patents. Supporting this petition and receiving the commission to install the Grand Lodge, was the only intervention that this person had in the Rite, for which he has been so much and so unjustly denounced.[5]

Their opponents agree with most of this account, except that, as already indicated, they consider the

---

[3] This was a common monarchical idea. While Washington was serving his first term as president of the United States he tried the same plan by placing Hamilton and Jefferson in his cabinet.

[4] Priestley, *Mexican Nation*, p. 265.

[5] Mateos, *op. cit.*, p. 16.

United States Minister, J. R. Poinsett, to have been the chief instigator of the movement. According to them:

Poinsett secured aid through the imbecile Victoria, who adopted his project; Zavala [because of whose later career his name has become that of a hero in Texas but anathema in his native land]; Alpuche, curate of Cunduacán and senator; the canon, Ramos Arispe, and other persons of sad memory.

Poinsett had arrived in Mexico in the time of Iturbide, who, informed who the Anglo-American was, made him leave the country.[6]

In the same group were Santa Anna and others of the rising young men of the day.[7] The rapid increase of this party (the *Yorkinos*) soon gave them a decidedly larger following than that of the *Escoceses*. Beyond doubt, one reason for this strength was the fact that the Spaniards, as distinguished from the *creoles,* were aligned with the former group.[8]

On the other hand, one of the outstanding leaders of the *Escoceses* was the Vice-President of the republic, Nicolás Bravo.[9] The members of that body soon

[6] Arrangoiz, II. 173-174.

[7] Mayer, *op. cit.*, I. 311-312.

[8] Mateos, *op. cit.*, p. 15.

[9] In the García Collection is a copy of Luís Pérez Verdía, *Compendio de la Historia de México.* In this work Genaro García, from whom the collection takes its name, interpolated his own ideas, apparently with the idea of a revision of the work. On pp. 370-371 is found the following (the phrases in parenthesis being the García interpolations):

"Bravo and the moderate party were the first to throw themselves into the lodges, establishing those of the Scottish Rite (origin of the Conservative Party) whose organ was the periodical *El Sol,* and following this unfortunate example the radical party, under the leadership of Guerrero, established, with the aid of the American Minister, the York Rite (organization of the Liberal party) founding *El Correo de la Federación.*"

realized that they were losing not only power and numbers but also that even more important factor, prestige. After a number of disturbances, Montaño, who was being used as a decoy by Bravo, announced his "Plan" on December 23, 1827, in the village of Otumba. It contained four points: the congress was to prohibit by law all secret societies; the President's ministers were to be dismissed; Poinsett was to be driven out of Mexico, and the constitution was to be rigidly enforced.[10] To a casual observer, the first provision may seem odd, but the reason is not hard to find. The President and his assistants, being *Yorkinos,* would be the first ones affected, and, the organization of the powerful enemy once destroyed, anything might happen in the rearrangement of affairs.

Bravo soon placed himself at the head of the insurgents, relying on the uprising, which he thought would sweep him into power. The government sent out Vicente Guerrero to meet the rebels. From the standpoint of bloodshed, one can hardly dignify the encounter which followed with the name of a battle. The two forces met at Tulancingo, thirty miles north of Mexico City, on January 7, 1828. In the skirmish, eight men were killed and six wounded.[11] The important fact was that General Bravo and his chief assistants were made prisoners.[12] This was the end of the *Escoceses* as an important political factor. Their downfall was so overwhelming and partook so much of

---

[10] Rives, *op. cit.,* I. 172-173; Bancroft, V. 37-40.

[11] This may be accounted for to a certain extent by the fact that the attack of Guerrero seems to have been delivered during a truce. Smith, *War With Mexico,* I. 38.

[12] Wilson, *op. cit.,* pp. 68-75.

the nature of *opéra bouffe* that, as a political party, they were little more than a laughing-stock in the future.

Such complete success proved a handicap for the *Yorkinos*, especially since it came just on the eve of the presidential election, then due. With no outside opposition to promote internal cohesion, the two chief men in the *Yorkino* party became candidates for the office. Both of these candidates had military support—a fatal thing in Mexico. One of them was the Minister of War under Victoria, Manuel Gómez Pedraza. Once a member of the *Escoceses,* he had joined in the great exodus to the *Yorkinos* when the latter came into prominence; also he had once been an officer in the old Spanish army. Before the election, he tried to build up a personal party with the support of such conservative *Yorkinos* as Victoria himself, Ramos Arispe, and Esteva.[13]

The second candidate was the logical one, the successful general who had overthrown the rival party in battle and who was grand master of the York lodges, Guerrero. Supporting him were to be found Alpuche, Zavala, and the United States minister, Poinsett. Popular feeling against the last two men soon reached such a pitch that, while Zavala was minister of the treasury, the legislatures of the good Church districts of Puebla and Michoacán asked that he be ousted from office and that Poinsett be forced to leave the country.[14] Under such conditions, the election took place on September 1. Gómez Pedraza secured ten out of the nine-

[13] Rives, *op. cit.,* I. 171.
[14] Zamacois, XI. 809.

teen state votes cast. At the same time, Anastasio Bustamante was elected vice-president.[15] In the congressional elections, the Guerrero party secured control of the Chamber of Deputies, in which all the members, in order to continue in office, had to stand for reëlection. In the Senate, where only half of the members were subjected to the popular will, the Gómez Pedraza supporters were still in the majority.[16]

With cries of fraud and violation of the wishes of the people, the standard of revolt was raised by the defeated party under the leadership of Santa Anna. Biased by a knowledge of his later acts, one wonders at this early alliance of Santa Anna with the more radical group in the liberal party. His actions about the time of the *Escoceses* debâcle had been very hazy,[17] but now, having espoused the winning side in the earlier contest, personal considerations probably drove him into opposition to Gómez Pedraza. The relations between the two were such that Gómez Pedraza a short time before had devoutly hoped that Santa Anna, then governor of Yucatán, would push forward with his proposed plan to capture Havana, saying that if the movement succeeded it would be a glorious one for

[15] These figures follow Priestley, *Mexican Nation*, p. 266. Arrangoiz, who was trying to make out a case for Gómez Pedraza, says that his vote was eleven out of eighteen. II. 185. In such a case, the original records not being available, it has been thought best to adopt the first figures given. The situation was doubtless a very complicated one. Alamán states: "In the disorder which there had been in the elections of the congresses and governors of the States, it was easy to find reasons to annul them, and thus it was done wherever it was suitable." *Op. cit.*, pp. 850-851. Specific references are then made to the cases of Vera Cruz, México, Jalisco, and Michoacán.

[16] V. J. Martínez, *Sinopsis, Histórica, Filosófica y Política*, pp. 141-142.

[17] See Bancroft, V. 38, for a discussion as to whether Santa Anna was concerned in the Plan of Montaño.

Mexico, while, if the leader perished in the attempt, Mexico would gain through the death of such a man.[18]

Santa Anna launched a *"pronunciamento"* (manifesto) September 11, 1828, insisting on the election of Guerrero. A majority of the Chamber of Deputies had already indicated that they favored the movement, but the Senate was the headquarters of the friends of Gómez Pedraza. Victoria took the field and defeated Santa Anna, only to have the latter win over his troops by shrewd promises. Immediately, there was a military revolt in the capital, which has become known by the name of the *Cuartelazo de la Acordada*. Gómez Pedraza, realizing that he could not hope to rule with such widespread opposition to his administration, left the country. The congress, now dominated by the friends of the successful leader, declared, on January 1, 1829, that, at the end of Victoria's term of office, Guerrero should be the president of the Republic with Anastasio Bustamante as vice-president.

During the same period, and more or less connected with the Masonic troubles, there was developing an interesting situation in the foreign affairs of the nation. The Mexican government had been making many attempts to secure recognition of its independence by Spain. Various schemes were suggested for bringing pressure to bear on the homeland for this purpose. One was to start a joint movement for liberty in both Spain and Mexico at the same time. It was thought that if Mexico would contribute one hundred and fifty to two hundred thousand *pesos* the project would succeed. Another plan was to proclaim the

[18] Martínez, *op. cit.*, pp. 146-147.

independence of Cuba, thus taking Spanish troops and attention from Mexico and allowing the latter country to carry on its own program.[19] The last plan met with a good deal of encouragement from the Mexican government. Victoria ordered a number of troops to Yucatán, that being the point nearest to Cuba, so that they would be handy for use. The internal conditions were such, however, that, in spite of the support of many of the leading *Yorkinos,* it was decided to be inadvisable to go on with an affair that would take so many troops away from home.[20]

Just at this point, the United States saw fit to give some advice to Mexico. To any observer, it was evident that Cuba was a point of immense strategic value, since it controlled the water approaches to Florida and Louisiana. Consequently, Henry Clay, then secretary of state, sent instructions to Poinsett declaring that the United States desired Cuba to remain in the hands of Spain and that, if a change of ownership was to be effected, the former country intended to be considered as a possible recipient.[21] Probably this warning was even more responsible for the change in the plans for the invasion of Cuba than was the internal condition in Mexico.

While the struggle between the Masonic factions in Mexico was in progress, *Yorkinos* of one kind or an-

[19] J. M. Torrijos and Juan Palera to M. E. Gorostiza, Mexican Minister at London and forwarded by him to Minister of Foreign Affairs in Mexico. Antonio de la Peña y Reyes, *Lúcas Alamán,* p. 33.

[20] Antonio de la Peña y Reyes, *La Diplomacia Mexicana,* in *Archivo Histórico Diplomático Mexicano,* Num. 1, p. 19.

[21] G. H. Stuart, *Latin America and the United States,* p. 142. It is in the same connection that Arrangoiz claims that this was really a movement on the part of the *Yorkinos* with the purpose of raising a Negro rebellion in Cuba to be aided by the Haitian blacks. II. 196.

other were in charge of the administration. Hence reforms were to be expected, especially in so far as the Church and the clergy were concerned.

Slowly the work of reform continued against the group of clerical privileges. The law of February 7, 1828, gave to the State of Chihuahua the building of the college of Jesuits which was located in its territory. On April 18 of the same year the *Desierto de los Carmelitas* was given to San Bartolo, Santa Rosa and San Bernabé, towns of the Federal District. On May 10, 1829 the sale of the temporalities *(bienes de temporalidades)* was ordered. This, together the property of monastic orders, the Hospitallers, Jesuits and the Inquisition which had been declared the property of the nation, ascended to 1,880,604 *pesos.*[22]

To be sure, several of these acts were purely local, but the results of such laws affecting ecclesiastical property were important. The movement was not an isolated one; with unrest from Chihuahua to the Federal District, the situation was becoming critical. Public opinion in general was being educated, so that, in the future, when such laws should be passed, they would no longer be met with popular outcry but would be more or less expected as a regular means of raising needed funds.

Writers have devoted much space to the relative strength and weakness of the Roman Catholic Church in Mexico before and after the Revolution. The number of the clergy, especially of the regulars, was undoubtedly reduced by 1825 when some would say that the number of ecclesiastics was only about two thirds as large as in 1800.[23]

[22] Bulnes, *op. cit.,* pp. 83-84.
[23] Rives, *op. cit.,* I. 68-69.

The suppression of the Inquisition had had some effect, but not so much as the driving out of the Jesuits and the consequent loss of their property; the forced contributions, which, whether enforced or not, had a very bad effect on the self-reliance of the clergy and on their prestige; and the aloofness with which many intelligent people now looked upon the ecclesiastics. Furthermore, during the Revolution and the period following, the Church made a great mistake in not keeping the clergy united on political issues. With the spectacle of clergymen leading the opposing military forces and bitterly denouncing each other on political issues, the people necessarily became disturbed, and their respect for the Church materially lessened.[24]   This should not be taken to mean that the Mexican nation was ready to throw off Catholicism. The mass of the people was temporarily bewildered, but as soon as the Church once more showed a united front, the rank and file were glad to fall into line, asking no questions and only too glad that the issue had been settled for them. On the other hand, many of the bolder spirits, such as Valentín Gómez Farías and his followers, once having been forced to face issues and think for themselves, continued to do so. It was these men that the Church would have done well to consider carefully. They, once aroused, would not be lulled again into fancied security.

Certain phases of the decline in the numbers of the clergy seem to have become exceedingly serious by the year 1830. The minister of justice and ecclesi-

[24] Otero, *op. cit.,* pp. 58-61.

astical affairs reported in 1831 that conditions were becoming worse and worse, so that even the larger churches were often unable to secure the necessary clergymen. The bishopric of Chiapas was in desperate circumstances, having had no bishop to preside over its affairs for nine years and being without many other ecclesiastics of high rank. The regular clergy were still declining in numbers, because few new men entered to take the place of the old ones. This was partly due to the expense attached to ordination outside of the republic, when most of the candidates were no longer from the upper classes but from the poor people of the country.[25] Though the decline continued for some years,[26] a reaction was actually setting in. Bishops were soon secured for the six dioceses of Michoacán, Puebla, Guadalajara, Durango, Chiapas, and Nuevo León.[27] The number of the secular clergy was increased, and the morale of the communities greatly improved with the active oversight of regular administrators.

Financially, the Church was increasingly prosperous in spite of the minor confiscations of property it had suffered. Just before the Revolution its property had been valued at sixty-five million *pesos,* but after the war its property was variously estimated at from one hundred and seventy-nine million *pesos* upwards. "So extensively were private properties mortgaged in favor of the church that it is said that there was hard-

[25] *Memoria del Ministro de Justicia y Negocios Eclesiásticos,* 1831, pp. 12-13.
[26] *Ibid.,* 1832, pp. 17-18.
[27] *Ibid.,* 15.

ly a big farm in the whole republic which was entirely free from some such incumbrance."[28]   The annual income of the clergy in 1829 also seems to have been quite satisfactory, if one can rely upon the figures in the report of the minister of justice and ecclesiastical affairs. In all probability this was an underestimate but included revenues derived from real estate, loans, investments and from special payments on a total capital amounting to more than 125,000,000 pesos.[29] [For a later and higher valuation see p. 250.] As yet the final betterment had not extended to the mission fields.[30] These had been neglected for so long that it was necessary to undertake a very active forward movement in the whole Church before such distant outposts could possibly be affected.

Due to the decline in the number of ecclesiastics while the quantity of Church property was increasing, there developed a condition of absentee landlordism, or the *latifundia* evil.[31]   Some would claim that even in prosperous times the Church authorities were not good business men and that their chief efforts were directed to the securing of rents and produce and not to the upbuilding of estates as such and for the benefit of the tenants.[32]   If this was ever true, it would be more particularly the case in Mexico in the last years of the decade from 1820 to 1830, when at one time, as

---

[28] McBride, *op. cit.*, p. 68.

[29] Otero, *op. cit.*, pp. 38-39.

[30] *Memoriá del Ministro de Justicia y Negocios Eclesiásticos*, 1832, p. 17.

[31] Parra, *op. cit.*, p. 71.

[32] Justo Sierra, *op. cit.*, II. 28.

was noted above, six bishoprics were without their proper executive officers.[33]

Regardless of whether hatred or dislike of the clergy was so great as some have represented, or applied only to a few of the leaders because of their having become embroiled in the political disturbances of the country,[34] the fact is, both the ecclesiastics and the army were attacked, and an association of the two denounced groups was formed in consequence.[35]

So long as the military acted as an instrument of the *Yorkinos* no one dared to speak either of their demoralization or lack of discipline; but scarcely had the army showed its inclination to resist the disorders of that same party, when there was raised in all parts an impassioned clamor asking its reform.[36]

Allied with these groups were the *hacendados,* private owners of large estates. They were all of the wealthy class; all had similar *fueros* and desired similar types of legislation for their benefit. Together,

---

[33] In the report of the minister of justice and ecclesiastical affairs for 1835 there is found on page 70 this summary of the convents of the nation:

Year	Men	Women	Girls	Servants	Difference Total
1829	1726	1905	820	1758	
1830	1688	1911	652	1714	
1832	1586	1847	696	1545	
1833	1449	1732	665	1474	
1834	1411	1448	627	1137	

Decrease of the last year over the first given:

	315	457	193	621	1586

The figures for 1831 were not given since the reports as rendered were not complete.

[34] Suárez y Navarro, *op. cit.,* II. 66-67.

[35] Molina Enríquez, *op. cit.,* p. 27.

[36] Suárez y Navarro, *op. cit.,* II. 66-67.

these elements made up the conservative party and, in general, opposed liberal measures whenever possible.[37]

As already observed, from the legal standpoint, there was little doubt that Gómez Pedraza was the duly elected president. The revolution, on the other hand, had had much popular support, and Zavala, the grand master of the York-Rite Lodge, was one of its leaders, to say nothing of Guerrero and his following. These leaders skilfuly fostered hatred of the Spaniards by the creoles and Indians.[38] Guerrero as president was to be expected to aid his old friends and give them the spoils of office. Perhaps, though, the most serious result of this succesful revolution was the fact that it established a precedent whereby a man or party, legally defeated at the polls, might feel justified in appealing to force to secure the presidential office.[39] When the leaders did not show a willingness to accept defeat in an election, the prospect ahead of Mexico was gloomy indeed so long as the people of that country insisted on an attempt to use a republican form of government.

By way of a reaction, there arose the beginnings of a political party, based chiefly on the principles of a legal republican administration. Its first purpose was the accomplishment of a negative act; i.e., the ousting of Guerrero. A conservative group, its membership was said to be composed "of the remnants of the *escoceses* and of all the respectable folks who had been among the *Yorkinos*", including representation of the

[37] McBride, *op. cit.*, pp. 41-42.
[38] Mayer, *op. cit.*, I. 314.
[39] Rives, *op. cit.*, I. 176-177.

clergy, the army, and the property owning class. They adopted the name of *hombres de bién*. At all events, they rapidly came together, or were thrown together, by the force of circumstances.[40] In the national government itself, furthermore, they had a member in the person of the Vice-President, Anastasio Bustamante.

On December 4, 1829, their plans were completed, and the Plan of Jalapa was announced by Bustamante. Its plea was for the reëstablishment of the constitution and of all laws violated by the assumption of power by Guerrero.[41] Among other prominent men who joined them was the later historian, Lúcas Alamán. The rebels rapidly secured control of the country, except for the region to the southward, whither Guerrero had fled and taken up his headquarters among friends. He was finally betrayed and delivered to his enemies. On February 14, 1831, he was shot.[42]

Before entirely dismissing the Guerrero régime, short and stormy as it was, there is one liberal act that remains to be noted. While no real slavery existed in the country, a few remnants of it were still to be found here and there. Guerrero, being invested with

[40] Alamán, *op. cit.*, V. 850-851; Zamacois, XI. 832; Arrangoiz, II. 198-199.

[41] Alamán, *op. cit.*, V. 847.

[42] Mateos, *op. cit.*, pp. 44-50; Pérez Verdía, *op. cit.*, p. 378. This incident has given to the Mexican people one of their strongest adjectives of disdain and contempt; *i.e.*, "picalugano". Francisco Picaluga, a Genoese captain, was the man who, pretending to be a friend of Guerrero, enticed him on board his boat. Then he delivered him to his enemies for fifty thousand *pesos*. (Zamacois, XI. 849-873, discusses the incident at length). The derivation of "picalugano" is obvious and carries the imputation of being a scoundrel and a "Judas". Suárez y Navarro, *op. cit.*, II. 45, note 3.

extraordinary powers, issued a decree at the insistence of Deputy Tornel forever abolishing all slavery in Mexico. This decree was signed September 15, 1829, and proclaimed the next day. Apparently the only demur came from Coahuila and Texas, where putting it into effect would have worked a real economic hardship upon the people. This decree, while as legal as were any of the acts of the government, was not enforced, for, on April 5, 1837, another law was passed to the same effect, except that it provided compensation to owners of slaves, the revolted Texans being denied this favor.[43]

The downfall of Guerrero marks the end of the Masons as outstanding political factors in Mexico. The *Escoceses* had been scattered, and the *Yorkinos* split. The *Rito Nacional Mexicano* was formed August 22, 1825, and spread fairly rapidly, till, in 1831 and 1832, it was seen to be absorbing many of the old *Yorkino* members.[44] However, it never became particularly prominent in politics. From time to time, its lodges formed convenient centres from which to issue propaganda, but when references are made to any of the Masons in the future it will be seen that they were allies of the liberal movement and were not the primary political leaders, having others to assist them.[45]

[43] Bancroft, V. 79-80.

[44] Mateos, *op. cit.,* pp. 44-50.

[45] Something of an exception occurred in 1856, when the liberals under Álvarez came into power, but this seems to have been due, in part, to coincidence. A sample of the attitude of certain groups may be seen in the following dialogue taken from an anti-masonic pamphlet dated 1861 and entitled *Algo de Masones,* by Villaseñor Cervantes:

Canuto. . . . what remedy is there against those clubs, societies or lodges?

With the incoming of the conservatives under Bustamante, the Church at once secured power, and organized attempts were made to stamp out all liberal and heretical ideas.   The government aided the clergy whenever possible by "concessions that virtually restored their former influence".[46]   A frequent argument, and one that was very effective in view of the conditions in Europe, was that the coming in of Protestantism meant the introduction of a riot of sects, each of which would follow its own whims or fancies and would try to enforce them on its neighbors.   The result, it was claimed, would be religious anarchy.[47] Tolerance of other faiths would mean:

Tecla.   The best is to flee from them.
Canuto.   And against those who attend them?
Tecla.   Good people, the Cross and Holy Water.
Canuto.   Well, what things do those abominable people hate?
Tecla.   Three: voluntary poverty, the state of chastity and a life of obedience [the three chief vows of the regular clergy].
Canuto.   Who are cowards in their opinion?
Tecla.   Those who do not lose their temper, or approach it.
Canuto.   And those philosophers, Masons, well-known folk and libertines, where ought they to be, and are they, proscribed?
Tecla.   In heaven, on earth and everywhere.
Canuto.   Blessed and praised be the Holy Sacrament.   Embrace me a thousand times, Madam Tecla.   You are a teacher, and most worthy of being one.   I am going home to write what you have so wisely taught me; I will not delay two days in seeing you so as to learn again, and then write again.

A further extract is this:

Canuto.   What sign do they [the philosophers and Masons] hate?
Tecla.   The Holy Cross.
Canuto.   Who is a fanatic in their eyes?
Tecla.   He who is chaste in words, works, and thought.
Canuto.   What do they commonly ignore?
Tecla.   The Creed, Commandments, prayers, and sacraments.
Canuto.   From whom do they flee?
Tecla.   From our Mother, the Holy Church, ruled by the Holy Spirit.

[46] Bancroft, V. 105.

[47] José María Guerrero, *Dictamen Teológico,* p. 25.

. . . the sacrileges and scandalous free love *(amance-bamientos)* of the leaders of the reform, who from time to time justify that sentence of St. Jerome, "heretics seldom love chastity", the eighty thousand public prostitutes which we were told were found in London alone four years ago; drunkenness, of which St. Augustine says that it is a *soft demon, a sweet poison* and that *he who is in such condition is not master of himself, he who admits it does not admit sin, for then all is sin,* the very frequent suicide, the last result of the great overthrow of customs, the—but when would we finish? . . . We would see the temples of the Living God desecrated, robbed, and burned; the virgins consecrated to the Lord outraged, persecuted, and violated . . . Sedition, disorder, cruelty, blood, and death are the terrible effects of Protestantism.[48]

According to this philippic, tolerance would bring with it promotion of schism, destruction of the ecclesiastical organization, the establishment of Protestantism, an admission to the ranks of Christianity of all sects who receive the revelation, acknowledgment that these sects also offer salvation, and the preference of Protestantism to Catholicism.[49]

Financially, the administration of the conservatives under Bustamante was both efficient and successful. The internal debt was reduced; arrangements were made to satisfy foreign creditors; the expenses of the government were provided for, and a neat surplus was accumulated, amounting to nearly a million *pesos,* over which the next administration could quarrel.[50] Such a record the liberals would have done well to follow when their turn came. Possibly this success was to be expected in a measure, since the conservatives

[48] José María Guerrero, *Dictamen Teológico,* pp. 49-52.
[49] *Ibid.,* pp. 3-4.
[50] Alamán, *op. cit.,* V. 852-853.

represented those groups most accustomed to handling financial matters.

Smuggling and highway robbery, which had almost become honorable professions, so widespread were they, were put down at the same time that the taxes were being collected.[51] In spite of this, or possibly in part because of it, the army was materially reduced in size. In 1808 there were 40,000 men under arms in the country; in 1820, 85,000; in 1823, 30,000; in 1827 (under General Victoria), there were 33,565 active troops and 25,870 reserves, but under Bustamante there was a total of only 25,540.[52]

But peaceful developments were not destined to proceed. Already party alignments were being made that came to spell disaster for those in power. A plan of the government to have the Church aid the state by contributing to its support proved to be a fatal mistake. Santa Anna was quick to seize the advantage and at once appeared as the champion of the Church and of the legally elected Gómez Pedraza. This was the man who had helped to seat Guerrero but who now claimed that the latter had no right to the office after all! This seemed to be pure opportunism; yet on Santa Anna's behalf it might be urged that, during this early part of his career, he consistently supported the man who appeared to stand for the most liberal principles.

The attack at once began to be massed against those bodies whose natural alliance was at last generally recognized. "The clergy and the army now became the prominent objects of attack, the destruction of

[51] *El Partido Conservador en México,* p. 20.

[52] Alamán, *op. cit.,* V. table facing p. 956; *supra,* p. 49.

their influence being regarded as a policy that would tend to secure future peace and permanency of free institutions."[53]

The prominence of certain places as headquarters for the liberals and for liberal propaganda now began to be noticeable. The commercial rivalry of the merchants of Mexico City and Vera Cruz, observed by writers even before the Revolution,[54] may have had something to do with the fact that Vera Cruz was a place so frequently relied upon by would-be rebels for assistance. Another possible factor was the obvious advantages which that port would reap as a result of greater trading privileges with foreign nations. For hundreds of years these privileges had been curtailed from the seat of government in the New World, Mexico City. In addition to the friction so generated, there was a slow growing apart of the two urban centres. Vera Cruz, a prominent port, had been subject to the more or less liberalizing influence arising from contact with foreign peoples and ideas. No matter how heavy the restrictions, at a port such as Vera Cruz, which was the chief one of the country, individual sailors from all over the world would come and leave their mark. With its inhabitants at least not strangers to new ideas and trade rivals of the capital, Vera Cruz proved an excellent place from which to launch a liberal program. In addition to the attitude of the people, the strategic value of the port was so great that it was well worth while for any

[53] Bancroft, V. 127.
[54] Humboldt, *op. cit.*, IV. 54-55.

revolutionary leader to attempt to secure control of the city.

The other chief centre of liberal movements during this period was the Zacatecas-Durango district. In 1810, out of 3479 *haciendas* in the country, only 108 and 155 were to be found in Zacatecas and Durango respectively, while, of the 6684 *ranchos,* they contained 438 and 184.[55] Of the 4682 *pueblos,* or towns, in the whole of Mexico, Zacatecas could boast of only twenty-eight; Durango, of 168.[56] When it is recalled that in 1803 the number of inhabitants per square mile was only about nine for Zacatecas and one and a half for Durango,[57] much is explained, the increase between that time and the revolution having been inconsiderable. The figures for Durango are somewhat misleading. In the southern section it was similar to Zacatecas, though its average population was much reduced because of the sparse settlement of the north. For years the people in both these states had been leading a hard and stern life. They had had to deal with one of the worst series of Indian wars that is to be found in Mexican history. These Indians were not the docile natives of the Mexican valley region, who quietly sank into a hopeless condition of peonage; they were a fiery warlike folk that virtually caused the settler to carry his gun in one hand while he worked

[55] McBride, *op. cit.,* pp. 63, 89-90. The terms *hacienda* and *rancho* as used here refer to land-holdings of a thousand *hectares* and above and to those of less than a thousand *hectares,* respectively. Of course this classification, as McBride points out, is subject to more or less variation from time to time. (A *hectare* is equal to 2.471 acres.)

[56] *Ibid.,* p. 131.

[57] Humboldt, *op. cit.,* I. 283-286.

with the other. When racial intermixture took place, a vigorous product resulted. Another fact to be considered is, that this region could not become a great agricultural district because of the lack of large tracts of arable land. The settlers who engaged in farming were necessarily small landowners, who tilled their own fields and were their own masters. Mining was one of the leading industries in many communities and resulted in the arrival of other vital spirits and vigorous characters. Writing before the period in which this part of the country started to play a part as a great liberal center, Humboldt said:

This struggle with the Indians, which has lasted for centuries, and the necessity in which the colonist, living in some lonely farm, or travelling through arid deserts, finds himself of perpetually watching after his own safety, and defending his flock, his home, his wife and his children against the incursions of wandering Indians; and, in short, that state of nature which subsists in the midst of the appearance of an ancient civilization, have all occurred to give to the character of the Inhabitants of the north of New Spain an energy and temperament peculiar to themselves. To these causes we must no doubt add the nature of the climate, which is temperate, and an eminently salubrious atmosphere, the necessity of labour in a soil by no means rich or fertile, and the total want of Indians and slaves who might be employed by the whites for the sake of giving themselves up to idleness and sloth. In the *Provincias Internas* the development of physical strength is favored by a life of singular activity, which is for the most part passed on horseback. This way of life is essentially necessary from the care demanded by the numerous flocks of horned cattle which roam about almost wild in the savannas. To this strength of a healthy and robust body we must add great strength of mind, and a happy disposition of the intellectual faculties. Those who preside over seminaries of education in the city of Mexico have long observed that the young people who have most distinguished themselves for their rapid progress in the exact sciences, were for the most part natives of the most northern provinces of New Spain.[58]

It should be borne in mind that Jalisco, in 1810, was the name of the district now known as the state of Guadalajara and that the statements made above applied in large measure to it also. The Masonic struggle was particularly bitter there. The character of the people would also appear to have been partly the cause and partly the result of the fact that under the Spanish régime education and all other privileges were there to be found at their maximum. "It is sufficient to say that the greater part of the events happening on Mexican soil, whether favorable or adverse to the republic, have all had their origin in Jalisco."[59] After July, 1832, it was under the dominance of bitter anti-Church radicals. In the south, the liberal movement was chiefly confined to districts very similar in character, as regards both country and people, to Zacatecas and Jalisco.

The Texas liberal movement should not be confused with the one in Mexico proper. The outstanding characteristic of the agitation in Texas was the fact that it was dominated by citizens or ex-citizens

[58] *Ibid.*, II. 241-242.

[59] Suárez y Navarro, *op. cit.*, II. 79-82. It is in references to this part of the country that the terms *chirrin* and *cucha* are found. *Chirrin* was the nickname of an uneducated man who attempted to play the *gran señor y literato*. The anti-Church party used the term in derision to designate their opponents. *Cucha* was the name of a coarse beggar who earned his living by entertaining the public with his mimicry and feigned weeping. The Church party chose him as typical of their opponents and so dubbed the latter *Cuchas*. *Ibid.*, II. 75, note.

of the United States. While the loss of the territory and the resulting war will necessarily be mentioned repeatedly, because of their effects on Mexico, still they can hardly be considered as a vital part of the democratic movement in that country. The Texans, chiefly immigrants from the north, may have affected that movement, but they could hardly be said to form a part of it, even though they did lend their support to it for a short time.

With these widespread centres of dissatisfaction coöperating for the time being, there is little wonder that the Gómez Pedraza forces were able to take over the government with little difficulty. The legality of the election and the skilful appeal to the Church were sufficient to secure adherents, even in such a strong pro-Church community as Puebla.[60] On the other hand, the liberals were plausibly saying:

In the introduction of all political and religious improvement prudence advises that one prepare, convince, persuade, and illuminate the mind, and then the outcome is certain; this is the pleasing hope that animates me and stimulates me to put forth my ideas concerning religious toleration, so that it may be established in future times, since the force of superstition and ignorance does not permit us to enter into the immediate enjoyment of the incalculable advantages which it produces.[61]

Some of the more radical were actually to be found in office, and there was no objection to the support of those who had offered on June 20, 1831, in the fourth congress of the state of Zacatecas, a prize of a gold medal and two thousand *pesos* to the author of the

[60] Zamacois, XI. 916.
[61] Vicente Rocafuerte, *Ensayo sobre Tolerancia Religiosa,* pp. 5-6.

best dissertation concerning the settlement of the questions pertaining to ecclesiastical fees and property.[62] The work that won the prize was by a Dr. Mora. Supported and advertised as it was, it was read throughout the nation and had a really great effect on the country. One of the men most concerned in the publication of this volume was Valentín Gómez Farías. He was in the legislature of Zacatecas and was in a certain sense responsible for the fact that, in 1831, when nearly all the nation was satisfied with the government then in power, the Jalisco and Zacatecas discontents could still find a rallying-point.[63]

When Gómez Pedraza assumed office as president, on December 24, 1832, for his short term of three months and seven days, everyone realized that this was little more than an *ad interim* appointment to bridge the gap till the liberals came into power under one of their own unquestioned leaders. Gómez Pedraza, at heart not a liberal, nevertheless delivered an inaugural address calculated to satisfy them. Among other liberal sentiments expressed by him was this: "But since the people recovered their rights of what have they to complain? Men speak and write freely

[62] Mendieta y Núñez, *El Problema Agrario,* p. 78, says: "In the dissertation the following questions were to be settled: 'If the civil authority is able, without exceeding its rights, to enact laws concerning the acquisition, administration, and investment, of all kinds of ecclesiastical rents and property; if it is able to fix all the expenses of religion and to assign the contributions with which to meet the said expenses; if having this power, it possesses it exclusively, or if its laws and provisions concerning these objects need the approval or consent of the ecclesiastical authority to be obligatory; and, finally, if it belongs exclusively to the civil power, ought it to belong to the States or to the General Congress'."

[63] Zamacois, XI. 885.

what they think; property is respected, jails are occupied by the real criminals, and the homes of citizens are sacred and inviolable."[64] His opponents insisted that such statements were for effect only and that even then he was scheming to build up a personal following.[65]

Meanwhile, the Texas situation was becoming ever more serious and was demanding the attention not only of the parties in Mexico but of the people of the United States and of certain countries in Europe. As early as December 26, 1829, there was an active trade being carried on between such points as Fayette, Missouri, and Santa Fé, New Mexico. One party of traders was reported as coming into Fayette with returns from an expedition to the amount of $248,000, their average profits having been one hundred per cent. That England and France were carefully watching this region was an open secret. The London *Times* as early as December, 1829, said:

Without going deep into a delicate subject, we will say that the United States have got far enough to the southward and westward on the gulph of Mexico, and that it is for the interest and safety of our colonies, to have Mexico rather than the United States for their neighbor. The province of Texas ought to remain Mexican, as it is, and not to be swallowed up, like the Floridas and the whole course of the Mississippi, by any grasping government.[66]

In 1833 the state of Chihuahua was recorded as having a population of about 145,000. When it was made a

---

[64] Suárez y Navarro, *op. cit.*, II. 41.

[65] *Ibid.*

[66] *Niles' Register*, XXXVII. 277 (December 26, 1829).

state, ten years before, its population was less than 113,000.[67] Much of this increase was in the part of the state known as Texas. Since the power of the Mexican missions had declined and the requirement that new settlers be Roman Catholics[68] was generally ignored, there were few if any of the bonds of race, language, religion, laws, customs, traditions, and similar essentials of nationality to bind the Texans to Mexico.

Of course the Mexicans knew that the Texans were not Catholics, and many were insisting that the country to the northward be settled under Mexican auspices and by citizens of their own country, since this might possibly save the northern region from absorption by the United States.[69] It was even pro-

[67] Suárez y Navarro, *op. cit.*, II. 73.

[68] Austin's interpretation of this restriction as given by Rives is: "I wish the settlers to remember", he said in a manifesto issued just after his return to Texas, "that the Roman Catholic is the religion of this nation. I have taken measures to have Father Miness, formerly of Nachitoches, appointed our curate; he is a good man and acquainted with the Americans. We must all be particular and respect the Catholic religion." Rives further comments that it is quite possible that not one of Austin's settlers was a Roman Catholic. In fact, according to a report of the Texas Veteran Association, of the earliest settlers: forty-one were natives of New England and the middle States; eight, of Louisiana; nineteen, of foreign countries; 107 of the Southern Atlantic States, and 137 of the Ohio and Mississippi valleys. *Op. cit.*, I. 142-143. For the official lifting of this restriction see Zamacois, XII. 58-59.

[69] During the period the United States maintained an official neutrality, which was, at least in part, offset by the normal desire for expansion of a healthy and aggressive people. This desire was spurred on by such articles as the following copied by *Niles' Register*. L. 123 (April 16, 1836), from the *Commercial Bulletin*:
"The land of Mexico is generally much superior to that of the United States. Almost all the productions of other climes grow there in rich luxuriance.
The produce of maize is wonderful. An acre has been known to yield 200 bushels, and some stems are twenty feet high with five or six large ears.

posed to enter into contracts for the entrance of emigrants from England. This would have introduced the hated Protestants, it is true, but the north would be developed and the advance of the United States checked, for these settlers would have no affiliations with the northern republic to qualify their allegiance to their adopted country.[70]

Practically all of the territory of Texas came under the head of public lands, or *terrenos baldíos*. Official acts after 1823 in regard to public lands are said to have been dominated by three factors: rewards to the military, concessions to foreigners, and the adjudication of public lands to the citizens of nearby towns. As early as August 18, 1824, certain definite restrictions were laid down to prevent the assembling of large estates on the frontier with the consequent *latifundia* evil. The same law forbade new inhabitants to allow their property to fall into mortmain.[71]   On April 6, 1830, the congress passed another law to foster colonization, especially to the northward. It provided that those Mexican or foreign families who wished public

Wheat grows well only on the table land, but there it commonly yields 25 for 1. In the irrigated lands of Mexico it has yielded 50 to 1, while in Europe only 10 or 12 to 1 is considered the average production, and the best lands in Kentucky yield only 22 for 1.

To produce 1,000,000 pounds of sugar, only 150 laborers are required, while 300 are requisite in Cuba and Louisiana.

The production of coffee is still easier in Mexico; 20 men can attend 200,000 trees, which on an average produce 500,000 pounds.

Cotton also, of a quality far superior to ours, can be purchased [?] in many parts of Mexico, in greater quantities by one-third, than can be obtained from the best lands in Louisiana.

The silver mines in Mexico are perhaps inexhaustible; 3,000,000,000 of silver have been drawn from them during 300 years past, averaging $10,000,000 per annum."

[70] Rocafuerte, *op. cit.*, pp. 62-69.

[71] Mendieta y Núñez, *op. cit.*, pp. 70-71.

land might be given it, and that Mexican families should be provided with funds on which to make the trip to their land, supplies (*manutención*) for a year, and tools.[72] In spite of this encouragement there seems to have been no great rush of Mexican settlers to the frontier. If this was to be considered as a counter move on the part of the conservatives in order to save the frontier, it must be regarded as a failure, for, by 1840, of approximately one hundred thousand people in Texas, about eighty thousand were from the United States.[73]

[72] *Ibid.*, pp. 71-72.

[73] For migration from the United States to Texas see *Niles' Register*, LVII, 337. (January 25, 1840). Article copied from *Galveston Gazette* of December 6, 1839.

CHAPTER IV

A PREMATURE LIBERAL MOVEMENT

Bustamante, in spite of all that he could do for the country, was not destined to remain in office for long. The liberals throughout the nation rose, and, in a short time, he was forced out of office.[1] Gómez Pedraza, as has been seen, also tried to adopt an attitude that would satisfy his supporters, consequently he chose associates of a liberal stamp. Among them was his minister of the treasury, Valentín Gómez Farías. The latter was born February 14, 1781,[2] as a member of the upper middle class, his father being a *pulque* merchant of some standing in Guadalajara. Though he studied for the medical profession, he appears to have had a leaning toward political preferment from his early days. In 1822 he was well started on such a career as deputy for Zacatecas. Soon he became quite prominent in the ranks of the liberals as one of their most important leaders and spokesmen, consistently denouncing the *Borbonistas* and the *Escoceses*.

The new position that he was called upon to fill was a hard one. The surplus funds left over from the Bustamante administration had been used up in the disorders of the day before he took office.[3] Not only

[1] *Supra*, pp. 73 ff.

[2] There is some debate on the point, though Zamacois asserts the birth certificate bore this date and the Christian name of José María Valentín. Zamacois, XII, 25n, note.

[3] *Ibid.*, pp. 13-14.

that, but he was hardly the man for the place. Even his opponents admit that he was scrupulously honest— no small compliment at that time[4]—nevertheless, he was more of a political theorist and idealist than a financier, and neither by training nor inclination a man to delve into the intricacies of refunding old loans, floating new ones, establishing a banking system, ousting grafters, and the like. While he did not correspond to either Jefferson or Hamilton in United States history, he resembled the former more than the latter. Liberty, equality, and similar general ideals appealed to him, but not the routine of the financier's office, unless he through this office could attack the entrenched enemies of his ideals, *i.e.*, the Church and the privileged classes.

A sample of the liberal demands familiar at the time is a list submitted by Lorenzo de Zavala, governor of Mexico. On July 31, 1833, Zavala wrote to the governor of the state of Nuevo León saying that he expected to resign his position so as to go as a delegate to the congress about to assemble. He urged that a convention should be held at Querétaro or Guanajuato to deal with the following questions: (1) preservation of the federal system; (2) popular elections; (3) absolute liberty of the press; (4) freedom of religion; (5) abolition of *fueros;* (6) reorganization of the army; (7) moving of the seat of government from Mexico City; (8) introduction of free trade throughout the union; (9) economies in salaries; and (10) a statement of the political rights of the people.[5]

[4] Arrangoiz, II. 214.

[5] Lorenzo de Zavala, governor of Mexico, to governor of Nuevo León, July 31, 1833. Gómez Farías Papers, García Collection.

It now began to appear that an ardent admirer of
Iturbide was not far wrong, when he said that the
overthrow of the Emperor really meant that the civil
government would no longer enforce the payment
of tithes by the people, that Church property would
no longer be safe, that monastic institutions would fall
to pieces, that education would be secularized, that the
Spaniards would be driven out, that missionaries would
be recalled, and that the whole Church system would
be weakened.[6] Such were the desires of the liberals,
except for the fact that they did not wish to destroy
the Church, since they were in nearly all cases pro-
fessing Roman Catholics themselves. In fact, they
were making active efforts to secure Roman Catholic
colonists for Texas and were actually able to send out
two lots of one hundred and thirty-three, and one hundred and seven military settlers (*presidiarios*) within
a year.[7]

As soon as the new congress took office, it proceeded to open the ballots of the state legislatures for
the election of a president and vice-president. Of the
eighteen votes cast by the states, Santa Anna received
sixteen for the presidency, while Gómez Farías secured eleven for the second office. Santa Anna was on
his estate, *Manga de Clavo* (Clove Spike), and could
not get to Mexico City by the date set for the inauguration. From April 1 to May 16 the Vice-President
acted as the chief executive of the nation.[8] This trick
of being absent was played so often by Santa Anna in

[6] Navarro y Rodrigo, *op. cit.*, pp. 198-199.

[7] *Memoria del Ministro de Justicia y Negocios Eclesiásticos*, 1833,
p. 8.

[8] Zamacois, XII. 42-43.

later years that many have said that he was never in
earnest as a liberal but was simply using his Vice-
President as a foil by causing him to start a progressive program and feel out public sentiment. Then, if
public opinion was in a hesitant or dangerous mood,
Santa Anna could appear and act accordingly. However, he had never yet held the position of chief executive, and, considering his passion for preferment, it
is hard to believe that he deliberately exercised so
much self-restraint in the face of such an overwhelming vote. At least one well known historian comes to the
conclusion that Santa Anna was well aware of the
sentiments of his Vice-President and that he left him
in charge because he agreed with him and felt that
matters would be safe in his hands.[9]   On April 13,
1833, he wrote to Gómez Farías and, in commenting
upon the necessity of caring for the public debt, said
that for the time being only such sums should be paid
as were absolutely necessary for the maintenance of
the good name of the nation. "Among which [sums]",
he continued, "I do not include the loans made in the
times of Bustamante and Musquiz." This may have
been for effect, but, taken at its face value, it does not
sound like the statement of a man who sympathized
with the conservatives.[10]

[9] Cf. Suárez y Navarro, *op. cit.,* II. 55.

[10] Antonio López de Santa Anna to Valentín Gómez Farías, April
13, 1833. Gómez Farías Papers.

The following letter may be cited in the same connection:

"Manga de Clavo, March 16, 1833.

Exmo. Sr. D. Valentín Gómez Farías

My dear sir and appreciated friend:

Your pleasing letter of the ninth inst. has just arrived, and, in fact,
I have seen the articles (*impresos*) of which you speak, and certainly

There is further evidence to indicate that the chief executive and his first assistant corresponded with each other with apparent frankness in June of this year and that they were in seeming harmony in not forcing the issue at that date. Santa Anna wrote to the Vice-President on June 3, 1833:

The editors of the *Demócrata* ought to be persuaded of the inconvenience which would result in the present circumstances of suspending discussions on ecclesiastical matters, which, as has been demonstrated, do not suit at this time.

Finally, in my opinion, the progress of free men ought to be just, prudent, tolerant, and always in accord with the laws so that the Radicals (*Serviles*) should be confounded, and the people should know the difference which exists between one and the other.

On the fifth of the month Gómez Farías answered:

I have recommended repeatedly to the editors of the periodicals that they do not agitate any question on religious issues; but one cannot stop them from answering the imputations of impiety with which you know the government is calumniated without ceasing.[11]

there is nothing to be surprised at from their too-well-known authors.

I am writing now to my friend, Sr. Pedraza, and to you I repeat that it is impossible for me to go up [to Mexico City], since having started a cure, as a result I am in a state where I cannot even put on my shoes, the effects of irritations and past events.

You, my good friend, can assume charge, taking it for granted that you will be the vice-president elect if the election should fall on me [.] nothing will [then] remain for the Mexicans to desire or for their liberties to fear. Count on our good friends the reliable Messrs. Pedraza, Parres etc.

Until I, in better health, have the pleasure of seeing you and placing myself at your disposal as your affectionate friend, Q. B. S. M. (who kisses your hand)."

(Signed) Anto. López de Santa Ana.

[11] Santa Anna to Gómez Farías, June 3, 1833; Gómez Farías to Santa Anna, June 5, 1833. Gómez Farías Papers.

While these extracts may sound conservative, one must not forget that the congress then in session was dominated by the radicals of the day. It had been elected by the country under the influence of a wave of liberal success and so formed what has been referred to as "the reddest Congress Mexico had had up to that time". It is stated that many of the delegates put on evening dress and gloves for the first time in their lives when they appeared at the formal opening of the congress.[12] It soon became known that the conservatives could expect little mercy, for at once the congress exiled fifty-one of its erstwhile opponents. After so much disorder in the country, it was not to be expected that the delegates would be the wisest and most tolerant of their party; certainly the contrary was the case now, and those in office were determined to crush their opponents while they had the chance.[13]

The leaders of the congress were men of considerable ability. Among them were such men as Andrés Quintana Roo, Juan Espinosa de los Monteros, Bernardo Couto, José de Jesus Huerta, Juan Rodríguez Puebla, Manuel Crescencio Rejón, and Dr. José María Luís Mora. These, Gómez Farías formed into a sort of private council to aid him with their advice and particularly with their prestige throughout the nation.[14] With their endorsement, his acts would be assured of a sympathetic hearing by all the people, or at least by all the liberals.

[12] Arrangoiz, II. 216.
[13] Zamacois, XII. 15.
[14] Suárez y Navarro, *op. cit.*, II. 59.

Some feared a merciless persecution of the Spaniards, but this would have demanded a steadily pursued policy and would have taken considerable time. Also Santa Anna at heart probably sympathized with them, because of his training and ambitions. Be that as it may, he stated on May 30, 1833, that other matters had been so pressing that he had been entirely unable to attend to this.[15]

The attack on the Church, on the other hand, was not long in materializing. On June 6, 1833, a warning was sent to the clergy which may be considered as the first peal of thunder of the approaching storm. On that day the Minister of Justice issued a circular advising them that they were not to deal with political affairs from the pulpit and were to restrict their preaching to the Roman Catholic religion only.[16] The movement rapidly gathered momentum, and on the nineteenth and twenty-fourth of October, laws were passed completely secularizing public education. In the future, this was to be a governmental function, even if the government was not prepared to exercise it. The University of Mexico was suppressed, on the ground that it was entirely dominated by the priests who composed its faculty, while all other colleges were made subject to a bureau known as the *Dirección de Instrucción Pública*.[17] Greek, heretofore not taught, and the modern languages were to be introduced. If native teachers could not be found,

[15] Santa Anna to Antonio Echeverria, May 30, 1833. Gómez Farías Papers.

[16] Mendieta y Núñez, *op. cit.*, pp. 77-78.

[17] Arrangoiz, II. 223.

foreigners were to be secured.[18] The opposition
aroused can easily be imagined.[19] The public good had
been injured, and the clergy and pro-Church party
were given splendid arguments, which they knew full
well how to use.

On the twenty-seventh of the same month, the congress came to the conclusion that the government
should no longer enforce the collection of Church tithes
and that these should be left strictly to the conscience
of the individual. The income from tithes had suffered
a distinct decrease since before the war for independence; for in the five year period from 1806 to 1810,
the income from this source amounted to 10,691,300
pesos, whereas in the five year period from 1829 to
1833 they brought in only 5,211,628 *pesos*.[20] The
Church was very much afraid that even this amount
would be seriously decreased if something drastic were
not done to block the proposed legislation or prevent it
from going into effect. Half of the tithes, to be sure,
was divided equally between the bishop and the ecclesiastical chapter; the other half was divided into nine
parts, of which two were given to the public treasury,
three to certain uses of the cathedral church, and the
rest distributed to the parishes, though it did not always

[18] *Niles' Register,* XLV. 410-411 (February 15, 1834).

[19] The chapel of the University was actually used as a *pulque* shop.
This would not create the impression in Mexico in 1833 that would have
been created in the United States by the opening of a saloon, even
before the days of the eighteenth amendment. But to open the chapel
for any kind of a business enterprise was of course considered an
insult to the Church. A brief summary of most of these laws may be
obtained from Alamán, *op. cit.,* V. 860-863.

[20] *Memoria del Ministro de Justicia y Negocios Eclesiásticos,* 1844,
appendix, table 2.

reach its theoretical destination.[21]   The fear that tithes
would not be voluntarily paid was well founded, because of the fact that they were a heavy burden on
the farmers, a class widely scattered and hence difficult to collect from.   They had been collected "in
kind" on the gross crop, not on the net produce. Under
such circumstances, the burden was almost unbearable
in poor crop years, when the farmer was not even
making expenses.   It was also claimed by the opponents of the Church that, with its superior marketing
facilities, it secured the best price and flooded the market so that the prices were ruined for the farmer
himself.[22]   To lay all of this blame on the Church was
unfair, for the small producers usually sold their produce as soon as the harvest permitted; if the market
was glutted, they shared in the blame.

The work of reform, once begun, went merrily on.
On November 3, the support for prebends (*provisión
de prebendas*), which had been provided for canoni-
cally, was formally abolished.   This step attacked more
especially the upper part of the Church system, with
which the congress had little or no sympathy.

On the sixth of the month, the congress struck still
deeper and passed a law allowing members of monastic orders to forswear their vows and reënter secular activities.   This act applied to both sexes, and, to a
strict Roman Catholic of the day, was a blow at the
very heart of the Church system.   For a young girl
who had taken vows as the "bride of Christ" to forswear those vows and enter into family life as a wife

[21] Parra, *op. cit.,* p. 56.
[22] *Ibid.*

and mother was not only indecent; it was repulsive and sacrilegious in the extreme.

By the laws of the seventeenth of December, 1833, and the twenty-second of April, 1834, furthermore, the patronage was taken from the Church. This right had been held by the Spanish king as long as the colonies remained in the hands of Spain. When Mexico revolted, however, it was maintained by the Church that this right reverted to it and could only be alienated by a specific papal grant to the Mexican government or to some other party.[23] It was emphatically denied that the right was inherent in the civil government and so passed from that of Spain to that of Mexico by virtue of a successful war for independence.

Another reform was the beginning of a more general secularization of Church property.[24] Not content with arousing opposition among small groups and in special sections, the gauntlet was now thrown down to the whole organization. As has been noted, the missions of the Church in California had been declining in efficiency for some time; now it was decreed that they should be formally secularized. The Indians were to be released from their servitude, the Pious Fund to be confiscated, and mission property in California was to be divided among the settlers and the natives. This affected some 23,025 people, divided as follows: men, 10,272; women, 7632; boys, 2623; girls, 2498.[25] It was hoped that this division of property, together with the other inducements offered, would help to fill

[23] *Memoria del Ministro de Justicia y Negocios Eclesiásticos,* 1835, p. 22.

[24] Alamán, *op. cit.,* V. 860-863.

[25] Mayer, *op. cit.,* II. 368-369.

California with settlers from Mexico. However, little seems to have come of it for some time.[26] As might have been expected, a considerable amount of the land confiscated fell into the hands of a few private individuals as official spoils and through speculation, one of the chief offenders in this respect being General José Figueroa, commanding officer of the district.[27]

This attempt to secularize Church property brought up the questions of the reasonableness and legality of the action. If, as was argued, property was a natural right, antedating the enactment of laws in Mexico, then the Church owned its holdings, since it had held property from the beginning. On the other hand, if such legislation was held to precede property rights, then the Church still owned its holdings, since it had acquired them in accordance with the laws of the land.[28] Possibly a more telling argument against the confiscation of the property was, that experience proved very little of the value of these possessions ever reached the treasury of the nation, certainly not enough to employ persons (as was now being proposed in this new situation) to take the place of those driven out.[29]

The repeated orders of the government[30] to the clergy to the effect that they must not preach on any political matters only added fuel to the flames. Occa-

[26] McBride, op. cit., p. 91.

[27] MSS copy of a protest addressed to the Minister of War, signed "Y. M. P.", dated June 3, 1835. Gómez Farías Papers.

[28] F. Castillo, Exposición que el Gobernador del Obispado de Oaxaca dirige al Supremo Gobierno . . ., p. 7.

[29] Ibid., pp. 10, 13-14.

[30] El Telégrafo, November 3, 1833.

sionally there was an indication that the Church was making concessions, either for the sake of policy or otherwise. For instance, some ecclesiastical corporations of the Federal District offered to make the government a loan of fifty thousand *pesos* per month for six months.[31] If this was voluntary, it was certainly the exception to the rule, for the general attitude was one of bitter opposition. In 1847, the Bishop of Michoacán frankly stated that the opposition of the Church to the state began in 1833, at the time when the latter refused to continue its financial support.[32] The position of the clergy was briefly put by the Bishop of Monterey, writing to the Governor of Tamaulipas: "To assert, then, that the arrangements for ecclesiastical revenues, and the assignment, in consequence, of a portion of them to the ministers of the Church, is a civil power, is not only beyond question but [is] clearly heretical."[33]

The effect of these attacks on the already weakened Church system can be more fully appreciated when it is realized how large was the number of parishes with *ad interim* appointment of priests. The report of the minister of justice and ecclesiastical affairs for 1833 shows that of 1007 parishes in the country, 781 were regularly filled (*servidas en propiedad*), while 226 were served by temporary appointment only (*en interinato*). As might be expected, in the bishoprics of Mexico, Puebla, Michoacán, and Oaxaca, containing 744 out of the total number of 1007 parishes,

---

[31] *Ibid.*, March 3, 1834.

[32] *Protesta del Illmo. Sr. Obispo y . . . Cabildo de Michoacán contra la lei de 11 de Enero de 1847*, p. 10.

[33] *El Mosquito Mexicano*, supplement, March 8, 1834.

there were only 120 provisional appointments, while
in the bishoprics of Nuevo León, Guadalajara, and
Durango, with 263 parishes, 106 were improperly
cared for.[34]

The bitterness aroused by the above decrees affected the clergy to such an extent that a number of them,
led by the Bishop of Puebla, denounced the government vigorously. A letter marked private (*reservada*)
addressed to the Vice-President on February 11, 1834,
indicates that the country folk[35] were very much disturbed over the situation.[36] The Bishop of Puebla became so prominent in the reactionary forces that he
had to leave the country. The order for his expulsion
stated that every provision was to be made for his
comfort, but care was also to be exercised that there
should be no disturbance or undue demonstration. To
insure this, his transfer to the port of embarkation
was not to take place till plenty of troops were on
hand to carry it out successfully.[37] Other priests were
also driven out of the country, especially those of
Spanish birth.[38]

To leave the impression that the whole country
supported the liberal movement and that only a few

[34] *Memoria del Ministro de Justicia y Negocios Eclesiásticos,* 1833,
table 3.

[35] The term used is *"los amilpas".* Amilpa means a corn-patch, hence
the meaning of the term is "corn-patch folk" and refers to the small-
farmer class.

[36] Francisco G. Pavón to Valentín Gómez Farías, February 11, 1834.
Gómez Farías Papers.

[37] MS of the order is in letter form, from Gómez Farías to Cosme
Furlong, dated March 29, 1834. This, together with an acknowledgment
of the order by Furlong, dated the next day, is to be found in the
Gómez Farías Papers.

[38] *Niles' Register,* XLV. 266 (December 21, 1833).

of the clergy were active for the conservatives would not be fair to either party. As a matter of fact, the masses of the people scarcely knew what the agitation was all about. The pleas of the liberals sounded well, and so some called themselves liberals. On the other hand, the habits of a lifetime were strong, especially when supported by such newspapers as *El Mono, La Verdad Desnuda,* and *La Antorcha.*[39]

The army, regularly an ally of the conservatives, came once more to their support, not only because of the determination of the Vice-President and of the congress to reduce the size of the army, but more especially because of the movement to take away the particular *fueros* heretofore enjoyed by both army and Church. As a visitor expressed it, "If the masses [in this case Congress was their spokesman] would prey upon the Church, it was the policy of the Church to support the army; if the people [congress] desired to destroy the army, it was the interest of the army to support a church which could control by conscience or bribe by money the miscalled representatives of the people."[40]

With the completion of the union of the two groups, there was sounded forth the battle cry of *"religión y fueros".*[41] After March, 1833, the masses of the people, because of interest or principle, slowly gathered about their old leaders, the military and the clergy.[42] One can hardly conceive of a much stranger and yet more accurate commentary on the condition of

[39] Suárez y Navarro, *op. cit.,* II. 44 and note.
[40] Mayer, *op. cit.,* II. 158-159.
[41] Zamacois, XII. 28-29; Arrangoiz, II. 220-221.
[42] Suárez y Navarro, *op. cit.,* II. 48.

Mexico than that of a mob of common folk, ignorant, illiterate, and the plaything of those who could play most successfully upon its passions, howling for more privileges to be granted to their masters and consequently for a longer period of tyrannical domination for themselves.

Liberty of the press having been granted as a matter of principle by the liberals as soon as they assumed control, there was no restraint on the inflammable material issued for public consumption.[43] All of the reforms, but especially this last, were broadly advertised and created quite an impression abroad.[44]

Just at this time the Texans chose to make their plea for separate statehood because of the widespread dissatisfaction arising from the joint-state arrangement by which they were united to Coahuila.[45] Idealists and radicals, as the congressmen may have been, they had no intention of allowing a group of immigrants to run their own affairs in the name of the Mexican government. The issue was very neatly dodged by recommending that the legislature of Coahuila and Texas handle the affair while they, the national congressmen, did nothing at all for Austin, the Texas representative, except to repeal the old law of April 6, 1830, which had forbidden further immigration from the United States into Texas.[46] Inciden-

[43] Suárez y Navarro, op. cit., II. pp. 44-45 and notes.

[44] Lorenzo de Zavala to Gómez Farías, January 3, 1834. Gómez Farías Papers.

[45] These national reforms were also reflected in acts of the individual States, such as that of Nuevo León which attempted to regulate parochial dues. See Un Cura de Michoacán, Tercera Impugnación a la Representación del Sr. . . . Ocampo, p. 21.

[46] Rives, op. cit., I. 224-225.

tally, it is probable that the chief reason for this repeal was a vigorous protest from Washington and not the desires of the Texans.

Anyone who is acquainted with the conditions in Mexico in 1833 and who reads over the reforms introduced stands amazed at the audacity of the plans just mentioned, all of which were actually accepted by the congress. Gómez Farías, with a working majority in both houses of the legislature and with the support of many of the state governors and legislatures, was responsible for most of the work.[47] He and his advisers, swept away by their enthusiasm, seemed to forget that a nation does not change in a few short months. "Nothing more courageous or ill-timed could have been attempted by a party only recently come into power."[48] The real liberals who could be relied upon for support in time of trouble were a small minority of the Mexican people, who were ready to break with the past.[49] On the other hand, with skilful leading, the masses of the people were slowly but surely induced to believe, more or less with one of the great conservatives of the day, that, "All the most arbitrary and unjust things that the most absolute oriental despot could imagine while in a state of insanity is what composed the collection of decrees of that legislature."[50]

As the tide began to turn, the position of the President, Santa Anna, became of more and more importance. While certain actions in his career up to this

[47] Suárez y Navarro, *op. cit.*, II. 69-70.
[48] Priestley, *Mexican Nation*, p. 270.
[49] Parra, *op. cit.*, p. 8.
[50] Alamán, *op. cit.*, V. 857.

time were none too clear, as has been seen, he had been fairly consistent in his support of liberal principles. If he did not approve, certainly he had made no particular effort to block the religious reforms that were being passed by the congress.[51] It is true that he was not acting as president during the whole of this period, but he most certainly was for a very considerable part of it. It would seem that he was just about neutral in the whole matter and was carefully watching the signs of the times. In order to do this the better, he retired repeatedly to his estate. As a result, Gómez Farías was in charge during the following periods: April 1, 1833-May 16, 1833; June 3, 1833-June 18, 1833;[52] July 5, 1833-October 27, 1833; and December 16, 1833-April 24, 1834.

By the last date the sentiment of the country had become crystallized, and further delay was unnecessary. The President's mind was made up, though a new leave of absence granted by the congress had not yet expired. He returned to the capital and took charge of the government. The Vice-President must have known with whom Santa Anna had been associating and should have known fairly well what his purposes were. If he possessed the knowledge he did not act upon it. Gómez Farías has been severely criticised for not seizing his chief and taking charge in his own

[51] Arrangoiz, II. 226.

[52] This short absence was while he set out ostensibly to overthrow some rebels. To all appearances, he was captured by his own men and forthwith, by them, offered a dictatorship. A rebellion in the capital at the same time was not successful. Santa Anna then escaped and returned to Mexico City. In spite of the opposition of Gómez Farías, the drastic *Ley del Caso* was passed, which exiled large numbers of the rebels.

name. However, he kept entirely within the law and turned the government over to Santa Anna quietly and without a stain of illegality or corruption on his record, even though such action meant the sacrifice of the immediate possibility of success of the liberal program. On the other hand, a friend of the Vice-President spoke of the situation thus:

> The clergy being greatly heartened by the defection of Sr. Santa Anna, the army being deceived by them, the Spaniards being hopeful of a change which would be favorable to them, and the ambition of the innumerable parasites which the revolution has produced being excited, there is formed a colossus of power which overthrows everything in accordance with its will.[53]

One of the first acts of the President was to abolish both houses of the congress. Then, by a series of executive decrees, he proceeded to overthrow the laws controlling ecclesiastical patronage, to restore the fugitive bishops to their seats, to lift the ban on those who had been banished, to reopen the University, and to enter on a full-fledged conservative régime.[54] These decrees were to be approved by a congress, which, it was announced, would assemble later.[55]

On May 23, 1834, the Plan of Cuernavaca was announced. This plan specified the planks of the conservative platform and called upon Santa Anna to put them into effect by acting virtually as a dictator till the constitution could be amended and a new congress

---

[53] Anonymous letter signed "He who visited you in Alpolleca (?)" to Gómez Farías, September 4, 1836. Gómez Farías Papers.

[54] Smith, *War With Mexico*, I. 46-47.

[55] Zamacois, XII. 45-46.

called into being.[56]   On May 2, the old congress, dominated by Santa Anna, had passed a law declaring that
"in him resided, by the will of the nation, all the extra-
constitutional powers necessary to make as many
changes in the constitution of 1824 as he should think
needful (*conveniente*) for the good of the nation, without the hindrances and delays (*trabas y moratorias*)
which that instrument prescribed."   He was limited
only by not being allowed to change the articles "which
establish the liberty and independence of the Republic, its religion, form of government, liberty of the
press, and the division of the supreme powers of the
Federation and the States."[57] On September 22, a new
congress formally announced the death of the old
bicameral system and assumed, as a single body, the
duties and rights of the old Senate and Chamber of
Deputies.[58]

Santa Anna, now on the crest of a wave of popularity, was considered to be the savior of the Church[59]
and of the conservatives in general.   The liberals, so

[56] Rives, *op. cit.*, I. 228.

[57] Arrangoiz, II. 229.

[58] *Ibid.*, II. 230-231.

[59] An evidence, chosen from many, is this bit of verse at the end of a
long song of thanks to be found in *Acción de Gracias del clero y pueblo
Mexicano al Todopoderoso por el triunfo de la religión*, by "M. B.", p. 3:
  ¡Oh Santa Anna! tú has sido en nuestro suelo,
Del cismatico [Farías and associates] el angel de esterminio [sic];
El cielo te corone de laureles
Inmarcesibles, en su patrio olimpo;
¡Con qué placer recordarán tu nombre
Los Hijos, con ardor de nuestros hijos!
Tus proesas [sic] en la historia quedarán
Escritas con perpetuos coloridos;
Y tú en el templo excelso de los héroes,
Ocuparás asiento distinguido,
Y eternamente en la mansión de Dios,
Escucharás angelicos himnos.

recently dominating the situation, were denounced on all sides as heretics and dangerous citizens. Gómez Farías was forced to leave the country with his entire family. This repudiation of the liberal leader was both national and local; for instance, the governor of Toluca issued a decree nullifying for that state certain acts of the old government and insuring the fact that this arch-fiend, as Gómez Farías was then considered, should not be recognized as vice-president, and even taking from him the title of *Benemérito del Estado,* granted in his days of prosperity.[60]

For some time Gómez Farías remained securely in hiding, and, on July 4, 1835, Barragán, the acting president, wrote to General Martín P. Cos, authorizing him to give the old Vice-President and his family safe con-

[60] The official decree is to be found in the *Boletín del Ejército Protector de la Religión y Fueros,* July 9, 1834. In the midst of all this vituperation and abuse it is peculiarly refreshing to find this letter from one of the outstanding conservatives of the day (the original MS is in the Gómez Farías Papers in the García Collection):

"At your home (*Casa de U.*) Mexico, September 7, 1834.

My respected friend and companion:

I know that you are on the point of going away, and I would do violence to my feelings if I did not bid you the farewell of an old friend[ship]. We have differed in our opinions, but not in our love for each other; we have both sought the happiness of the Nation although by different means, but we both have been patriots. I know also that you are going with your wife ill. Because of this and because you are going to a country where Nature shows herself harsh, especially in the winter season, I counsel you that you do not embark except in a large, safe boat with all of the accommodations possible in order to make more tolerable the trials of navigation.

Here I remain at your service because I have been your personal friend, and not that kind of a friend who has filled the term with meaningless phrases. In this sense command me as your appreciative friend who offers to your wife his humble respects and attentively kisses your hand.

Carlos Mª Bustamante.

Sr. D. Valentín Gómez Farías."

duct to any port they might choose, all towns in Texas being excepted.[61] The hatred of the people, once so thoroughly aroused, was not easily burned out, as is evident from the references in *El Mosquito Mexicano,* where he is referred to even after retiring from office as a wild beast in both cruelty and destruction.[62] It was said that he was in hiding in the west, where he was stirring up Indian raids and plotting with the rebels of Texas—in other words, acting the part of a most despicable traitor.[63] Shortly after this, he and his family were able to get away. On September 11, an editorial commented on the news that the ship on which the exiles had sailed was wrecked, but all lives saved. One of the Gómez Farías children was thrown into the water but was saved by a man on board. The editorial continued:

Oh, how much better it would have been that the father and not the child, should have passed through that shock and salt bath, so deserved by his malice and cruelties . . . But not by what has been said is it to be understood that we desire to amend the plan of the Omnipotent, whose incomprehensible wisdom, we, though confounded, respect.[64]

Another example of this bitter hatred of the liberals is a statement in the latter part of 1836 commenting upon the death of Lorenzo de Zavala: "what would we give that such a man should not have been born! But now that he does not exist, hallelujah!"[65]

[61] M. Barragán to Martín P. Cos, July 4, 1835. Gómez Farías Papers.
[62] *El Mosquito Mexicano,* January 30, 1835.
[63] *Ibid.,* July 21, 1835; May 31, 1836.
[64] *Ibid.,* September 11, 1835.
[65] *Ibid.,* December 23, 1836.

Of the four parties striving to elect delegates to the new congress called by the conservatives, that composed of the clergy and military would seem to have been the most skilful at maneuvering in a complicated field. They carried the elections in spite of the combined opposition of the old Federalists, the *Escoceses,* and the *Santanistas,* or partisans of Santa Anna. He himself had favored the *Escoceses,* so, when the result of the elections became known, the Dictator offered his resignation. It was not accepted, but he was given a temporary leave, while M. Barragán was selected to assume control during his absence.[66] It would seem, if appearances are to be trusted, that Barragán was a very different kind of temporary executive from Gómez Farías. In fact, he is generally said to have taken little responsibility and to have acted only after receiving advice from Santa Anna.[67]

In the south, in the village of Texaca, Juan Álvarez still proclaimed his faith in liberal principles and called upon the inhabitants to follow him. On the other hand, Canalizo, the governor of Querétaro, called upon his people to rally to the support of "the sacred religion, the venerable clergy, the well-beloved (*benemérito*) permanent army and the best and most worthy of the citizens" of the nation.[68] Álvarez was said to be fostering *sansculottism.* This, of course, was an attempt to condemn him with a foreign word and with all of the implications that such a word of French Revolutionary fame—or infamy—carried. It not only

[66] Bancroft, V. 143.
[67] *Ibid.;* Arrangoiz, II. 226.
[68] *El Mosquito Mexicano,* April 10, 1835.

called to mind the hated Frenchman, who had recently overrun the mother country, Spain, but also carried its implication to the conservatives with reference to the violence of the French Revolution, the destruction of orderly government, and the overthrow of the Roman Catholic Church itself.[69]

Sentiment in favor of a centralized government to take the place of the discredited federal system grew rapidly. The Plan of Toluca had expressed this desire and clarified it.[70] This "plan" was a typically conservative document calling for a union of the "sword and the cross"[71] such as would appeal to the ambitious Santa Anna and to those who loved pomp and ceremony. As the year 1836 drew to a close, a new constitution was published, December 30. This is generally referred to as The Seven Laws (*Las Siete*

[69] Santa Anna to Victoriano Morelos, September 21, 1837(?). Gómez Farías Papers.

The following is a view of the Federalists as seen by the Conservatives of the day, taken from *El Mosquito Mexicano*, July 21, 1835:
"*Pintura verdadera, aunque triste, del estado de la república, bajo el sistema federal, significada en el siguiente*

SONETO

Un conjunto de muchos abogados,
 Una reunion de empleados espantosa,
 La escuela de asuntos achacosa,
 Pero á este paso todos bien pagados:
Tanta oficialidad, como soldados,
 De estraños una suma escandalosa,
 Y nuestra pobre hacienda mas gravosa
 Con tantas sanguijuelas condenados.
He acquí, lector, el cuadro, aunque en embrion,
 De la suerte que hoy todos cabalmente
 Tristes lloramos en la federación,
Mientras que Filadelfia, felizmente
 es mas preponderante en su nacion
 Por ser á sus leyes consecuente.

[70] Mayer, *op. cit.,* I. 321.

[71] *Niles' Register,* XLVIII. 342 (July 18, 1835).

Leyes), from the number of laws that made it up. Law Number 1 specified the rights and duties of Mexican citizens and granted the franchise to adult males with an income of a hundred *pesos* per year, provided they were not disqualified for some other reason. Law Number 2 provided for a fourth branch of government to be known as the Supreme Conservative Power (*Supremo Poder Conservador*). It was to control the three regular branches and to be the especial guardian of the constitution. It was to be composed of five men, each forty years of age or more and with a minimum yearly income of three thousand *pesos*. But, like other theoretical bodies of the sort, it lacked the actual power needful to make its decisions effective.[72] Law Number 3 provided for a bicameral legislature, the senators to have at the time of their election an income of at least twenty-five hundred *pesos,* while the deputies were required to have fifteen hundred. The system of election to the senate was quite complicated, but practically resulted in a choice by the state assemblies. The deputies were elected by popular vote. Law Number 4 provided that the president should serve for an eight year term, be eligible for reëlection and be named as follows: The Chamber of Deputies was to select three candidates out of nine names submitted to them. Of these three the state legislatures were to choose one. His yearly income, as a qualification, had to be at least four thousand *pesos*. He was provided with a council, to be composed of thirteen members, two of whom were to represent the Church and two the army. These

[72] Zamacois, XII. 102-103.

councilmen were to be selected by the deputies from a list compiled by the president, which had, in turn, been chosen from a list selected by the senate. Law Number 5 provided a court system. On paper, at least, it appears to have been fairly free from interference on the part of the other branches. Law Number 6 abolished the old state governments provided in the constitution of 1824 and adopted the French system of division into departments. In each department there was to be an assembly to submit a list of names from which the president of the republic was to choose the governor. The town governments were also centralized. Law Number 7 provided for amendments.

As is so often the case, that which appeared to be wanted by all in theory was liked by few in practice. As one writer said:

This constitution failed to satisfy any of the parties. The progressionists saw retrogression in it. The clergy were displeased because certain principles had not been expunged, which were at a future day to bear a bitter fruit for them, causing the loss of their influence and property. The army could not find in the law any power, entirely dependent upon bayonets.[73]

A sop was thrown to the Texans in the shape of an offer to separate them from Coahuila and make them into a new department.[74] Under the old federal system, their chief demand had been for a separate organization, but to offer it to them under a centralized government was to grant the shadow with none of the substance. What good could a departmental status

[73] Bancroft, V. 146.
[74] Ibid., V. 145, note.

do them if all of the chief officers were to be selected
by Mexican officials in the capital?

An attempt was made to secure the support of
chieftains scattered through the country. These men
had strong local followings and could keep up guerrilla
warfare almost indefinitely. To suppress them all
would have been next to impossible. Adopting the
policy later so successfully used by Porfirio Díaz, the
new administration made many of these men national
officials and charged them with keeping the peace in
their own districts. The scheme seems to have worked
fairly well, and many localities heretofore difficult to
control were rapidly pacified in this way.[75]

As soon as the conservatives were in the saddle, a
most welcome type of recognition was extended to
Mexico. The pope, in 1837, for the first time recognized Mexico and sent over an *internuncio* as his representative. The papal funds were so low that an officer
of higher rank was out of the question, and the *internuncio* was only sent on the understanding that he was
to be comfortably supported by the Mexican government. This recognition was most gratefully received,
for it added much to the prestige of the conservatives
and gave them greatly needed moral support at a
time when all was not going well internally. The congressmen were frequently absent from their posts, and
for periods as long as a week at a time no votes could
be taken because of the lack of a quorum.[76] One is
tempted to suspect that the real cause of the absence
of so many members was that they felt that they were

[75] Bulnes, *op. cit.*, p. 393.
[76] *El Mosquito Mexicano*, February 10, 1837.

doing nothing anyway. The President was doing the real work, regardless of whether they were present or absent.

As the time for the election of 1837 drew on, it was seen that the chances for Santa Anna were quite slim. Two years earlier he was the hero of the nation, hailed not only by the Church and the army but also by the common people. In the meantime he had led the Mexican army into Texas to reconquer that troublesome region. The first part of his campaign was successful, but at the battle of San Jacinto the tables were turned completely. His army was soundly defeated and the General himself taken prisoner. Because of the atrocities committed during the campaign by the Mexicans under his command, his life was in serious danger. Houston, the Texan general, however, protected his prisoner and then secured from him a very satisfactory treaty—for the Texans. Santa Anna ordered his second in command to retreat at once. This was done. The treaty looked forward to a definite settlement in which not only was the independence of Texas recognized, but most of its boundary claims were presumably to be approved as well. Santa Anna, when released, went to Washington, and from there to Mexico, reaching home in the later part of 1837. Rumors and reports were already widespread throughout the country, containing more or less of the truth, as to his questionable conduct in connection with the treaty. These rumors killed his presidential aspirations for the time. Even those who were once his ardent supporters were now asking awkward questions.[77]

[77] *El Mosquito Mexicano,* March 3 [4], 1837; June 7, 1836.

Knowing the temper of the Mexican people thoroughly, he retired to his estate, claiming that he was a misjudged and mistreated patriot. Later, on March 9, he announced that he loved his country so sincerely that he felt impelled to withdraw from his beloved(?) retirement again to take the oath as a general to support the existing administration.

The chief candidate was Anastasio Bustamante, who had been exiled by the liberals and had always been a popular man. His exile had only served to make him more popular by adding an atmosphere of martyrdom to a name already well liked. When contrasted with Corro,[78] the acting president, he showed up so well that there was little opposition to him. Accordingly, he was elected to act as the executive for the term of eight years, taking office on April 19, 1837.[79]

---

[78] Barragán, who was very well liked and who was doing his best to handle a difficult situation, died while in office. The Chamber of Deputies met and chose José Justo Corro to take the office of acting president from February 27, 1836 to April 19, 1837. This was most unfortunate for the nation, as Corro was anything but a decisive character. He was timid, some say overly pious, and knew nothing of military affairs. A natural result was a steady decrease in the efficiency of the national government at the very time that a strong hand was particularly needed.

[79] Arrangoiz, II. 239.

CHAPTER V

BUSTAMANTE AS PRESIDENT

One of the first and most important problems faced by the new executive was the financial condition of the country. It had been going steadily from bad to worse through the years from 1833 to 1836. An illustration is furnished by the comparative expenses of the office of the minister of justice and ecclesiastical affairs. In 1833 it had received 20,170 *pesos,* but in 1835, with only one addition to the staff, the amount granted was 25,420 *pesos.*[1] Under a centralized republic, moreover, the national government had to assume, not only the debts of the old administration, but also those previously borne by the states. Then, due to the internal disorders and the Texan war, all funds that could possibly be raised went to the army, and for six months not a single civil employee was paid. In October, 1837, the entire ministry resigned in a body, for, as one writer expresses it, "nobody cared to support so heavy a load when there was no chance to steal or even to get paid."[2] It was reported that in Zacatecas the mines were closed, all business was at a standstill, and people begging for the actual necessities of life.[3]

Many schemes were used by which to raise funds. Whether because of pressure brought to bear or be-

---

[1] *Memoria del Ministro de Justicia y Negocios Eclesiásticos,* 1833, 1835.

[2] Smith, *War With Mexico,* I. 48.

[3] Cayno Murguia to Gómez Farías, August 26, 1837. Gómez Farías Papers.

cause of real interest in the government does not appear, but on March 3, 1834, the Minister of Justice and Ecclesiastical Affairs announced that certain "ecclesiastical corporations and pious establishments" of the Federal District had offered the government a voluntary loan of forty thousand or more *pesos* a month for six months.[4] This loan was gratefully accepted, but the record does not show that it was all paid. On December 4, 1835, also, a special tax of one per cent. of its valuation was placed on all city property, excepting only convents, institutions of public welfare, and those homes which were personally inhabited by the owner and whose value did not exceed five hundred *pesos*.[5]

The rates of interest paid by the government showed plainly that all investors considered loans to it in the light of a gamble. The bonds issued for a loan on April 10, 1835, to raise five hundred thousand *pesos* in specie, were sold at forty-five per cent. of their face value. Another loan, floated on the twenty-seventh of the same month, was for two hundred thousand *pesos* and bore an interest rate of not over four per cent. a month, the loan to run from four to six months. On November 4, a third loan for a million *pesos,* was made at four per cent. a month, for five months.[6] The congress also authorized the government to take over half the income of the departments, it being estimated that this would yield about four million *pesos* a year. Still the revenue was insufficient for running

---

[4] *El Telégrafo,* March 3, 1834.

[5] Decree to be found in *El Mosquito Mexicano,* December 4, 1835.

[6] Zamacois, XII. 67-68, 72.

expenses and for carrying on the war; so, on February 8, 1836, Congress authorized another loan of six hundred thousand *pesos,* to bear interest at three per cent. a month.[7] Among the taxes attempted was a forced annual contribution of three *pesos* on every one thousand *pesos* worth of rural property owned.[8] The possibilities of the personal type of forced loans were not overlooked, and an attempt was made to raise two million *pesos* in this fashion. The amount secured from any one individual was not to exceed one thousand *pesos,* and the certificates given to the contributors were to be redeemed by the government at the end of one year as satisfactory payment for any tax.[9]

Another complication in the financial system was the flooding of the country with copper money. From 1833 to 1837 so much of it was coined that the legal total amounted to more than five million *pesos.* In addition, much was smuggled into the nation in various forms,[10] to say nothing of the vast quantities of counterfeit money that were produced. Business was badly crippled thereby, for this, the money of the common people, was passing current at a discount of some fifty per cent.[11]

One of the bright spots in the financial history of 1837 was the real advance made in connection with the British debt. This was refunded into "active" and

[7] *Ibid.;* Arrangoiz, II. 231-233.

[8] *Niles' Register,* LI. 20 (September 10, 1836).

[9] *Ibid.,* L., 365 (July 30, 1836).

[10] Juan Tlascaltleca to Gómez Farías, August 17, 1833. Gómez Farías Papers.

[11] Arrangoiz, II. 249; also *El Mosquito Mexicano.* Nearly all through volume III (1836), there are references to these conditions.

"deferred" bonds at five per cent. and six per cent. respectively. The difference between the two was that the second type were to bear no interest for ten years, during which time they could be exchanged for public lands in Texas, Chihuahua, New Mexico, and California at the rate of about one and a quarter *pesos* per acre. The total face value of each of these two kinds of bonds was 46,239,720 *pesos*.[12] With France, however, financial and even political relations were by no means harmonious. Baron Deffaudis, the French Minister, was a very unfortunate choice for the position he was called upon to fill. He supported the most radical claims of his fellow countrymen against the Mexican government.   One of these claims gave the popular name to the so-called war that followed. A baker claimed sixty thousand *pesos* damages as a result of a local disturbance incident to the political unrest of the time. The sum was so preposterous that when trouble broke out over the claims in 1838 it was commonly referred to as the "Pastry-Cook War". The Mexicans had to accept any terms that they could secure, since they could not think of fighting France. It was agreed that the entire amount due should be six hundred thousand *pesos,* but when France tried to distribute this to its claimants, only four hundred thousand *pesos* could be disposed of.[13]

Turning now from financial to religious conditions at the beginning of Bustamante's administration, it is easily realized that the people would be restless after the much advertised reforms and attempted reforms of

---

[12] Payno, *Mexico and her Financial Questions,* p. 10.

[13] Pérez Verdía, *op. cit.,* p. 392; Zamacois, XII. 129-130, 151.

the preceding few years. One phase of the situation appeared in connection with the army chaplains. The Minister of Justice and Ecclesiastical Affairs reported in 1835 that chaplains were being paid such a small sum, twenty-nine *pesos* per month, that reasonably efficient men could not be procured. He recommended a salary increase to fifty *pesos* in order to secure better men and better service. This was done September 30, 1836, with the result that two years later the Minister could report an increase in the number of chaplains, though something of a shortage still existed.[14] The restlessness was increased by a steady propaganda, including such "pithy paragraphs" as the following, which were used to fill odd corners of the conservative newspapers: "MONKS. Philosophers and democrats hear the word *monk* with the same disgust, hatred, and rage as that with which all good men hear that of *democrat;* and perhaps this is the best praise that ever has been given to monks."[15] Sport was made even of the most sacred ideas of the Christian faith. For instance, in the theatre *de los Gallos,* a bitter satire on the incarnation and death of Christ was presented for the amusement and ribald jesting of the audience.[16]

The judicial system at such a time could do little to stabilize matters. With rapidly changing laws and a new executive every few months, the judges, never any too efficient, let matters take their course, provided the court fees and perquisites were not interfered with. Equality before the law was little more than a

[14] *Memoria del Ministro de Justicia y Negocios Eclesiásticos,* 1835, p. 30; 1838, pp. 28-29.

[15] *El Mosquito Mexicano,* September 8, 1835.

[16] *Ibid.,* February 14, 1837.

catchword, for he who had cash usually secured the judgment desired.[17]

It was under these conditions that Bustamante took office on April 19, 1837. As was to be expected, his first steps were conservative, until he could secure control of the situation. He was not destined to have much time in which to get his bearings, for at once the demands of the French Minister, backed by a French fleet, had to be considered.[18] Such an opportunity was just what the opponents of the new administration hoped for. Rebels in Tampico, together with dissatisfied local chieftains in other places, at once attacked the national government just when it had need of all of its resources. This attack was so successful that when the treaty with France was finally signed the rebels had captured and were holding the ports of Matamoros, Tampico, Tuxpán, and Soto la Marina. This was the end of their advance, however, for the government now focused its attention on them and by July 19, 1839, had recaptured the ports. The ship of state appeared to be fairly safe after having weathered two severe storms.[19]

In the meantime, Bustamante was dealing with the mother country and attempting to bring about a set-

[17] *Ibid.,* April 28, 1835.

[18] An example of the way in which the Church made capital of the events of the day is seen in the *Pastoral Letter of the Bishop of Puebla,* dated December 16, 1838, (pp. 1-2). In this the good Bishop maintained that the capture of Vera Cruz by the French, the high cost of living, and other troubles were visitations of the Almighty because of the irreligion of the Mexican people. This, he further said, was the result of reading books that denounced the doctrines of an everlasting hell, the immortality of the soul, the sinfulness of gratifying the desires of the flesh, etc.

[19] Zamacois, XII. 172-173, 179-180, 193.

tlement with it. While advancing money from his private funds to pay the army and maintain its loyalty, he carried through the negotiations to a successful conclusion. Spain officially recognized the independence of its revolted colony, Mexico, in the early part of 1837.[20]

In spite of these successes at home and abroad, discontent was widespread and based on fundamental differences between the conservatives and liberals. The feeling of dissatisfaction was seen on all sides and expressed itself in various ways. Revolutions which proved abortive were undertaken in Puebla by José de Jesus González; in Sonora, by General José Urrea; and in Michoacán, by Gordiano Guzmán, to mention only three of the many attempted.[21] Valentín Gómez Farías, though in New Orleans, was kept posted and was assured in November, 1837, that affairs were just about ripe for a change and that he should return to Mexico to take charge of the movement to bring it about.[22] In this connection, a letter of Juan N. Cumplido from Guadalajara states in part:

You should know that here as everywhere, in spite of the misfortunes which we have suffered, there are many and well disposed friends, who always hope for a system of government under which some day we can be happy. The lack of communications . . . is that which has made many apathetic, for they never take their eyes from their immediate surroundings

[20] Bancroft, V. 181.

[21] Zamacois, XII. 121-122.

[22] Juan ———— to Gómez Farías. Several other letters written about November 1837 while Gómez Farías was in New Orleans are also available. Gómez Farías Papers.

(del centro), and the simple reading of newspapers never replenishes their hopes.[23]

Not all the discontented elements at once resorted to plots by which to overthrow those in power. Some lawful measures were adopted. At least one petition, with eight hundred and fifty names attached, reads:

The undersigned protest before the whole Nation, and before Your Excellency that it is their will

1st, That the Constitution of the year '24 be reëstablished; a general congress, popularly elected, reforming it within a period of six months,

2nd, That all the citizens from the greatest to the least have a right to vote in the present reform.[24]

Serious complications arose also from the Texas question and from the condition in which Santa Anna had left matters there. Originally, the Texans had desired liberty but not independence. So ardent a patriot as Gómez Farías had written in November, 1835, from New Orleans: "it is false, most false, that they [the Texans] wish to dismember the Mexican territory."[25] With the change from a federal to a central republic, and the consequent change of the object for which the Texans were fighting from liberty to independence, the breach was seen to be irreparable. Bustamante realized that Texas could be reconquered only by a fully equipped army and at enormous ex-

[23] Juan N. Cumplido to Gómez Farías, July 12, 1838. Gómez Farías Papers.

[24] This petition is to be found in the Gómez Farías Papers. It should be noted that the exact wording of the first article of the petition varies slightly from sheet to sheet, though in no case does the meaning differ materially. Many of the sheets are dated December 2, 1838.

[25] Valentín Gómez Farías to General Estevan Moctesuma, November 7, 1835. Gómez Farías Papers.

pense. To admit the independence of Texas, however, was impossible, for such an action meant certain overthrow. Consequently, he did the next best thing and signed a treaty with the United States to develop trade and bring about more harmonious relations with it.[26] This indirect approach, he hoped, would have beneficial results.

Partly because of foreign complications, but especially as a result of the internal situation in Mexico itself, the Minister of Justice and Ecclesiastical Affairs, after commenting on the educational value of the press, came to the conclusion that the constant abuses of the freedom that had been accorded justified its abolition. This was not surprising, in view of the publication of scathing denunciations of the authorities, to say nothing of the fact that revolutions were actively being fostered thereby.[27] Restrictions were made more and more severe, until even private correspondence was not secure. One man wrote from Aguas Calientes: "Friend, because of the lack of newspapers we are in the dark; and desiring to know what is happening, I and other friends beg of you, if your troubles and business permit, that you tell me something of what is happening in an anonymous letter, so as to see what one ought to do."[28] On April 8, 1839, Santa Anna, who had just been made temporary executive, issued an order that all writers or other persons who disturbed the public peace should be arrested "without distinction of

[26] *Mexico; the Country, History and People*, pp. 182-184.

[27] *Memoria del Ministro de Justicia y Negocios Eclesiásticos*, 1838, p. 12.

[28] Cayetano Guerrero to Gómez Farías, May 5, 1839. Gómez Farías Papers.

class or *fuero*".[29]   Such papers as were not suppressed existed in daily fear of what the morrow might bring forth.[30]

While there is no doubt that the state during this period was friendly to the Church and was allowing it to recoup its losses of 1833-1834, still there was no attempt to get the government to collect tithes, as had originally been done as a matter of course.[31]   One more reform had become permanent. Also it would seem that the clergy did not place unbounded confidence even in this government; for, according to a United States correspondent writing in the early part of 1838, the clergy were opposed to granting the executive extraordinary power. Opposition, the writer continued, was based on a fear that the president, once having such power, would use it for the confiscation of Church property to pay the expenses of the upkeep of the army and the prosecution of the Texan war.[32]

It was just at this time that Santa Anna appeared on the scene again. Bustamante wished to march against the rebels at Tampico. Morán, the president of the council, was sick and could not take charge of affairs. Hence, with the approval of the Council and the Chamber of Deputies, Santa Anna stepped in as temporary executive, February 18, 1839. As usual, he did not stay in power very long, but retired to attend to his private affairs, July 10, 1839, leaving the office in the hands of General Nicolás Bravo. At the end of

[29] Zamacois, XII. 183-184.

[30] *El Mosquito Mexicano,* January 31, 1840.

[31] *Memoria del Ministro de Justicia y Negocios Eclesiásticos,* 1838, p. 27.

[32] *Niles' Register,* LIV. 226 (June 9, 1838).

nine days President Bustamante was back and had assumed office once more.[33] During this temporary incumbency, Santa Anna once more endeared himself to the Mexican people. In the defense of Vera Cruz against the French he had lost a leg and was still suffering from the wound. Hearing that the rebels were approaching Puebla, he secured a permit from the council to go to that city, even though he had to be carried there in a litter. In spite of this, he reached the city just in time to defeat the rebels in a sharp engagement.[34] This was enough to make him a hero again in the eyes of the masses, who were rapidly forgetting his debâcle in Texas.[35]

One would expect that, by the end of 1839, with the collapse of these internal disturbances, the conservatives under Bustamante might have counted on a period of comparative peace. On the contrary, one of the most vigorous revolts that the liberals had engaged in up to that time was just about to be undertaken. Twenty-nine of the leading liberals of the day, including Valentín Gómez Farías, José Urrea, Manuel Andrade, Felipe Briones, Manuel Crescencio Rejón, Ignacio Arista, A. Zerecero, Antonio Fuentes, José María Ocampo, and Manuel Duran, signed a series of articles, one of which states:

In the reforms which shall be made to the Constitution of twenty-four [1824] the following principles will be respected: 1st, the Roman Catholic Apostolic religion which will be protected by wise and just laws. 2nd, the representative, popular, federal form of government. 3rd, the division of powers. 4th,

[33] Zamacois, XII. 174, 192.
[34] *Ibid.*, XII. 184-186.
[35] Arrangoiz, II. 243.

political liberty of the press without previous censorship for either printing or publication of articles. 5th, the organization of a land and naval force which will form the army and navy of the Republic.[36]

They embody a carefully planned scheme, with Gómez Farías and Urrea as the ringleaders. The former had little ready cash for such an undertaking, for only a month earlier he had been trying to secure a loan of five hundred *pesos* from a friend.[37]

On the morning of July 15, General José Urrea seized the President in his palace. Then he "invited" Gómez Farías to join him. According to Urrea himself, they proposed to Bustamante that he remain in office, using the constitution of 1824, which the liberals were to reform, as the basis of his government.[38] This offer was refused. Shortly afterward, the President escaped from his captors and kept up the struggle,[39] aided by about thirty-eight hundred troops, among whom were one hundred and sixty lads from the military college.[40] The rebels were able to count on a few regulars and on such assistance as might be rendered by more or less disorganized bands of citizens.

The struggle, begun on July 15, lasted for twelve days. As will be remembered, the first principle laid down by the liberals was the protection of the Church. This their early actions bade fair to live up to. In a

[36] Found in Gómez Farías Papers.

[37] V. G. F. to Felipe Neri del Barrio, June 13, 1840. Gómez Farías Papers.

[38] José Urrea to Juan Ávarez, July 15, 1840. Gómez Farías Papers.

[39] Arrangoiz, II. 244-245.

[40] MS. report of Vincente Filísola to Minister of War and Marine, Juan N. Almonte, September 15, 1840, p. 38. Gómez Farías Papers.

personal letter to Gómez Farías, the Archbishop assured him that the Church had not been despoiled in any way and that it had not even been asked for funds. Furthermore, he said that the convents had been used very little, if at all, as strategic points by the soldiers after his requests to the contrary, and that the members of the clergy had been treated with all due respect.[41] Such a letter from the Archbishop to a liberal leader, and above all Gómez Farías, is worthy of note. However, an attempt on the part of that prelate to bring about peace failed.

The liberals found themselves steadily growing weaker. Santa Anna and other generals were hastening up with government troops. This was an ideal situation, enabling him again to pose as the savior of the nation while the Puebla episode was still fresh in the minds of the people. Both parties knew and feared this. Speculation as to his probable course was rife, as may be seen by a letter from one of the rebel leaders to Bustamante, answering his offer of peace terms:

You speak to us of the coming of Santa Anna: we have been told that he comes as a mediator; but even though it should not be so, do you not see that his arrival will complicate [the situation of] our opponents more? Do you believe that General Santa Anna will work for Sr. Valencia [the loyal general] or for Sr. Bustamante?"[42]

Obviously Santa Anna was considered so shifty that the rebels did not hesitate to make the suggestion that he might turn against them and might also choose the

[41] Manuel, Archbishop of Mexico, to Gómez Farías, July 22, 1840. Gómez Farías Papers.

[42] Gómez Farías and José Urrea to Carlos María Bustamante, July 25, 1840. Gómez Farías Papers.

man, Valencia, and ignore the master, Bustamante. This letter could easily be regarded as a bit of desperate propaganda, sent out by the rebels when they were facing disaster, were it not for the action of Bustamante, showing that he did not want an outside mediator, especially if Santa Anna were to play the rôle. In order to forestall this situation, very favorable terms were granted to the revolutionists on July 26. They were to be allowed to keep their property and even their positions under the government with amnesty for all past offenses. Fewer than five hundred men took advantage of the terms,[43] while the two leaders of the rebels, not appearing to place any too much faith in the promises of the government, went into hiding.

With the administration more or less discredited, an excellent opportunity was available for the monarchists to attempt to secure public favor once more. The man who crystallized the ideas of the group was Gutiérrez de Estrada, who had held numerous public offices and who was popular with the masses. Feeling that he could rely upon the property interests and on the old "Iturbidists", he published one or two very able pamphlets advocating monarchy. He claimed that he was a true republican at heart, but that a republic was not practicable for Mexico at that time.[44] He declared that the constitutions of both 1824 and 1836 contained grave faults, which could best be remedied by a new instrument[45] to be put into operation under a prince from a foreign country, who would not be

[43] Bancroft, V. 220-223.
[44] Gutiérrez Estrada, *Carta Dirigida al . . . Presidente de la República*, p. 90.
[45] *Ibid.*, pp. 15-16.

handicapped by local jealousies and rivalries. The success of the United States as a republic was offset in his mind by the lack of success of the French republic and by the further thought that the Mexicans were more like the French than the Anglo-Saxons in temperament.[46] The pamphlets created a furor in the capital. Disapproval was so outspoken and approval so timid that the author was constrained to go into hiding for a time and later to escape from the country. This outburst might indicate that the Church and the army were not as strong as was commonly thought.[47] Possibly a more balanced conclusion is, that, due to the kaleidoscopic changes of the times and the poor system of communications, a united opinion did not have time to form on any one event before another situation served to bring about a new alignment of time-serving individuals in charge of the various detachments of the army. Without the support of the army, the clericals feared to go on with the movement, even though they approved of it.

For a second time the great leader of the liberals decided that he would do well to leave Mexico. He was entirely without funds and with a wife and three children to support; so his friends opened a subscription for him, showing a total of about sixty-four hundred *pesos* donated.[48] Part of this was given to him while in Mexico and the balance forwarded to the

[46] Gutiérrez Estrada, *Carta Dirigida al . . . Presidente de la República*, pp. 22-23, 37-40.

[47] *Ibid.*, pp. 51-52.

[48] Quite probably more than this amount was raised. In fact, *El Mosquito Mexicano*, September 1, commenting on the sailing of Gómez Farías, stated that the President had subscribed to the fund. On the available lists, however, the name of Bustamante does not appear.

United States. On June 5, 1841, he wrote that he was leaving three days later from New York for Yucatán.[49] Again the reason given was lack of funds, though this time his opponents might be inclined to doubt its validity, since the Yucatecs had just drawn up a new constitution and were actively threatening to withdraw from Mexico if their demands were not granted.[50] Futhermore, on July 22, 1841, the government of Tabasco offered its resources to Gómez Farías provided he would lead a revolt for them in favor of the constitution of 1824.[51]

The revolt in Mexico City safely disposed of, Bustamante found himself faced with three ambitious generals, Valencia, Pedraza, and Santa Anna, the first and last being inclined to coöperate. They found ready popular support because of the heavy taxation that was being enforced. Among the chief items of this were: an increased tax of fifteen per cent., after 1839, on the internal circulation of imports, an increase in the tax on real estate, and a direct tax of from one *real* to two *pesos* per person.[52] The army had not been any too well treated by Bustamante, so he found that the troops were ready to desert his cause to follow any popular general. On September 28, 1841, the Plan of Tacubaya was announced, by which a dictatorship was practically offered to Santa Anna. He was to select two deputies from each department. These, in

[49] Gómez Farías to Julio F. Uhink, June 5, 1841. Gómez Farías Papers.

[50] Bancroft, V. 242.

[51] Justo Santa Anna to Gómez Farías, July 22, 1841, a transcript (corrected) in Gómez Farías Papers; also Manuel Rejón to Gómez Farías, July 22, 1841, an uncorrected transcript found in same collection.

[52] Bancroft, V. 226-227.

turn, were to meet, select a provisional president, and issue a call for a convention to amend the constitution. Bustamante and Almonte, his minister of war, decided on a last desperate move. On the twenty-ninth they announced that they favored a federal system[53] and called upon the people to support them in reorganizing the government. Failing to realize the strength and popularity of their opponents, they fought on in vain for several days and subjected the City of Mexico once more to the horrors of civil war. Within a week the situation was seen to be hopeless, and the President withdrew his troops from the city. Arrangements were made for the revolting generals to assume control of affairs, their armies absorbing the few remaining troops of Bustamante. The latter left the country, "attended by the respect of all parties for his frank and kind-hearted character and his unselfish and honorable record as a public man". A sympathizer of the ex-President reported that when Santa Anna entered the city "not a solitary *viva* was heard. . . . Those who knew Bustamante best, . . . agree on one point; that the true motives of his conduct are to be found in his constant and earnest desire to spare human life."[54]

[53] Mme Calderón de la Barca, *op. cit.*, pp. 346-348.
[54] *Ibid.*

CHAPTER VI

SANTA ANNA IN POWER AND BEHIND THE SCENES

The inaugural address of Santa Anna as provisional president, delivered October 9, 1841, contained these words:

Placed for the third time in this elevated position, which is also a precipice, I state as a citizen, and swear as a soldier, that all my desires shall be directed to the enhancement of the grandeur of the nation, to the establishment of principles worthy of this time in which the human race is progressing.

Representatives of the people, my acknowledgment of your great favor is equal to the obligations which you place upon me on this day of reconciliation and of hope. I have spoken.[1]

Unfortunately, the President's acknowledgment of the favors of the army was destined early to take such concrete form that it came into severe conflict with the spirit of progressive administration indicated in the first paragraph quoted. A none too friendly observer wrote that colonels were made "by hundreds" and generals in "batches", eleven of the latter being created in the division of Paredes alone.[2]

[1] *El Mosquito Mexicano,* October 15, 1841.

[2] Mme Calderón de la Barca, *op. cit.,* p. 354. These promotions are all the more striking in view of the following written eight years before: "Most Excellent Sr. Dⁿ Valentín Gómez Farías

Arroyo S(L?)ario, July 27, 1833.

One of the principal causes of the discredit into which the undesired administration of Bustamante fell was the profusion with which it scattered promotions; all principles of justice were then ignored, and awards which only ought to be given to the truly meritorious and for positive services were lavishly bestowed upon the inept and often upon the infamous, who found themselves decorated with the insignia of

As soon as the new administration was in office, the attention of those interested in public affairs turned to the constitutional convention, which was to be called in accordance with the Plan of Tacubaya. In spite of all Santa Anna could do, the convention was dominated by federalists, whose ideas of government were by no means in harmony with those of the Provisional President. On both the second and third days of the session, members of the ministry were present and desired to take part in the deliberations. They were most positively informed that this was impossible.[3] As the congress proceeded with its work, the public was kept informed of all its acts and of the proposals introduced as well as of many that were not. This being the case, the government had little difficulty in fostering revolutionary movements in various quarters as protests against those articles it disliked, thus creating an impression of almost unanimous popular disapproval of the congress.[4] Knowing the attitude of the executive, the newspapers had no hesitation in saying: "The Constitution of 1824 was bad; that of 1836 was worse, and

honor; but in order for such an award to be appreciated it is indispensable that he who obtains it can say with an honest face, *I do not owe it to favoritism or to intrigue.* Let us then be moderate, my friend. in the distributions of military promotions and honors; so that only those whom distinguished services recommend may receive them, and that fidelity may not be considered as merit . . . since it was only a duty, and a most sacred duty at that. Above all let us act just the contrary to the *picaluganos;* it is necessary to reduce the army and not to create more chiefs and officers, especially when there are more of these than of soldiers.

. . . .
(signed) Anto. López de Santa Ana."
Gómez Farías Papers.

[3] Zamacois, XII. 273-274.

[4] *Ibid.,* XII. 286-287. *El Mosquito Mexicano,* October 18, 1842.

that of 1843 is going to be the worst of all."[5]   Nor
was the excellent rallying cry of religion ignored.
"However much the delegates may wish to hide their
intentions", it was said, "that [religion] is the target
of their impiety or apostasy."   The congress had provided that liberty of the press was only to be restricted in case of a direct attack on religious teachings
or public morality.   This was held to mean that all
indirect attacks would be justifiable and permitted.[6]

As the month of December wore on, the deputies
realized that the congress was in serious danger of dissolution by the government.   Their deliberations, accordingly, took on a hectic appearance, and their plans
were rushed through; on some days ten and even twelve
articles were adopted.[7]   All of this was to no avail,
for on the nineteenth the deputies found the hall they
had been using closed by the orders of the government.[8]   Knowing that resistance was useless, they dis-
banded and went to their homes, protesting against the
treatment they had received.

Santa Anna had not remained at the seat of government for this whole period, for to have done so might
have endangered his popularity in certain sections.
He had left Bravo, the president of the council, in
nominal charge to carry on the contest with the congress, while he looked on from such a distance that no
blame could attach to him.   His absence lasted from
October 26, 1842, to March 5, 1843.   As soon as the

[5] *El Mosquito Mexicano*, December 6, 1842.
[6] *Ibid.*, December 13, 1842.
[7] Zamacois, XII. 285.
[8] *Ibid.*, XII. 287-288.

delegates had gone to their homes, Bravo called together an "Assembly of Notables" to take their places,
January 6, 1843. This body was composed of eighty
leading centralists, who could and would work in harmony with the administration. They worked rapidly,
knowing exactly what was wanted of them. By June
they were through, and on the thirteenth of that month
a new constitution was adopted with all due ceremony.[9] Under it the departments were highly centralized and controlled from Mexico City; the franchise depended on an income of not less than two hundred *pesos,* and deputies to departmental assemblies
were required to have an income of five hundred *pesos,*
while those to the upper and lower legislative branches
of the national government were required to have incomes of two thousand and twelve hundred *pesos,*
respectively. Though high ecclesiastical officers were
not to be allowed seats in the Chamber of Deputies,
the Roman Catholic Church was the only one allowed in the country. Furthermore, the *fueros* of the
Church, army, and other special bodies were con-
firmed.[10] "The new Constitution was, therefore, in
several respects more obnoxious and anti-liberal than
that of 1836."[11]

For the promulgation of the new instrument, Santa
Anna of course came out of his retirement. With
much *éclat* he appeared as master of ceremonies. The

[9] Bancroft cites this date as the twelfth of the month, *op. cit.,* V. 256.
Contemporary records and Priestley accept the later date. *Mexican
Nation,* p. 295.

[10] Rives, *op. cit.,* I. 462; Thompson, *op. cit.,* pp. 180-186; Arrangoiz,
II. 250-251, 255, and Noll, *op. cit.,* pp. 140, 141, 144-145.

[11] Bancroft, V. 257.

new council (*consejo de gobierno*) contained some
very prominent men, among them being Gabriel Valencia, J. M. Bocanegra, J. M. Tornel, C. M. Bustamante, and Manuel Crescencio Rejón.[12]   After remaining at the seat of government for a short time,
the Executive once more retired to *Manga de Clavo,* his
country estate.   This time his departure was doubtless
due to the fact that the new congress was to choose the
permanent executive, and Santa Anna had no desire to
remain at the seat of government, where his popularity
might be discounted by all the petty irritations that
were constantly arising.   On his retirement, October
4, he left behind him his lieutenant, General Valentín
Canalizo, a man wholly devoted to him and little better
than a pawn in his hands.[13]

When the vote for president was announced, it
was seen that Santa Anna's schemes had been entirely
successful, for he had secured nineteen of the twenty-
one votes cast.   His opponents then tried to oust his
puppet, Canalizo, but again met with overwhelming
defeat.[14]   The best they could hope for now was that
the President would stay away from the capital as
long as possible.   In this they were not entirely disappointed, for he did not return till June 4, 1844, and
then remained for little more than three months, when
he again retired, leaving the faithful Canalizo in
charge.[15]   This absence was destined to be more event-
ful than the first, for the congress was bitterly hostile

[12] *El Mosquito Mexicano,* July 25, 1843.
[13] Arrangoiz, II. 257.
[14] Bancroft, V. 259.
[15] Arrangoiz, II. 260.

to Canalizo and his ministry. Resenting such implacable opposition, the temporary executive decided that it would be wise to adopt the dictatorial methods of Santa Anna and to do away with the obstacle. Accordingly, on November 29, Canalizo prorogued the congress.[16]

The opposition, which had meanwhile become outspoken throughout the nation, immediately started an active revolution with support in the capital itself.[17] In the northwest a serious movement was set on foot by Paredes. Here the initiative for the return to the Plan of Tacubaya was taken by the departmental assembly of Jalisco, quickly followed by the four departments of Zacatecas, Aguas Calientes, Sinaloa, and Sonora.[18] Santa Anna, in truth, had made the mistake of thinking himself invulnerable and of concluding that his name was an "open sesame", by the invocation of which he could realize all his desires and quell all opposition. His inordinate love of flattery probably contributed to this blindness on his part, for blindness it must have been when all over the country the most scathing denunciations were being published, many of which were so sure of popular approval that they were not even issued anonymously.[19] The most effective of these criticisms were of the short, incisive type that delighted the public. One such was a list of words entitled *Santa-Anna's Dictionary*, some extracts from which are:

[16] Arrangoiz, II. 261.
[17] *Ibid.*
[18] *Niles' Register*, LXVII. 273 (January 4, 1845).
[19] Cf. Smith, *op. cit.*, I. 54.

Army—A collection of automatons which are moved like the pieces on a chess-board at the will of the player. When they lack bread give them false finery and they are content. When they become uneasy, discipline them and they are silent.

Patriotism—The art of deceiving the public, giving it false facts *(sic)*.

Oath—A ridiculous formula which I am accustomed to go through with, and which I break daily.

Native Country *(Patria)*—A large area of land, of which I am able to dispose at my pleasure, as of my own house.

Mexicans—Poor devils whom I have deceived whenever it suited me, and whom I control by kicks.[20]

The Mexican love of a pun, furthermore, could not resist this rearrangement of the letters of the names of two of their outstanding men: *Iturbide,* rearranged into *Tu vir dei; Lópes de Santana* (a common spelling), rearranged into *Pelón de Satanas.*[21]

At this point, it is interesting to note the activities of Valentín Gómez Farías, who had been so prominent in the early movements and activities of the liberals. While in the United States, in virtual exile, he was kept fully informed of what was going on. Such information, if detected, would mean that the sender would probably face a firing squad. Several letters went through in code,[22] giving ample details. One of

[20] *Boletín de Noticias,* No. 9, December 29, 1844.

[21] "Pelón" means either a "bald-headed fellow" or a "block-head", either meaning giving the desired touch of humor and derision. *Boletín de Noticias,* No. 14, January 7, 1845.

[22] By a most fortunate chance a scrap of paper with the vowels, a, e, i, o, u, and beneath them a row of symbols, all in pencil, was in the bundle of letters containing this code material. This may have been the work of Sr. García, who collected the material, or it may have been in one of the original letters. By substitution of the symbols for the corresponding vowels it was found that, when decoded, the letters were in very good, though somewhat phonetic, Spanish. The sender seems to

them affords many sidelights on the life of a rebel
and on the existing conditions:

Mexico, thirty-first of August, eighteen hundred and forty-
four. friend never have the affairs of your country been in
such a condition as to-day; Santa Anna is obliged to leave the
capital, he is threatened with assassination from one moment
to the next; the troops which are in tacubaya are under arms
day and night, the cannon loaded, the horses saddled, and all
the troops in barracks. The destruction of the Congress is
rumored, but all the forces on which he [Santa Anna] relies
are going to rebel, no one can talk to him because he fears
everyone; within four days he is leaving for vera crus [his
estate near Vera Cruz], Senor herrera remains as president
for fifteen days while Canalizo comes from san Luis, and in
place of canalizo general arista [also in the plot] is going to
take command of the troops which are found in san luis potosi.
In short the revolution is going to break out at any moment,
certainly within two weeks . . . the people ask for you
and even individuals who were your enemies in the year thirty-
three have said that they recognize their mistake and confess
that you are the only man who is suitable to control [affairs].
Things are very warm and all that I write you now is heard
publicly on the streets, . . . and as I have stated not only
the people but also men who have been your enemies wish to
proclaim you; but I counsel you that you do not put faith in
your friends, especially in jauregui, because he is not a man of
good faith but a fool of the worst kind, very false and hypo-
critical as some day I will prove to you verbally. It is said
that some correspondence which you sent to olaguibel has been
captured and has reached the hands of Santa Ana [.] I would
regret exceedingly his securing any letter for me since there
have been those who have told me that I was in correspondence
with you. As a result I have manufactured *(finjido)* a letter

have been one Bernardo Othon, for at the end of one of his regular
letters to Gómez Farías there is a short postscript in the same code
and the same script.

as though it had been sent to me by you and I have showed it
to some so that Santa ana will order me to let him see it,
. . . Do not doubt that within two months you will find
yourself and all your family back in this country . . . but
do not forget what I tell you, do not put faith in your countrymen because they deceive one and only when I write can you
believe that the revolution has broken out, not before; and
then you can come within all confidence [.] all the houses [of
congress] are opposed to the man [Santa Anna] because the
minister of the treasury department has stolen *eleven* millions
of pesos, it is said with the knowledge of Santa ana, . . .
tomorrow I leave for Queretaro employed with Senor Zenteno
whom you know, send me the letters as I advised before, soon
we shall see each other, regards to all.[23]

A later code letter says in part:

I take my pen to let you know that general paredes has issued
a "pronunciamento" in guadalajara. cortazar in guanajuato,
and arista in san Luis Potosi; all against santa ana, demanding
his separation from the government.[24]

The adherents of the ousted congress supported
Herrera, chief of the council of state, for president
and coöperated with Paredes. Santa Anna rushed to
take the field, knowing that, with the liberals in the
northwest and those who supported the congress in the
central portion of the country, there was also Juan Álvarez in the south, one of the most successful and
consistent of all of the guerrilla chieftains of the
liberal cause.[25] But all magic power seemed to have

[23] The original of this is to be found in the Gómez Farías Papers.
[24] MS of this is likewise in the Gómez Farías Papers.
[25] *Boletín de Notícias,* No. 15, January 9, 1845. The conduct of
Juárez during this period has been the subject of much controversy.
Bulnes claims that he was a time-server and very unstable in his principles. *Op. cit.,* p. 133.

deserted the name of Santa Anna, and, after some minor battles around Mexico City and Puebla, he was captured and banished from the country. Many of the fickle populace as well as of the more thoughtful leaders demanded his execution,[26] but a policy of mercy prevailed. He went to Havana after delivering a heartrending farewell to the Mexican people from a man in "extreme age [he was fifty years old], mutilated and surrounded by a wife and innocent children," as he went to "bury himself, . . . seeking an exile among strangers".[27]

Due to complications arising with the United States as well as to the lessons learned in 1833, the liberals took no rash steps immediately. Most of their efforts were directed toward tax relief and the stoppage of leaks in the revenues. In fact, Gómez Farías, who was back in the country, seemed to be decidedly conciliatory to the Church.[28] Minister Slidell presented the claims of the United States so forcefully that, December 14, 1845, Paredes, with the undoubted encouragement if not the direct aid of Gómez Farías,[29] put forth a manifesto in San Luís Potosí against President Herrera, on the ground that he was planning to

[26] Arrangoiz, II. 262.

[27] Zamacois, XII. 383.

[28] Gómez Farías to Francisco de Paula Vázquez, May 28, 1845, and Joaquín Rangel to Gómez Farías, September 9, 1845. Gómez Farías Papers. It is true that a loan of 15,000,000 *pesos* from the Church was proposed, but it received little support and came to nothing.

[29] Gómez Farías to General Mariano Paredes, October 1845, marked "strictly personal" (*muy reservada*). On the letter Genaro García has noted that the body of the letter is in the writing of Benito Gómez Farías but that the name of Paredes is in that of Valetín himself. Gómez Farías Papers.

alienate Mexican territory. This argument appealed
to all Mexicans, rich or poor, conservative or liberal.
On the thirtieth of the same month, General Valencia
in Mexico City followed the lead of Paredes. Herrera
realized that opposition was hopeless and turned the
government over to the rebels.[30] For some time Paredes had been one of the most popular and successful
generals of the country. It was only natural that he
should be the next executive, chosen by the representatives when they met, presided over by the Archbishop,
on January 3, 1846.[31] Dominated by conservative
ideas, he established one of the most complete dictatorships that the country had ever experienced. At
once, he set himself vigorously to bring order out of
chaos in financial affairs and to guarantee the safety
of human life from the wellnigh omnipresent bandits
ravaging the country.[32] Though he was a stern ad-
ministrator and certainly ambitious, there is little doubt
that his personal honesty was entirely above re-
proach.[33] As soon as he became president, the monarchists took heart and prepared for the European
prince that he himself had ardently advocated and
that they had so long desired.[34]

While the government was striving to secure resources that were badly needed and to get a constituent congress to draw up a plan for the administra-

[30] Zamacois, XII. 398.
[31] *Ibid.,* XII. pp. 408-409.
[32] Bancroft, V. 293-294.
[33] *Boletín de Noticias,* No. 27, January 29, 1845.
[34] Bulnes, *op. cit.,* pp. 135-136; Pérez Verdía, p. 400; Manual Gon-
zalez Cosío to Gómez Farías, November 7, 1845. Gómez Farías Papers.

tion of the country, it became obvious to every one
that war with the United States was imminent. But
even this danger could not prevent Vera Cruz, Querétaro, and other sections, which were becoming more
and more pronounced in their federalist doctrines,[35]
from intriguing for the overthrow of an administration generally thought to be tending toward monarchy.

Through all of these plots and counter plots ran
the thought of war with the United States. Periodically, demands had arisen for money and men with
which to invade Texas.[36] New taxes were levied with
this as an excuse.[37] Gradually such persistent propaganda, which was aimed either directly or indirectly
at the United States, began to bear fruit. Having
talked about it for so long, the Mexican people really
began to think of the people of the United States as of
an inferior race. Hence, when the level-headed Juan
Álvarez wrote as follows, the people of Mexico were
far from agreeing with him:

So far as Texas is concerned, I do not expect to reincor-
porate it into the Republic [of Mexico] under any administration or institutions, and only powerful efforts on the part of

[35] J. Ignacio de Basadre to Gómez Farías, September 27, 1845.
Gómez Farías Papers. Another letter found in the same place dated
March 11, 1845, from Bernardo Othon to Gómez Farías has the following postscript: "In the city lampoons appear every day which cry
'long live the federation, or death to the army!!!'" All but the first
phrase of this postscript is in the same code as that referred to above.

[36] Introduction to *Dictamen Sobre la Cuestión de Texas*, . . .
This *dictamen* was read to the senate, June 3, 1844. *Archivo Histórico
Diplomático Mexicano*, Num. 8, pp. 195-196.

[37] J. H. Smith, *Annexation of Texas*, pp. 362-363; Arrangoiz, II. 259;
El Mosquito Mexicano, December 8, 1840; December 22, 1840; March
19, 1841.

Mexico aided by abundant resources, will oblige the United
States to release the prize. Money, money, and more money are
the three things which are needed in order to recover that territory, to save California in order to define our interior departments and even to preserve our nationality.[38]

Whether the United States was justified in all its
acts in connection with the Texas question or not,
there can be no doubt that many people in that country favored a policy of expansion. The press had
adroitly awakened the avarice of the covetous, the
bigotry of the religiously intolerant, and the race hatred of the non-Latin for the Mexican, to say nothing
of the fear of those who dreaded the encroachment of
England or France through an independent Texas.[39]
Nor was this last an idle fear, for the two European
powers would have been delighted to have had under
their protection a cotton-producing area for use as a
make-weight against the cotton plantations of the
United States.[40]
Considering the enormous territorial loss at the
end of the war and the fact that the issues involved
provided subjects of political discussion in Mexico
for several years thereafter, a brief consideration of
the causes of the war may not be amiss. While Mexico
had been making spasmodic efforts to induce settlers

[38] J. Alvarez to Gómez Farías, November 11, 1845. Gómez Farías
Papers.

[39] *Niles' Register*, LII. 113 (April 22, 1837); LVII. 80 (September,
28, 1839).

[40] Smith, *Annexation of Texas*, pp. 389-390, 413, 419. For the attitude of the press see *Niles' Register*, LVII. 150 (November 2, 1839);
LXX. 25-26 (March 14, 1846).

to go to the frontier provinces,[41] the United States had
not only sent thousands of home makers into Texas
but had carefully fostered and deliberately developed
through governmental protection an active trade with
Texas and northern Mexico. This policy had started
at least as early as 1829, when a caravan came into
Fayette, Missouri, from Sante Fé, with goods valued
at two hundred and forty thousand dollars, which
yielded a high profit. The same year four companies of
United States troops were detailed to accompany such
expeditions "as far as our limits would permit" for
protection.[42] By 1839, the process had spread through
Arkansas from New Orleans to Chihuahua. One expedition alone carried goods worth three hundred
thousand dollars.[43] Many of these were under convoy
of United States soldiers.[44] In 1843 the trade suffered
a set-back, due to the restrictions laid on various custom-houses in Mexico by the national government.[45]
At the demand of Washington, the custom-houses were
reopened the next year, and apparently commerce went
blithely on thereafter till the outbreak of the war.[46]

In the minds of the Mexicans, the constant Indian
raids into the northwestern departments were associated with the traffic in question, for it was currently
reported that the traders incited the Indians and then

[41] *El Mosquito Mexicano,* December 22, 1843.

[42] *Niles' Register,* XXXVII. 274 (December 26, 1829).

[43] *Ibid.,* LVII. 216 (November 30, 1839).

[44] *Ibid.,* LVI. 261 (June 22, 1839).

[45] *Ibid.,* LXV. 166 (November 11, 1843) ; J. D. Richardson, *Messages and Papers of the Presidents,* IV. 262-263.

[46] *Niles' Register,* LXIX. 416 (February 28, 1846) ; LXVI. 276 (June 29, 1844).

supplied them with arms. As early as 1835 this accu-
sation was also made against the permanent settlers
of Texas and the southwest of the United States.[47]
In 1841 the raids became worse and reached as far
south as San Luís Potosí. These last outbreaks were
made, not because the Indians were being incited from
without so much, but because the national troops had
been withdrawn from the frontier to take part in revolutions.[48] Nevertheless, the Mexicans felt the danger
more and more, attributing it largely to the assumed
or potential enemy to the north. Furthermore, the
interest manifested by the United States in the ill-
fated Santa Fé expedition sent out by the Texans to
invade Mexico was taken much` amiss by the Mexi-
cans, who considered it to be undue interference in the
internal affairs of a friendly nation.[49]

Because of the vague and ill-defined boundary lines
of the United States, moreover, officials were none too
careful about the exact extent of their jurisdictions.[50]
In any region near the border a man was likely to claim
either United States or Mexican nationality as the
immediate need demanded.[51] Migration from the
southern states to Texas was heavy, and the attitude
of the whole Southwest toward it correspondingly
friendly. Radicals, therefore, felt free to say: "There
is no depending (sic) interest of the United States of
half so much importance as the prevention of the sub-

[47] *El Mosquito Mexicano,* August 4, 1835.

[48] Zamacois, XII. 217-218.

[49] *Niles' Register,* LXII. 48 (March 19, 1842).

[50] G. W. Featherstonhaugh, *Excursion through the Slave States,*
p. 118.

[51] *Ibid.,* p. 123.

jugation of Texas. It is a country absolutely essential to our security and interest, and it must, sooner or later, become a part of the Union, at whatever cost."[52]   Such utterances had their effect, not only in increased volunteers for the Texan armies and in the creation of a sentiment favoring annexation, but also in an increased bitterness throughout Mexico toward the United States.   It was said that "peace in Mexico will never exist unless *our states* increase the number of stars" in the flag of the United States.[53]   Articles such as the following, copied from New York or New Orleans newspapers, received wide circulation in Mexico:

UNITED STATES OF AMERICA

New York, October 31, 1835.

Texas Affairs

Those who have offered, or who may wish to offer themselves, to join the Texas volunteers are asked to meet the commission in the arcade this evening at six o'clock, in order to take measures and to be organized before their immediate departure.   For this they will receive arms and supplies, and their transportation will be paid to Natchitoches.

NOTE The commission, composed of Messrs. James H. Caldevell [Caldwell?], W. Bogart, W. Bryan, Jas. N. Niven, W. S. Hodge, Thomas Banks, James Ramage, and W. Christy, will receive donations of rifles of various kinds and supplies. Those who wish to aid the cause by means of subscriptions can do so by seeing any of the members of the commission.[54]

[52] Letter of Langdon Cheves to *Charleston Mercury* in September, 1844.   Found in pamphlet, *Southern State Rights, Free Trade and Anti-Abolition*.   Secured by courtesy of Professor Yates Snowden of the University of South Carolina.

[53] *El Mosquito Mexicano,* May 19, 1835.

[54] *Ibid.,* January 5, 1836.

Even cabinet members, by speeches to Congress in open session, had early fostered the feeling of resentment.[55] Officially also much dissatisfaction on the part of the Mexican government was shown at what it considered to be the very unneutral attitude of the people of the United States toward Mexican attempts to reconquer Texas.[56] Strong protests had been made on the basis of the constant newspaper reports as to the number of men leaving Kentucky and other states for the war in Texas.[57] The answer of the United States, that it could not prohibit emigration or disarm emigrants, was not very effective in soothing the ruffled feelings of Mexican officialdom.

Another reason for the bitterness of many of the people of Mexico was the realization that in 1830 and thereafter much of the liberal northwest of their own country had sympathized with the Texans and that it would have taken very little pressure to cause the whole section to revolt.[58] Now that Texas seemed definitely lost, they were horrified at the thought of the further possible loss of this same region through absorption, not into Texas as an independent nation, but into Texas as a part of the United States. The fear was only too well founded.[59] Furthermore, the rebellion in Yucatán in 1841 was attributed, at least

[55] *Niles' Register*, LII. 248 (June 17, 1837).

[56] Manuel de Gorostiza to Secretary of Foreign Affairs, May 30, 1836. *Archivo Histórico Diplomático Mexicano*, Num. 8, pp. 148-149.

[57] Manuel de Gorostiza to John Forsyth, July 21, 1836. *Ibid.*, pp. 127-128.

[58] *Niles' Register*, LI. 34 (September 17, 1836).

[59] James Buchanan to John Slidell, November 10, 1845. *Sen. Ex. Docs.* (509) 30 Cong., 1 sess., VII. No. 52, pp. 77-79.

in part, to the expansionist policy of the northern republic, which found its expression in attempts to secure an option on the Tehuantepec route as a means of easy communication between the oceans.[60]   Just how much coöperation there was among parties in the United States, Texas, and Yucatán is not clear, but certainly the rebels in Texas, as late as 1841, were quite closely in touch with the Yucatecs.[61]

The conduct of General Gaines on the east Texas border has been so frequently discussed that it will not be dealt with here further than to say that it not only met with opposition in the United States[62] but with repeated protests from Mexico also.   Later the situation in California became so acute that an Irish Catholic priest, planning to plant a colony of his countrymen there, could write to the Mexican government about 1845:

I have a triple object in my proposal. I wish, first, to advance the cause of Catholicism; second, to promote the happiness and thrift of my countrymen; and, thirdly to put an obstacle in the way of further usurpations of that irreligious and anti-Catholic nation—the United States. And if the plan which I propose be not speedily adopted your excellency may be assured that before another year the Californians will form a part of the American nation. The Catholic institutions will become a prey of Methodist wolves, and the whole country will be inundated with cruel invaders.[63]

[60] *El Mosquito Mexicano,* August 3, 1841.

[61] Martín F. Peraza to Gómez Farías, October 19, 1841. Transcript of letter in Gómez Farías Papers.

[62] *Niles' Register,* L. 377 (August 6, 1836).

[63] W. Butler, *Mexico in Transition,* pp. 87-88.

While this does not dovetail exactly with the statements of the United States Minister,[64] there is enough similarity to make it apparent that a number of plots were on foot and that in all probability the Mexican government knew in a general way of their existence. In addition, the premature attack of Commodore T. A. C. Jones on the California coast in October, 1842, while duly apologized for, nevertheless added fuel to the flames of popular hatred.

In regard to the resentment arising out of the United States claims against Mexico, it can be said that if the Congress of that country was growing restless,[65] the Mexican people on their part were feeling the direct burden and could be far more easily aroused on the question. The centralist government of Mexico, at all events, decreed a forced loan to pay the sum due. This was to amount in all to two and a half million dollars, to be paid in slightly more than five years. Each department was required to turn in a sum varying from one thousand four hundred *pesos* a year for Chiapas to one hundred and seventeen thousand six hundred *pesos* per annum for Mexico.[66] Such an item, added to the burdens of a department already suffering from excessive taxation, would receive far more than its proportionate amount of blame from the taxpayers.

Moreover, in choosing ministers for the post in Mexico, the United States was peculiarly unfortunate. In the eighteen-twenties, J. R. Poinsett was the repre-

[64] D. D. Barnard in *The American Review,* IV. 11.

[65] *Niles' Register,* LII. 30 (March 11, 1837).

[66] *Ibid.,* LXIV. 260 (June 24, 1843).

sentative. In Mexico he seemed to have an eye open
for both public and private interests.[67] His relations
with the York-Rite Masons have already been noted.
The Mexicans considered his having been authorized
by Jackson to try to buy Texas as little less than an
insult;[68] and, when he left for home, the official newspaper commented:

On Sunday, the famous Mr. Poinsett left Mexico, after
having filled his diplomatic mission wonderfully well. This
renowned founder of Yorkism, on flying from amongst us,
was accompanied by millions of curses, and by the Deputy
Zerecero, who will remain without [with] his lord and best
friend.[69]

[67] An interesting example of this is the following letter, the original
of which is in the possession of Professor Yates Snowden, of the University of South Carolina:

"Mexico
4th June 1825.
Dear Cambreleng
You will no doubt have heard of my arrival here long eer (sic) this
by the public prints. . . .
I have gone through the ordeal of a public reception. The room was
crowded to suffocation with the magnates of the land, and I made a
speech in Spanish, which I enclose done into English. This exposition
of the potential (?) course of this country, became necessary from the
speech of the President to the British Chargé, which I suppose you will
see. I sent a copy to the department and one to Mr. Walsh. It is
abominably English. I have been sent here at least one year too late—
this entre nous—I will do my best to recover the lost ground. . . .
The English are employing an immense capital here. Fortunes will
be made and lost in mining—It is gambling—There are still open some
of the most profitable speculations, more of that anon—Could a company with a capital of 100,000 be formed with a certain prospect of a
profitable investment ?
I have been writing to the honble Henry Clay until my fingers are
cramped.
Good night
Yours truly
(signed) J. R. Poinsett."
[68] Arrangoiz, II. 196.
[69] Niles' Register, XXXVIII. 4 (February 27, 1830).

Poinsett was followed by Anthony Butler. Public opinion was aroused to such a pitch by the crass and blundering performances of that individual that even Santa Anna, master of crowd psychology though he was, was repudiated for a while, after his tentative treaty with the Texans and his interviews with President Jackson in Washington.[70] From this period up to the decade of the eighteen-forties, petty bickerings, charges and counter charges, claims and counter claims were the order of the day. In 1844 Thompson was sent to Mexico as a "bearer of Despatches", but he at once conferred with Santa Anna and appears to have been authorized to offer from six to ten million dollars as an offset to the United States claims and for territory varying in extent from that of Texas alone to that of Texas and California.[71] The low standard of public morality as to bribery, the misappropriation of funds by officials in both countries,[72] the difficulty of travel, which made a trip between Mexico City and Washington last three weeks,[73] and the rapid changes in the Mexican government added further complications and made diplomatic representation of the first class next to impossible.

One other item of apparently minor importance, yet liable to produce far-reaching effects on the liberal party in Mexico as well as to incite official hatred for the United States, was the fact that the latter country

[70] Antonio López de Santa Anna, *op. cit.,* p. 41.

[71] Smith, *Annexation of Texas,* p. 289.

[72] Buchanan to Slidell, November 10, 1845. *Sen. Ex. Docs.* (509), 30th Cong., 1st sess., VII. No. 52, p. 80.

[73] *Niles' Register,* LXIII. 96 (October 8, 1842).

was a customary haven of refuge for Mexican political exiles.[74]   Even though the individuals who happened to be in control of home affairs at the time might themselves have once enjoyed the hospitality of the United States in that manner, the mere fact that their enemies were now congregated there served to replace gratefulness for past favors with fear of present or future injury.

In March, 1845, the joint resolution for the annexation of Texas was passed in Washington.   Following this, diplomatic relations were severed, and, though Mexico offered to renew them[75] in January, 1846, matters remained at a tension.

Such was the condition of home and foreign affairs when Paredes accepted the office of provisional president.   The assembly of notables which had selected him was composed of conservatives and included a number of clergymen.   The Bishop of Chiapas was selected as minister of justice and ecclesiastical affairs.[76]   The call issued for the new congress provided for the most complete class representation.[77] Under an executive whose monarchical inclinations were so well known, the movement for establishing a kingdom grew apace.   A newspaper, *El Tiempo*, (*The Times*), edited by Lúcas Alamán and others, was founded to disseminate the idea.[78]   The movement was sufficiently serious to give the federalists grave con-

---

[74] Zayas Enríquez, *Benito Juárez, Su Vida—Su Obra,* p. 50.

[75] M. M. Quaife, ed., *The Diary of James K. Polk,* I. 91.

[76] Arrangoiz, II. 270-271.

[77] Zamacois, XII. 420-421.   It was said to be the work of Alamán.

[78]*Ibid.,* 419, 429, 488; Arrangoiz, II. 271.

cern.[79] They pointed out that a monarchy meant aristocracy and that a Mexican aristocracy would inevitably be chosen from the generals and local leaders of the country. The rivalries of these would lead to internal disorder and not promote harmony.[80] It was declared also that the establishment of a monarchy would mean almost certain intervention by the United States, an aggressive republic which had never had to depend upon a monarchy for success and which hated the aristocratic system.[81] Probably one of the factors that most seriously injured the cause of the monarchists, however, was the death of the Archbishop, who had been one of the strongest supporters of their faction.[82]

The whole issue was soon lost sight of because of the war, which drew rapidly on. It is true some Mexicans of the time felt that the United States was a home of religious freedom and a great example to be followed.[83] In later years it has even been admitted that Texas was never geographically a part of Mexico and that its absorption by the United States was inevitable.[84] This is a recent attitude, however, and does

[79] Florentín Gómez to Gómez Farías, February 9, 1846. Gómez Farías Papers. Sr. García has written on this letter that it is from Manuel Crescencio Rejón, though his reason for the statement is not clear.

[80] Haro y Tamariz, Esposición . . . sobre la Monarquía Constitucional, pp. 21-22.

[81] Ibid., pp. 29-33. Needless to say, the monarchists argued to the contrary, maintaining that a monarchy would provide a strong central government that would be able to save the country from its aggressive neighbor. Gutiérrez Estrada, op. cit., pp. 55-58.

[82] Niles' Register, LXX. 242 (June 20, 1846).

[83] Rocafuerte, op. cit., pp. 15, 36-38.

[84] Molina Enríquez, op. cit., pp. 45-47.

not indicate the feelings of the mass of the Mexican people in 1846, when they firmly believed that in explaining the origin of the war "it is sufficient to say that the insatiable ambition of the United States, favored by our weakness, caused it."[85]   Central America, also, felt much the same way, as was shown by the invitation of Honduras to its neighbors to join in the war to aid Mexico.[86]

At this point appears that shadowy character, Atocha, who is usually heard of by the title of "colonel". This person, in touch with Santa Anna, acted as a sort of go-between for him and President Polk. In June, 1845, he had an interview with the latter, reappearing in February, 1846, to urge that the United States keep a strong military and naval force available for Mexican service, so that the Mexican government would be able to represent to the people that they "had been forced to agree" to a treaty for the readjustment of the boundary line.   He stated that Santa Anna's last instructions were: "When you see the President, tell him to take strong measures, and such a treaty can be made, and I will sustain it".   For his maintenance in power after signing the treaty, Santa Anna wished to be provided with cash to the extent of half a million dollars.[87]   Commander Alexander Slidell Mackenzie, of the United States navy, also had an interview with Santa Anna at Havana and secured a similar statement from him.   To Mackenzie the Mexican recommended that General Taylor advance to San Luís

[85] A. C. Ramsey, ed., *The Other Side*, p. 2.
[86] *Niles' Register*, LXXIII. 10 (September 4, 1847).
[87] *Diary of James K. Polk*, I. 222-225, 228-230.

Potosí so as to defeat Paredes and secure his [Santa Anna's] recall. This advice was to be kept a profound secret, "since his countrymen not appreciating his benevolent intentions to free them from war and other evils might form a doubtful opinion of his patriotism." He also advised the capture of Tampico and the fortress of San Juan de Ulloa guarding Vera Cruz, but advised against an attack on Yucatán, since that province could be relied upon to support him in any event.[88]

Meanwhile, Santa Anna was in touch with the situation in Mexico and was planning to hoodwink the liberals and come back into power through their aid. By March, 1846, he had reached the conclusion that the good will of Valentín Gómez Farías was essential for his success.[89] Toward the end of the next month he had sufficiently prepared the way by indirect negotiations, and so he proceeded to write a long letter to that individual, expressing a wish to renew friendly relations and to secure coöperation for the development of his own plans.[90] On May 7, while the enemy troops under Taylor were advancing on the Rio Grande, a revolution was started by Tellez at Mazatlán in favor of Santa Anna.[91] Other plans proceeded apace, and by the end of the month Fermín Gómez Farías, a son of Valentín, could write to Santa Anna:

[88] Rives, op. cit., II. 234-236.

[89] M. C. Rejón to Crescencio Boves, March 9, 1846. Transcript of letter in Gómez Farías Papers.

[90] Santa Anna to Gómez Farías, April 25, 1846. Transcript of letter in Gómez Farías Papers.

[91] Zamacois, XII. 485.

Guadalajara has revolted and the triumph there has been complete. Mazatlán has done the same, and, according to good information, Zacatecas, Durango, Guanajuato and Puebla will soon support them. Our friends who are still at liberty [his father had been arrested] continue working actively, for they will not rest till they accomplish their purpose.[92]

On June 9 Santa Anna sent a letter of credit for the use of Valentín Gómez Farías and expressed sympathy for him in his captivity, assuring him that all would soon be well.[93] A month later he wrote again saying that he had received the offer of the troops of Yucatán in his undertaking,[94] and, on August 3, the garrison at Vera Cruz rose in his favor. Meanwhile, Paredes left the government in the hands of General Nicolás Bravo on July 29, while he hastened to take charge of a division of the army.[95] On August 4 a *pronunciamento* was issued from the fortress of Ciudadela by General Salas in favor of the constitution of 1824.[96] Among the first five names, of about one hundred and sixty on it, is that of Gómez Farías.[97] On the fourteenth, his son, Benito, wrote from Vera Cruz, where he was awaiting Santa Anna, that all was going well with their plans.[98] The United States fleet had

[92] Draft of letter in writing of Fermín Gómez Farías to Santa Anna, May 29, 1846. Gómez Farías Papers.

[93] Santa Anna to Gómez Farías, June 9, 1846. Transcript of letter in Gómez Farías Papers.

[94] Santa Anna to Fermín Gómez Farías, July 9, 1846. Gómez Farías Papers.

[95] Arrangoiz, II. 275.

[96] Zamacois, XII. 492 ff.

[97] MS of the *pronunciamento* with the signature of the leaders in the Gómez Farías Papers.

[98] Benito Gómez Farías to his Father, August 14, 1846. Gómez Farías Papers. Other letters were also sent to Gómez Farías from Vera Cruz by José Juan Landero on August 13, and by Fermín Gómez Farías on the fourteenth.

orders to allow Santa Anna to "pass freely" into
Mexico, so there was no danger from that source,[99]
and he duly made his arrival on the sixteenth of August.[100] At the same time, Juan Álvarez was actively
in revolt in the south.[101]

The combination of Santa Anna and Gómez Farías
was a particularly hard one for the administration to
handle. As Santa Anna wrote:

> . . . and I repeat now, we will succeed in overcoming all,
> uniting intimately by our respective influences the people and
> the army. For this I beg of you that you do not omit any
> means or effort, calming the excitement that may appear among
> the masses, as I, on my part, will quiet the fears of the
> military.[102]

Rejón and other liberals were outspoken in their praise
of Santa Anna[103] as soon as they came in personal
contact with him, but some there were who doubted.
For instance, Manuel González Cosío, Governor of
Zacatecas, wrote: "But speaking frankly, is success certain and sincere? Is your [Gómez Farías]
union with General Santa Anna true and honest?
These are the questions which we are all asking constantly; and this cruel doubt embitters the universal

[99] Rives, op. cit., II. 228-229.

[100] Santa Anna to Gómez Farías, August 16, 1846. Gómez Farías
Papers. Most Mexicans compliment Santa Anna most highly for his
shrewdness in reëntering the country, saying that if he deceived President Polk it was the deception by a patriotic Mexican of an enemy of
his country. Zamacois, XII. 507.

[101] Juan Álvarez to Gómez Farías, August 15, 1846. Gómez Farías
Papers.

[102] Santa Anna to Gómez Farías, August 17, 1846. Gómez Farías
Papers.

[103] Manuel C. Rejón to Gómez Farías, August 19, 1846. Gómez
Farías Papers.

satisfaction."[104]   Oajaca also was skeptical about such an alliance,[105] while Landero, in charge of the troops in Vera Cruz, wrote to find out if there was any truth in the report that Gómez Farías and the ministry were "at outs" with Santa Anna.[106]   The Masons had also been hesitant.   As a primary political factor, to be sure, they had disappeared, but they still had influence.[107]   They were none too enthusiastic in their support of Santa Anna, for they feared that he was dickering with the Church and army officials to secure control of the government.   Truly this was a heterogeneous group of rebels, containing those who supported the autocratic power of the soldier; the extreme democrats; "the regular troops and the National Guards, who loved each other as fire loves water;[108]   General Salas reluctantly taking orders from Citizen Farías, and both of them doing obeisance to Liberator Santa Anna, whom both distrusted; and all coöperating to

[104] Manuel González Cosío to Gómez Farías, August 31, 1846. Gómez Farías Papers.

[105] Franco Santoyo to Gómez Farías, August 31, 1846. Gómez Farías Papers.

[106] José Juan C. Landero to Gómez Farías, October 22, 1846. Gómez Farías Papers.

[107] Mateos, op. cit., p. 96.

[108] The National Guard had for years given much trouble. It was recruited in units in the various localities and was consequently ideal material out of which to form revolutions. Given local prejudices and a local leader, the result was almost a foregone conclusion. In a pamphlet by "Y. O." entitled, La Reforma Social de Méjico, on p. 9 are found the following suggestions for reforms of the Guard:

"To find a means by which each body of the National Guard will not represent one faction or party, but society in general.

To find a means by which the Guard will not acquire the vices, defects, and tendencies of the regular army.

To invent a way by which the officials and chieftains will not tyrannize over the Guard, will not be able to exploit it in the service of one faction or in their own particular interests."

revive a federal constitution which had been found in
practice unworkable, and needed, in the opinion of
everybody, to be redrawn."[109]

In spite of the anomalous character of the association, the plan worked as long as the several sets of
partisans were in opposition to a common enemy and
did not have to advance a constructive program, where
disagreement would inevitably occur. Since August
6, when General Bravo saw that he could not make
headway against the revolutions breaking out on all
sides, General Mariano Salas had been in charge of
the capital and of the nominal government. From the
first, he issued liberal decrees, such as that of August
9, which removed the restrictions on the freedom of
the press, even though a foreign war was in progress.[110] When Salas took charge, seven hundred thous-
and *pesos* remained in the treasury from a loan secured by Paredes from the clergy.[111] This sum stood
Salas in good stead, though it is said to have disappeared in fifteen days. Meanwhile, Santa Anna's
advance to the capital was almost a triumphal pro-
cession. On entering the city the President and Vice-
President of 1833 once more rode in the same carriage
and together received the plaudits of the throng.[112]
On September 14, the federal system was once more
formally established. Santa Anna supported General
Salas as president and turned his own attention to
the organization of an army with which to meet the
invaders in the north.

[109] Smith, *War with Mexico*, II. 1.
[110] Zamacois, XII. 504.
[111] *Ibid.*, XII. 503-504; Bulnes, op. cit., p. 148.
[112] Arrangoiz, II. 277-278.

The new congress, which met on December 6 at the call of Salas, was dominated by the liberals.[113] On the twenty-third, the election for president was held. Santa Anna secured eleven votes to nine cast for Elorriaga. A canvass of the individual deputies gave much the same result as had been secured with the delegations from each department entitled to cast a single vote; for, of the ninety-seven deputies present, fifty-two favored Santa Anna, thirty-seven were for Elorriaga, and eight were scattering. For the vice-presidency, Gómez Farías secured eleven votes, to eight for Ocampo and one for Elorriaga. Of the eleven departments voting for Santa Anna for president, nine voted for Gómez Farías for vice-president; while of the nine voting for Elorriaga for president, only two voted for Gómez Farías for vice-president.[114] From this it would appear that for the time being the fusion of the two groups was quite successful, in spite of the fears of the conservatives and moderates, both of whom had suffered severely the last time this combination was in office.[115]

[113] The following letter is quite interesting in this connection:
"Sor. Dn. Valentín Gómez Farías.

Vera Cruz, October 22, 1846.

My Most Respected and Dear Sir:

I hasten to write you to let you know the immediate necessity in which we are of choosing certain persons and placing them in positions from which they can influence the elections so that they will take the direction which we have proposed and [so that they can] prevent an unfortunate outcome through lack of supporters in the States.

Colonel Manuel E. Molina is recommended as an excellent person to act as Commanding General in Tabasco during the election.

(signed) Victorio V. Dueñas."

MS in the Gómez Farías Papers.

[114] Bulnes, op. cit., 167-168.

[115] Smith, War with Mexico, II. 5-6.

Santa Anna at once set off for the north with his troops, while Gómez Farías took over the administration of affairs.   In spite of the narrow majorities received, there was little immediate opposition.   For once, the pressure of foreign war seemed to be bringing about a certain amount of internal cohesion and coöperation in Mexico.

CHAPTER VII

FINANCIAL AND SOCIAL CONDITIONS

It has been said that all through its history the rising middle class of Mexico has been physically hungry and for that reason has been inclined to strive for public employment rather than for republican principles.[1] That this condition is cause and effect may be disputed, but there can be no question that economic forces have had great influence in the history of Mexico.[2] The masses of the Mexican people have always been peaceful and easily satisfied; they have not cared for fighting for its own sake. Only when discontented with their economic condition and without hope or prospect of improving it have they deserted their homes and followed some leader, himself usually ambitious for political preferment, into the vortex of civil war. One phase of that condition was financial.

The following figures indicate the condition of the national finances between 1839 and 1846:[3]

	Estimated Income	Estimated Expenses	Estimated Deficit
1839	4,431,474 *pesos*	20,378,792 *pesos*	15,947,318 *pesos*
1840	4,526,121 *pesos*	18,947,675 *pesos*	*14,421,554 *pesos*
1841	8,074,100 *pesos*	21,836,781 *pesos*	13,762,681 *pesos*
1842	14,650,000 *pesos*	19,326,475 *pesos*	4,676,475 *pesos*
1843	8,310,484 *pesos*	21,129,173 *pesos*	*12,818,689 *pesos*
1844	7,998,436 *pesos*	19,923,819 *pesos*	11,925,383 *pesos*

[1] Bulnes, *op. cit.*, pp. 109-110.
[2] Otero, *op. cit.*, p. 30.
[3] Sierra, *op. cit.*, II. 371.

1845........10,679,493 *pesos*   25,222,304 *pesos* *14,542,811 *pesos*
1846........10,247,760 *pesos*   24,310,030 *pesos* 14,062,270 *pesos*
* Very slight inaccuracies in these figures have here been balanced.—The Author.

They appear as estimates, since the actual figures for the sums collected are not available, owing to the lack of satisfactory records. The money collected from the people of Mexico was frequently more than the estimate for any given year, but the sum that reached the government was usually much less. For this diminution in actual revenue, the peculation of officials was largely responsible. Also it should be borne in mind that a considerable portion of the custom-house receipts was mortgaged for special purposes, such as the foreign debt, and consequently could not be counted on as a source of revenue available to the government. For 1841 the amount so hypothecated amounted to four million eight hundred thousand *pesos*.[4]

Government bonds were selling at ruinous discounts, while the value of mere promises to pay depended entirely upon who had issued them and the importance of their holders at any given time. One officer in the army, after having his accounts audited by the war department, "received a certificate that twenty-five hundred dollars were due him; after hawking it about amongst the brokers, he sold the claim for a hundred and twenty-five dollars, which was five cents on the dollar."[5]

Under these conditions men looked with longing eyes at that wealthiest of all the institutions of the

[4] Bancroft, V. 227.
[5] Thompson, *op. cit.*, p. 169.

country, the Church. In spite of the attacks that
had been made upon its property from time to time,
and especially in 1833, its holdings tended to increase.[6]
During the reaction in favor of the Church, a leader
lost popularity if he ventured to attack ecclesiastical
institutions. Even when Santa Anna was dictator of
the country, in 1842, his order for the confiscation of
silver plate previously deposited by the Jesuits in the
cathedral of Puebla brought him in only about seven
thousand *pesos* and seriously impaired his reputation.[7]
This act might have been explained away, since the
Jesuits had been expelled from the country, had it not
been followed up by others of the same general character. The Dominicans and Augustinians of Puebla
were each ordered to contribute twenty-five thousand
pesos to the government, while by the end of March
the Archbishop of Mexico had been forced to accept
drafts to the extent of one hundred and seventy thous-
and *pesos*.[8] These facts help to explain why, when
the Gómez Farías-Santa Anna alliance was formed
in 1846, the two men could not rely upon the friendship of the Church for either one of them. In the
election of 1846, also, when Santa Anna was chosen
president, the moderates were in favor of Elorriaga
and were distinctly opposed to the coalition.

It should not be supposed that Santa Anna had
made demands of the Church alone. In 1843 he faced
both a serious rebellion in Yucatán and the seemingly
ever-present Texas question. Also, the claims con-

---

[6] Thompson, *op. cit.,* p. 41.

[7] Zamacois, XII. 260-261.

[8] *Ibid.,* XII. 261-262.

vention just signed with the United States required heavy payments in specie, for promises to pay were no longer satisfactory at Washington. Consequently, as stated above, on April 20, 1843, the forced loan of two millions and a half was placed on the departments in proportion to their ability to pay.[9] This levy was passed on to individuals through an arbitrary assessment, which they were forced to meet, regardless of the justice of the amount demanded in each case. If they refused to pay voluntarily, their homes were entered and articles, such as coaches, pianos, and other furniture, were taken and sold to make up the required amount. Still the government needed funds, and money was repeatedly secured from the Church and its various institutions.[10] Import duties were raised twenty per cent. on April 6, 1843. This tax was particularly injurious to the merchants, whose support Santa Anna had been so anxious to secure in 1841 that he led them to believe that he would do all in his power to release them from the fifteen per cent. sales tax then in force.[11] Probably the sums collected by the government had never been so high as in 1842 and 1843, when Santa Anna, using to the full the powers granted by the Plan of Tacubaya, exploited all available resources. "According to the report presented by the Minister of the Treasury Department, Don Ignacio Trigueros, in 1844, the actual income amounted to 29,323,433 *pesos*. The sum was abnormal; but the expenditures amounted to 29,526,632 *pesos,* resulting in a deficit of 203,199

[9] *Niles' Register,* LXIV. 229 (June 10, 1843), contains a translation of most of the decree.

[10] Smith, *War with Mexico,* I. 52; Zamacois, XII. 297-299.

[11] *El Mosquito Mexicano,* April 9, 1841.

pesos. After deducting from the total all those items of income which were not taxes, the latter amounted to only 13,421,863 *pesos.*"[12]

It was a country with its finances depleted in this reckless fashion that went to war with the United States. The upkeep of a Mexican soldier was estimated at one *peso* per day. With an army of about thirty-five thousand men, this meant that slightly over a million *pesos* per month, or about twelve and a half millions of *pesos* per year, were needed for the maintenance of the military alone.[13] Because of the United States blockade of the ports of the country, the import duties decreased from about nine to five million *pesos* at the time of greatest need. In April, 1846, President Paredes adopted arbitrary methods to secure both men and funds. Vagabonds were to be seized and sent to the front, or wherever needed. Payment of all debts by the national treasury was suspended, while salaries and pensions were reduced. The "Church was called upon to contribute two hundred thousand dollars a month for the support of the government", which, however, it protested its inability to do.[14] In this connection, the Archbishop was advised that the share of his archdiocese was ninety-eight thousand *pesos.* He responded that the total revenue at its disposal did not amount to that sum.[15] Among other dioceses, that of Puebla was asked to pay forty thousand and Guadalajara two thousand.[16] In October a special war "con-

[12] Zamacois, XII. 271.
[13] *Ibid.,* XII. 543.
[14] Rives, *op. cit.,* II. 223.
[15] Bancroft, V. 297.
[16] *Niles' Register,* LXX. 228 (June 13, 1846).

tribution" was imposed as a direct tax on individuals. Some few paid it, only to find that a great majority of the people had ignored the demand, so that the loyal or timid souls were left with nothing to show for their patriotism except their empty pocketbooks. In November, another forced loan, to be laid upon the clergy, was proposed, but it met with so much opposition that little or nothing was collected on it. "The whole gamut of methods, even violence," was tried in vain.[17]

In view of these facts, an examination of the reports of the coinage of the mints yields something of a surprise. The largest amount coined under the Spanish régime was in 1805, when a total of slightly over twenty-seven million *pesos* passed through the mints in gold and silver.[18] During the decade from 1820 to 1830 this had fallen to an average of scarcely ten million *pesos* a year. After 1830, there was a steady improvement, with no marked fluctuations, as follows:[19]

From 1831 to 1835, 12,500,000 average.
From 1836 to 1840, 12,500,000 average.
From 1841 to 1845, 13,500,000 average.
From 1846 to 1850, 18,200,000 average.
From 1851 to 1855, 17,700,000 average.

Such a rate of increase might seem to denote a rise in prices and consequent prosperity for the nation, now that the old Spanish exactions that had taken so much

[17] Smith, *War with Mexico*, II. 7-8.

[18] Account of the Coinage in the Mint of Mexico from 1802 to 1821 inclusive, by José María Paría, July 15, 1822. J. R. Poinsett, *Notes on Mexico*, p. 85.

[19] C. Lemprière, *Notes in Mexico*, p. 215; *De Bow's Review*, IX. 43 (July, 1850).

specie out of the country were no longer in existence. Normally this would have been the case, but huge sums had to be constantly exported in order to secure necessary articles from abroad.[20]   Agriculture and other industries had been so disturbed that their products were being shipped in very small quantities and hence could not be exchanged for foreign supplies in any considerable quantity.

After 1841, the flood of copper seems to have receded slowly.   This was most fortunate, for, with copper at a fifty per cent. discount, a real hardship was worked on the laboring classes.[21]   Even newspapers were forced to announce that they would renew subscriptions only when paid in silver, or in copper at the rate of two for one.[22]   The government finally helped to relieve the situation by allowing certain fees to be paid two-thirds in copper and one-third in silver.[23] Also the fact that even copper was better than paper money and usually preferable to government bonds doubtless had a salutary effect on its acceptability as a medium of exchange.

From August to December, 1846, the British debt was refunded after wearisome negotiations.   For the old debt, which, with accumulated interest, amounted to £11,203,919, new consolidated bonds were issued to the value of £10,241,650.   These new bonds were to be guaranteed by twenty per cent. of the customs dues

[20] Mayer states that of the 13,732,861.04 *pesos* coined in 1844, nearly two-thirds, or 8,739,220, were exported. *Op. cit.,* II. 100.

[21] *El Mosquito Mexicano,* November 2, 1841; December 21, 1841; and August 27, 1841.

[22] *Ibid.,* November 30, 1841.

[23] *Ibid.,* November 26, 30, 1841.

collected at Vera Cruz and Tampico, by a duty on all silver exported from Pacific ports, and by one hundred and seventeen thousand *pesos* monthly to be secured from the government tobacco monopoly. If more was needed to pay the interest and provide five hundred thousand *pesos* annually for the sinking fund, the tobacco revenue was to be used still further for the purpose. On the whole, the transaction was beneficial to Mexico.[24]

On turning from the financial side of affairs to social conditions and their effects, the prominence of the Church, an opponent of democracy, in every phase of life becomes all the more apparent and calls for notice. Dissatisfaction was rife, otherwise the people would not have allowed the frequent spoliation of the Church by the executive. Even a paper that hated Gómez Farías, and the editor of which had been imprisoned by the liberal administration in 1833, stated that children supposed to be in schools were running loose in the streets; the Carmelite fathers, instead of going about in couples as formerly, were going alone and wearing well-shined shoes instead of sandals; the Augustinian fathers were accused of living in private houses with resulting scandal, and the Fathers of Mercy were also becoming lax.[25] A sympathetic foreigner noted the very poor educational system;[26] whereas one who disliked the Roman Catholic Church

[24] Payno, *Mexico and Her Financial Questions*, pp. 15-17. It is interesting to note that Benito Gómez Farías was attached to the Mexican commission that negotiated this settlement. Santa Anna to Gómez Farías, August 31, 1846, and Benito Gómez Farías to his Father, August 31, 1846. Gómez Farías Papers.
[25] *El Mosquito Mexicano*, May 19, 1840.
[26] Mme Calderón de la Barca, *op. cit.*, p. 179.

stated that the Indians, instead of being the Christians the priests were supposed to have taught them to be, were so poorly trained that they still regularly worshipped their old idols.[27] Reports were published from time to time to the effect that curates of some Indian charges regularly confessed their parishioners through an interpreter and actually deserted their charges and performed their duties through deputies in case a contagious disease was prevalent in the community.[28]

Moreover, the propaganda sowed by the liberals of 1833 was beginning to have effect in a more general opposition to anything that savored of compulsion in the collection of the formerly obligatory parochial fees.[29] Those who were inclined to criticize called attention to the fact that very few of the better class regularly attended the Church services. Even in the cathedral of Mexico, a lady who attended mass felt that it was advisable for her to change her garments after once kneeling upon the floor, which was filthy and had recently been occupied by vermin-infested Indians and *léperos*.[30]

According to the report of the minister of justice and ecclesiastical affairs for 1844, it appears that the number of monks in the country had decreased by two hundred and seventeen from that given for 1834,[31] while the number of nuns had increased by one hundred and sixty-one, and the girl pupils enrolled in

[27] Thompson, *op. cit.*, p. 189.
[28] *El Mosquito Mexicano*, May 19, 1843.
[29] *Ibid.*, March 13, 1840.
[30] Mme Calderón de la Barca, *op. cit.*, p. 50.
[31] *Supra*, chapter iii, note 33.

monastic schools had increased from six hundred and twenty-seven to nine hundred and ninety-five. However, in 1844, there were only twenty-six or twenty-seven novitiates in all of the nunneries in the country.[32] This would seem to indicate a slow but steady decline in the prestige of the clergy, which resulted in a consequent falling off in the number of persons who entered both the regular and secular branches.[33] There were, in 1843, 1123 parishes with 3179 ecclesiastics to take care of them. The large churches were naturally cared for first, so that whereas six hundred and forty-five parishes were regularly served, there were four hundred and thirteen with *ad interim* appointments of curates. Though the remaining sixty-five were presumably vacant, there appears to be no way to determine the matter. Among the bishoprics, Puebla had one hundred and sixty-three of its two hundred and fifty-five parishes with *ad interim* appointments. Due to its small size, however, this was nothing like as serious as for Nuevo León to have thirty-

[32] *Memoria del Secretario de Estado y del Despacho é Instrucción Pública*, 1844, table no. 4, and table headed "Estado General . . . de los Conventos de Religiosas".

Mayer, *op. cit.*, II. 131-132, gives the following figures:

Regular ecclesiastics: monks	....	1700
	nuns	2000
		3700
Secular clergy		3500
Total		7200

These figures are obviously approximate, if not simply estimates, from the fact that round numbers are used. For this reason the report of the secretary has been adopted, Noll (*op. cit.*, p. 191) to the contrary notwithstanding.

[33] *Opúsculo en Defensa del Clero*, p. 26.

nine out of its fifty-two parishes in the same condition.[34]

Beyond doubt, the work of many of the regular orders was excellent,[35] and that of some of them far-reaching, when a statement like the following from Guadalajara could be made: "The young folks of the present day are formed by the clergy and are so subjected to [the latter's] discretion, that nothing, absolutely nothing, can be expected of them, because through Jesuitism great care has been taken to keep them indifferent to public affairs". In spite of this, the same writer continued, the majority of the people in Jalisco, "as though by instinct", desired federalism.[36]

In 1841 the agitation became particularly strong for the reinstatement of the Jesuits. Pamphlets and newspapers took up the arguments pro and con. While education was admittedly in bad shape, it was said that the Jesuits were not needed to restore it.[37] *El Mosquito Mexicano* was one of the leaders of those supporting the order, praising its organization and work to the skies.[38] On June 21, 1843, Santa Anna

[34] *Memoria del Secretario de Estado y del Despacho é Instrucción Pública,* 1844: table inserted between tables 4 and 5, not numbered.

[35] Mme Calderón de la Barca, *op. cit.,* pp. 172-173.

[36] Pedro Zubieta to Gómez Farías, May 16, 1845. Gómez Farías Papers.

[37] Junta Departamental de Chihuahua, *Iniciativa* . . . *al Soberano Congreso,* pp. 4-5.

[38] *El Mosquito Mexicano,* June 18, 1841. A typical piece of propaganda is the following sonnet found in *El Mosquito Mexicano,* June 4, 1841. It purports to be the answer of a French Jesuit, driven from France to Genoa, when asked if he was an ex-Jesuit:
    No me nombres el EX por caridad
    Despues que lo adoptó la Convencion,
    Debió Europa á la Francia su invencion

decreed that the order might reënter the country to establish missions in the Californias, New Mexico, Sonora, Sinaloa, Durango, Chihuahua, Coahuila, and Texas for the evangelization of the Indians.[39] This was generally understood to mean that it could reorganize its mission work immediately and later expand in any way it saw fit. Two similar acts were those of September 15 and October 9, 1843. The first repealed a law of 1837, which prevented members of monastic orders from entering the republic, and the second authorized Sisters of Charity to establish themselves there.[40]

However, these were all minor encouragements for the Church. When other official acts of the reactionary government from 1841 to 1843 are taken into consideration, the restrictions laid are seen to outweigh the privileges granted. On February 8, 1841, the government once more assumed the right to administer the Pious Fund of the Californias. After October 13, civil permission was required for any bills of sale of Church property made by the regular clergy. On November 6, a circular was sent out calling upon

Y fué su primer fruto la EX-piedad.
Siguióse EX-trono, EX-rey, EX-orden, EX-lealtad,
EX-cura, EX-fraile, EX-monja, EX-devoción,
EX-papa, EX-cardenal, EX-religión,
EX-culto, Ex-templo, Ex-fé y EX-Christianidad.
    Mira si el EX, que me regalas hoy
Un EX fatal para tú patria fué;
Mas yo tambien otro EX buscando voy,
    Y do encontrarlo tengo suma fé:
Ya me parece que escuchando estoy
    EX-Masson, EX-citoyen, EX-impieté.—D.

[39] *Ibid.*, June 30, 1843, gives copy of the decree.

[40] *Memoria del Ministro de Justicia y Negocios Eclesiásticos,* 1844, pp. 68-69.

the regular clergy to report whether they had established the primary schools required by law and also the number of children attending the schools and the books used. On January 5, 1842, another circular was despatched, conveying the warning that if ecclesiastics entered the country without the necessary permit from the government they would be treated as any other foreigners who entered illegally. On June 27, a circular was issued, reënforcing the one of the previous October as to the civil transfer of Church property. October 24, the Church property in the Californias was entirely absorbed into the national treasury, this really amounting to confiscation. February 3, 1843, the restrictions of October 13, 1841, were extended to all clerical institutions. July 1, the law of the preceding February was explained and made more definite. On August 31, finally, the sale of jewels, silver plate, and other furnishings from houses of worship was absolutely prohibited; both buyer and seller were to be considered thieves.[41]

Some of these laws were objected to, but that of August 31, 1843, was regarded as particularly dangerous. The third Mexican ecclesiastical council gave to the bishops the right to approve all Church expenses, including those of monasteries exceeding twenty *pesos,* daily expenses being excepted. The new law preventing the sale of jewels and other precious articles was held to be in conflict with that right. All who had taken an oath to support the laws of the Church were, therefore, expected to oppose the national enact-

[41] *Memoria del Ministro de Justicia y Negocios Eclesiásticos,* 1844; Lázaro de Garza y Ballesteros, *Bienes de Iglesia,* pp. 35-36.

ment.[42] Complaints as to the harshness and even ruthlessness with which the laws were enforced and as to the way in which the Church had been despoiled by force were numerous, some of them being, beyond doubt, well founded.[43]

Closely associated with the condition of the Church and certainly a determining factor in the growth of democratic ideas, was the condition of education. Because of so much disorder in the country at the time, little consistent work could be hoped for. In 1842, however, by a decree of October 16, Santa Anna established a system of primary instruction. This system provided for the Lancasterian method of education, at least in theory.[44] In spite of this gesture, for it was little more, the next year there were only 1310 schools in the nation with a total of sixty thousand pupils enrolled. These schools were largely maintained by private aid, though some had government support. Of the entire number, only twenty-one, with an enrollment of 2012 pupils, were maintained by the Church.[45] Communities at a distance from the seat of power were begging and pleading for government support for their schools, but seem to have received little or nothing.[46] In 1846 the national budget assigned 29,613 *pesos* for the carrying out of the general plan for the establishment of a national system of primary education, while

[42] *Ibid.*

[43] *Memoria del Ministro de Justicia y Negocios Eclesiásticos*, 1845, pp. 26-27

[44] *Niles' Register*, LXIII. 225 (December 10, 1842).

[45] R. García Granados, *La Constitución de 1857 y las Leyes de Reforma*, p. 113.

[46] Martín de Villers to Gómez Farías, July 9, 1845. Gómez Farías Papers.

the same budget called for nearly twenty-two millions
for the army and navy.[47] One-third of a *centavo* per
capita for education and about two and three-fourths
pesos for the army and navy! Under such circumstances it is not surprising that, as late as 1843, a
crowd of country folk should carry a witch into Mexico City under heavy guard and demand her punishment.[48]

The enormous postal rates charged also seriously
impeded popular education in the broad sense of the
word. One lady visiting in Mexico City commented:
"We also received a number of old newspapers by
post, for which we had to pay eighteen dollars! Each
sheet costs a *real* and a half—a mistaken source of
profit in a republic, where the general diffusion of
knowledge is of so much importance."[49] Needless to
say, the people used the postoffice only in cases of dire
necessity. The situation finally brought about a revision in 1842, when the rates on newspapers were placed at about twenty-five per cent. of their earlier
amount.[50] Even this was exorbitant, and periodicals
were still forced to depend upon local sales. Travel
was slow, brain-racking, and body-racking, as well
as expensive. The danger from robbers was a serious
one. The trip from Vera Cruz to Mexico City was
made by a "diligence" which carried passengers and
parcels. The rates varied from time to time, but aver-
aged about fifty to sixty *pesos* per person.[51]

[47] Smith, *War with Mexico*, I. 14.
[48] *El Mosquito Mexicano*, June 30, 1843.
[49] Mme Calderón de la Barca, *op. cit.*, p. 171.
[50] *El Mosquito Mexicano*, June 3, 1842.
[51] A memorandum in the Gómez Farías Papers, indicating that such
a sum was used for the expenses of Valentín Gómez Farías.

Along with the desire for an improvement in the educational system of the nation, other social reforms were agitated. Among them was one calling for the limitation or abolition of the use of intoxicating beverages. From time immemorial, one of the besetting sins of the Indians and lower classes of Mexico had been the intemperate use of the fermented juice of the century plant, *pulque*. It was maintained that the *pulquerías,* or saloons, where this drink was sold, were a public nuisance, violating both morality and decency. Demands, accordingly, were made for the removal of all *pulquerías* from the city, or at least from the principal streets, and for strict supervision and limitation of the sale of the article even where permitted.[52] By March, 1843, some progress had been made, and the drinking-houses had been forced out of certain districts. Then the problem arose of itinerant vendors, who carried a jar "filled with a pulque, which, if it is not that in fact, at least goes by that name".[53] By 1847 the question appears to have been taken up still more seriously. At least one fairly complete study of the use of spirituous liquors was made and published in an attempt to check drunkenness. Here it was asserted that in England in 1833 the average consumption of spirituous liquors was about 11.7 quarts per capita annually; in Switzerland in 1838, 13.7 quarts; in the United States in 1828, 25 quarts, and in Mexico City 22.5 quarts,[54] or nearly as much as was used by the debauched and wicked race of the north, which, as

[52] *El Mosquito Mexicano,* March 9, 1841; June 4, 1841; March 7, 1843.

[53] *Ibid.,* March 14, 1843.

[54] Francisco Ortega, *Memoria sobre . . . la Embriaguez,* pp. 24-25.

all good Mexicans were said to know, was rapidly approaching its downfall. The enormous expense of such liquors was also held up as a reason for the limitation of their sale.[55] This agitation indicated real thought and an attempt to stimulate the same on the part of the people as a whole.

On the other hand, little or nothing is to be found by way of propaganda among Mexican writers for the limitation or prevention of gambling. Visitors stated that the vice was prevalent among both men and women in all grades of society. The great fête of San Agustín, semi-religious in its nature, was founded upon this passion for gambling in its various forms. Here *lépero* and general, street-wench and lady, priest and layman, came together and risked their little or their much, as the occasion demanded or their resources allowed, upon the whims of the goddess of chance.[56]

Turning to what may be regarded as part of the social work of the government as it related to the safety of business interests, the court system should be considered. Due to the rapid changes in the executive office, the tenure of judges was most insecure, and, even where the same judge remained in office, all too often his decisions were nullified by the incoming executive, who desired to make friends and supporters. At times, this was done by wholesale pardons granted to those condemned by the preceding administration. But perhaps the most serious trouble was that arising from time-serving judges, who rendered their decisions

[55] Francisco Ortega, *Memoria sobre . . . la Embriaguez*, p. 27.

[56] Mme Calderón de la Barca, *op. cit.*, pp. 163-164.

in accordance with the demands of those at the moment in authority, regardless of whether the local power happened to be that of a bandit or of the legitimate government.[57] Sometimes it was actually unsafe to prosecute a criminal, because of the revenge that was almost sure to follow.[58] An illuminating description of practices common in the best classes of society is given in an extract from a letter to Benito Gómez Farías:

> By my previous letter you will have seen that my lawsuit has become more serious than ought to have been the case, due to the unjust accusations of certain witnesses; but fortunately these [witnesses] are well known, and the judge (in confidence) has promised me that no harm shall come to me, at least in so far as he is concerned; . . .[59]

While Santa Anna was in office, he made a number of efforts to undertake internal improvements of a spectacular nature. Visitors often commented on the fact that the magnificent public buildings constructed under the viceroys, such as those of the Botanical Gardens and the Museum, had fallen into decay or were in sad need of repairs.[60] What interested Santa Anna more especially, however, was the promotion of public improvements that would cater more directly to his popularity with the masses. The city was already well supplied with theatres, but he built another, *El Gran Teatro de Santa Anna*, later called the National Theatre, at a cost of three hundred and fifty-one thous-

---

[57] *El Mosquito Mexicano*, March 31, 1843; October 27, 1843.

[58] *Mexico; the Country, History and People*, pp. 232-233.

[59] Gabriel Rufino to Benito Gómez Farías, March 13, 1845. Gómez Farías Papers.

[60] Mme Calderón de la Barca, *op. cit.*, p. 102.

and *pesos.* This was said to be the finest building of its kind in America at the time.[61] Large sums were also spent on the Iturbide Theatre. Another undertaking of his, which it is true had much greater prospect of benefit for the nation at large, was the railroad, built from Mexico City to San Angel.[62] This road involved large expenditures with little chance of immediate returns, so that its chief effect was to provide an ample outlet for the nation's funds.

In view of these expenditures, the government was all the more blamed for not preventing the serious Indian outbreaks that still occurred more or less periodically. As already noted, these began in the latter part of 1840 and continued in 1841. They affected the country from Tampico to Sonora, and even as far south as San Luís Potosí.[63] With the disturbed conditions resulting from the trouble with the United States, other raids began in the early part of 1845.[64] These raids started in Durango and Chihuahua and continued more or less constantly throughout the war.[65]

Regarding the social situation as a whole, it may be said that during the period of about twenty years since independence had been attained few changes had taken place. The equivalent of serfdom was hard to abolish and still persisted in the form of peonage,[66] despite the attempts to induce the poor of the nation to

---

[61] García y Cubas, *op. cit.,* p. 25; Marcos Arróniz, *Manual del Viajero en Méjico,* pp. 114-115.

[62] Zamacois, XII. 259.

[63] *Ibid.,* pp. 217-218; *El Mosquito Mexicano,* October 16, 1840.

[64] *Boletín de Noticias,* No. 16, January 11, 1845.

[65] Smith, *War with Mexico,* I. 376.

[66] McBride, *op. cit.,* p. 31.

go to the northern border, where land could be had for the asking. A friendly observer noted that, in the face of many obstacles, the condition of the Indian was improving as regards personal appearance and education. Schools were on the increase, and the natives were glad to support them.[67] In the cities, on the other hand, it is altogether possible that the *léperos* had degenerated as a result of the disorders of the times, when they were being catered to and humored by the politicians and generals who wanted their support. Certainly the servant problem was one that was consistently bad, so far as the quality of the work was concerned, even though the workers were humble, civil, and good-natured.[68]

As to the other extreme of the social scale, the clergy still held much of the invisible power, while the army held most of that which was visible; "wherever the bells ceased to ring, the roll of the drum could be heard".[69] However, there was slowly but steadily arising a new group. In it were a few merchants, but these were as yet of little importance, since most of the retailers were of minor ability, and a majority of the wholesalers were foreigners. The new group represented rather certain types of professional men, civil

---

[67] J. R. Poinsett in *De Bow's Review,* II. 169 (September, 1846).

[68] Mme Calderón de la Barca, *op. cit.,* pp. 148-149. Some typical wages given by the same writer are: a good porter, fifteen to twenty *pesos* per month; coachman, twenty to thirty *pesos;* a French cook, thirty *pesos;* housekeeper, twelve to fifteen *pesos;* major-domo, twenty *pesos* up; footman, six to seven *pesos;* chambermaid, five to six *pesos;* gardener, twelve to fifteen *pesos,* and sewing girls, three *reales* per day. *Ibid.,* p. 152. It should be noted though, that porters, coachmen, and gardeners expected to have wives and families in the house.

[69] Smith, *War with Mexico,* I. 8, 11.

officials, journalists, teachers, and others.[70] This was
the class in which lay the hope of Mexico.

A letter from Oajaca summarized the situation in
that department in 1846:

In my Department you have, for example, three kinds of
men: first, the rich, usually ignorant, without initiative
(serviles) and egotistical; second, persons more or less well
known, who are the only ones suitable to discharge public
duties, and who for this reason are almost all employed [in
public office]; and third, those absolutely without property,
who, destitute of all knowledge, are useless for public affairs.
Except, then, the second class and Oajaca will have to send to
the general Congress a representation of asses, or else ten good
clergymen to make up a delegation." For this reason do not
offend the second class.[71]

[70] Smith, *War with Mexico,* I. 5-6; Sierra, *op. cit.,* II. 192 note.

[71] Franco Bas[?]met to Valentín Gómez Farías, August 16, 1846.
Gómez Farías Papers.

CHAPTER VIII

THE END OF THE WAR

When Gómez Farías took up the reins of government on December 23, 1846, he found a difficult situation awaiting him. He was, at best, the choice of a scant majority of the Mexican people. Furthermore, everything he did was seen by the people in relief against the dashing figure of Santa Anna, who, though nominally in the background, was a far more striking personality than the Vice-President and was known as a man of action, such as Mexico needed in this hour of great danger.[1] Certain sections of the country failed to coöperate with the national government because of local conditions. Durango held back, owing to Indian raids; Ocampo did not allow Michoacán to render full support, on account of his inveterate hatred of Santa Anna; Jalisco did little, it is said, because of sympathy for her neighbor, Zacatecas, which had been crushed by Santa Anna in 1835.[2] The clergy hated Gómez Farías for his career as a liberal; they also feared the ambition of Santa Anna, which might lead him to aid them one day and to despoil them the next.

The great question facing the government, supported in this half-hearted fashion, was how to raise money to support the army and carry on the war. The most readily available source of money was the Church,

[1] Mayer, *op. cit.*, I. 367.
[2] Smith, *War with Mexico,* I. 376.

in spite of the failure of the attempt of the preceding November to raise funds by means of sight drafts drawn upon the clergy.[3] The position of Gómez Farías was doubted by none because of the record of his whole career, even though the ministers chosen to assist him at this juncture could not be classed as extremists.[4] The congress was predominantly liberal.[5] The instructions to the delegates of the department of Zacatecas show the sentiment of that community; it asked for a "republican, representative, popular, federal" system and called for a vigorous prosecution of the war with the United States, but also asked the congress not to allow Santa Anna to take over the government of Zacatecas as general-in-chief of the army.[6] The position of Santa Anna was in serious doubt. On January 2, 1847, he wrote to the Vice-President:

My esteemed friend and companion:

I have at hand your very pleasing letter of the 30 (?) of last month, and am impressed with its contents.

I know the difficult position of the government, and how exhausted the public treasury is; but my good friend it is necessary, absolutely indispensable to invent, create, and, in short, to seek out money wherever it can possibly be, and to take it legally for the expenses of the army, and the other needs of the nation.

To our mutual friend, Sr. Rejón, I write today approving his idea, and that of some of the deputies concerning a loan of twenty-five millions of *pesos* to be guaranteed by Church property, and I believe that at the present time one cannot place

[3] Rives, *op. cit.*, II. 308-313, 315-319.

[4] Bulnes, *op. cit.*, p. 144.

[5] Zamacois, XII. 545.

[6] Instructions sent to Gómez Farías as a deputy of Zacatecas to the Congress. Gómez Farías Papers. These were dated December, 1846.

his hand on any other resource that offers the supplies so needed. Hurry, and use all your influence in order that the project may be carried out as soon as possible; . . .[7]

All writers agree that the army was desperately in need of funds. Two days after endorsing the loan above mentioned, the Commander-in-Chief wrote that there was still a deficit of two hundred thousand *pesos* for the previous month, and yet the nation was demanding action. He added: "If I do not receive supplies immediately, I will find myself in the necessity of issuing a statement which will justify me and let it be seen that I am not responsible . . . Such a statement of mine would not only injure the government but would inform the enemy, at the same time, of our situation."[8] This could be interpreted as a threat and nothing else. Three days later he wrote that the new government had been in office two weeks and had sent no funds, apparently because it had forgotten the existence of an army of twenty thousand men facing the enemy, while "it (the government) engaged in the frivolous talk and stories of that accursed capital (*los chismes y cuentos de esa malhadada Capital*)."[9]

The Vice-President lost little time in applying to the congress for the loan of fifteen million *pesos* to be secured by mortgage or sale of Church property.

[7] Santa Anna to Gómez Farías, January 2, 1847. Gómez Farías Papers. The original of the letter to Rejón is also found here. It advises a twenty million *peso* loan and says conditions have changed since his (Santa Anna's) opposition to such a means of raising funds. See also Zamacois, XII. 551-552.

[8] Santa Anna to Gómez Farías, January 4, 1847. Gómez Farías Papers.

[9] Santa Anna to Gómez Farías, January 7, 1847. Gómez Farías Papers.

Strong opposition arose at once, for this was understood to be a kind of a "test case" to determine whether a liberal program based on the attempted reforms of 1833 was to be inaugurated.[10] With all the pressure the administration could bring to bear, the vote at the end of the general discussion stood only forty-four to forty-one in favor of the bill. Even so, the first article was subjected to amendments.[11] The bill was passed on January 11, 1847, and was published officially three days later.[12]   In order to gain popular support for the measure, the approval of Santa Anna for a twenty million *peso* loan was made known by the publication of his letter endorsing such an act.[13]   Three days later he still supported the administration program.[14]

The next question was how to put the act into effect.   It was decided to call upon the archbishopric of Mexico for one third of the sum, while to the bishoprics of Puebla, Guadalajara, and Michoacán were to be apportioned two million, one million two hundred and fifty thousand, and one million seven hundred and fifty thousand *pesos,* respectively.[15] The final one third of the whole sum was to be collected later from the remaining bishoprics.   The law provided that the property should be pledged, and, if necessary, sold, though the religious, charitable, and educational work of the clergy was not to be interfered with.[16]

[10] *Manifesto . . . [de] los Illmos. Sres. Arzobispo de México . . . y Obispos . . .*, p. 8.

[11] Zamacois, XII. 553-554.

[12] *Diario del Gobierno,* January 13, 1847.

[13] *Ibid.,* January 14, 1847.

[14] Santa Anna to Miguel Laro, and Santa Anna to Crescencio M. de Gordoa, January 14, 1847. Gómez Farías Papers.

[15] McBride, *op. cit.,* pp. 68-69.

[16] Smith, *War with Mexico,* II. 10-11.

With the publication of the law trouble began. The Church authorities not only refused to coöperate in any way whatsoever, but used every means at their disposal to prevent its execution. They refused to provide data as to property values, so the government had to make up its own estimates as best it could. One such report, dated February 13, 1847, was drawn up by Manuel Piña y Cuevas, later minister of the treasury, making out the value of the rural property of the Church in the department of Mexico to be 1,-193,278 *pesos*. This estimate appears to have been based on the income reported for the year 1838, assuming that it represented a return of five per cent. on the capital invested.[17] Necessarily many omissions and mistakes were to be found in reports compiled in this fashion, but they are the best available.

By no means all the opposition of the clergy was of this passive type. One of the first steps taken was to close the churches, on the ground that disorder was feared. The people at once became greatly excited, so the government ordered the buildings opened immediately.[18] This was done, but the protests of the clergy continued through newspapers open to them and even through political harangues delivered from the pulpits. The answer to such conduct was a law of January 16 forbidding any discussion of political questions under the guise of sermons.[19] Just why the bur-

[17] Manuel Piña y Cuevas, *Fincas Rústicas en Estado de México*. Report dated February 13, 1847. Gómez Farías Papers.

[18] Zamacois, XII. 557.

[19] John Black to James Buchanan, January 26, 1847. Gómez Farías Papers. Consul Black here refers to the decree in question, which was published in *El Monitor Republicano*, January 16, 1847.

den of this loan should fall on the Church alone and not proportionately on all the people of the nation was the question.[20] The Bishop of Michoacán protested that commerce, industry, and agriculture virtually owed their maintenance to the Church, so that if it was ruined the whole economic system would collapse.[21] Threats of revolution were heard on all sides; even personal violence was threatened against the leading reformers.[22]

From Querétaro, Governor Berduzco reported that through fear of mobs he had been forced to break up public meetings engineered by the clergy.[23] A week later, January 26, 1847, the Governor reported that he could not officially publish and enforce the law, because the members of the local legislature, his council, the town council, and others were bitterly opposed to it.[24]   However, on the thirtieth, the general in charge of the local troops said his supplies were low and that he thought he could handle the situation, which was calming down slowly, without additional troops.[25]   Toluca tried to bring up the idea of local option or states rights by having such departments as were opposed to the measure excused from its ef-

[20] *Representación del . . . Cabildo Metropolitano al Soberano Congreso,* p. 8.

[21] *Protesta . . . del Obispo de Michoacán . . . ,* p. 14.

[22] "un Católico" to Gómez Farías, January 20, 1847. Gómez Farías Papers.

[23] Francisco Berduzco, Governor of Querétaro, to Gómez Farías, January 19, 1847. Gómez Farías Papers.

[24] P. Barasorda to Gómez Farías, January 26, 1847. Gómez Farías Papers.

[25] *Ibid.,* January 30, 1847.

fects.[26]   The request of the legislature to this effect
was of course ignored.

The liberals of Zacatecas received the law with
approval and signified their intention of enforcing it.[27]
Similar cheering news reached the government from
Manuel Doblado, the enthusiastic liberal governor of
Guanajuato.[28]   He went further and stated that all
the central departments were determined to support
federal institutions to the uttermost.[29]

But all of this was getting neither cash into the
hands of the government nor supplies to the army.
Temporary expedients, for example, a government
lottery,[30] were able to do no more than tide over the
situation from day to day.   Santa Anna began to lose
patience and, long before the loan could become effective, wrote to Gómez Farías:

> I am astonished at such conduct on the part of the govern-
> ment [in not sending money], and I do not see how you can
> go to bed and sleep peacefully, knowing that you have an army
> of more than twenty thousand men to maintain and that in the
> month and more in which you have been in charge of the reins
> of power you have not sent a single *peso*.   Such conduct is
> incomprehensible to me.   I cannot believe that you intend to
> sacrifice me or to compromise this army to the end that you

[26] Eulogio Barrera and Ysidoro Ot-eras [?] to Gómez Farías, January 20, 1847. Gómez Farías Papers.

[27] Manuel Gonzáles Cosío to Gómez Farías, February 5, 1847. Gómez
Farías Papers. *Ibid.*, February 16, 1847.

[28] Manuel Doblado to Gómez Farías, January 29, 1847. Gómez Farías
Papers.

[29] Manuel Doblado to Ramón Adama, January 29, 1847. Transcript
in Gómez Farías Papers.

[30] *Diario del Gobierno,* January 22, 1847.

[or "I"] make a scandal which would bring on you the hatred of the nation . . .[31]

Two days later, he reported that he had mortgaged his private estate to the extent of one hundred and eighty thousand *pesos* and had also been forced to draw upon certain friends for aid.[32] Those who knew Santa Anna must have feared a revolt or *coup d'etat* on his part when he had the army at his back—an army devoted to him and which considered itself badly treated by the government as administered by its old enemy, the Vice-President. One of the first hints of this danger appears in a letter written from Vera Cruz by Ignacia Uhink, daughter of the Vice-President, an unusually clear-headed young woman. She said that in Vera Cruz all were fearing a *pronunciamento* from the army in favor of a dictatorship, and that then "the innocent Don Antonio [López de Santa Anna] will say that he finds himself obliged to accept"; that he would then proceed to join the clergy, revoking his approval of the law for the confiscation of their property.[33]

During February, reports from the departments and towns continued to come in with varying degrees of alarm and reassurance. On March 4, Joaquín Zarco

[31] "Ese comportam^to es para mi incomprensible, y no puedo suponer q. se intente sacrificarme, ó comprometer á este Egército á q. dé escándalo q. le atraiga la animadversion nacional." Santa Anna to Gómez Farías, January 26, 1847. Gómez Farías Papers.

[32] Santa Anna to Gómez Farías, January 28, 1847. Gómez Farías Papers. The use of private funds in this manner was not at all unusual. In fact it was customary for a general to use any cash available, and then present his bills at the end of the campaign.

[33] Ignacia F. de Uhink to Señora Gómez Farías, January 28, 1847. Gómez Farías Papers.

reported from Texcuco: "I have to work every minute to avoid a *pronunciamento* by these people who are directed by the priests".[34]   Olaguibel, governor of the department of Mexico, reported that he approved the stand of the administration but that the deputies of the local legislature could not be relied upon.[35]   From Morelia and Jalisco came reports that all was well and that the situation could be handled,[36] but from the Church stronghold of Puebla, the governor, Domingo Ibarra, wrote that he could not send aid to Mexico City, since he had only one hundred and forty men available with which to handle the discontented elements led by the clergy and members of Congress.[37]

As events proved, the reports from the department of Mexico were the most important. Here were the headquarters of the Church, and here the largest amount of the money was to be collected. The clergy positively refused to coöperate in any way and, when asked for the keys to their treasures, each man responded in writing that he did not have them.[38]   As a

[34] Joaqn. Zarco to Gómez Farías, March 4, 1847. Gómez Farías Papers.

[35] F. M. de Olaguibel to D. I. B. Alcalde and B. I. Comonfort, March 4, 1847. Gómez Farías Papers. Another note from Toluca, with the same date, stated that the National Guard was being undermined by the use of money and the work of the priests. This was signed "Suyo Amigo" and addressed to Guillermo Valle, deputy to the General Congress. After the signature someone, presumably Sr. García, has written that this was from Francisco M. de Olaguibel. However, the paper used, the writing of the secretaries, and the rubrics do not correspond at all with those of Francisco M. de Olaguibel as found on the first letter.

[36] Ramón Valen[?]zuela to Gómez Farías, March 8, 1847, and José Manuel Yáñez to Gómez Farías, March 9, 1847. Gómez Farías Papers.

[37] Domo. Ibarra to Gómez Farías, March 5, 1847. Gómez Farías Papers.

[38] Francisco Patiño to the Minister of the Treasury, March 10, and March 16, 1847. Transcripts of letters in Gómez Farías Papers.

result, Lieutenant Colonel Manuel Luís del Fierro was commissioned to take witnesses and a sufficient number of men to carry on the work while he entered, by force if necessary, into the various religious establishments and appropriated such funds as he could find, making a record of them.[39]   On one such raid, 3878 *pesos* were secured; on another, 5283.[40]   The clergy, having had repeated warnings, had obviously removed their funds from harm's way and were able to look on calmly while the government "ran amok" with public opinion. The people could not be expected to remain quiet when armed troops were breaking into the most holy places. To those who gave thought to the matter, it might seem strange that the Church should have relatively ample funds with which to carry on its work and yet could not assist the government to repel actual invasion.[41] But the masses, when aroused on the subject of religion, rushed to extremes and repeated after the most conservative of the clergy the statement that the demands were so exorbitant that none of them should be paid.[42]

It is true that nominally a million and a half of *pesos* was secured from the Church in the latter part of the year. The clergy, however, "appear to have taken up indirectly at a discount of forty per cent. the drafts of which this donation consisted".[43]   Their

[39] Transcript of authorization to Colonel Fierro to search the convents, dated March 16, 1847. Gómez Farías Papers.

[40] Transcript of report of Fierro and associates, March 21, 1847, with an earlier report of March 10, 1847. Gómez Farías Papers.

[41] *Reflexiones sobre la ley de 17 de Mayo del Corriente Año*, p. 7.

[42] *Representación del . . . Cabildo al Soberano Congreso*, p. 16; *Niles' Register*, LXXII. 1 (March 6, 1847).

[43] Smith, *War with Mexico*, II. 254.

action is one of the reasons why extremists said with so much bitterness, "the clergy loved their own institution and its interests, their own prerogatives and privileges; . . . the nation was little to them, public interests and civil society, nothing; . . ."[44]

Thus stood affairs when Santa Anna began the battle of Angostura (Buena Vista) against the United States troops under General Taylor. At the same time, February 22, the revolution of the so-called *Polkos*[45] started in Mexico City against the Gómez Farías administration. Each party had about six thousand men in the city for the contest.[46] On the twenty-seventh, M. de la Peña y Barragán issued circular letters to the leading men of the nation, calling upon them to join in the demand for a government under the leadership of Santa Anna.[47] The next day he wrote to Santa Anna, accusing the Vice-President of incapacity and of diversion of funds from the army and asking Santa Anna to take direct charge of affairs.[48] Olaguibel attempted to mediate between the contestants in Mexico City so as to present a united opposition to the foreign enemy, but this effort came to nothing.[49]

[44] Parra, *op. cit.*, pp. 39-40.

[45] Probably a name derived from a popular dance of the period, the *Polka*. There appears to be no connection with the name of President Polk of the United States. Arrangoiz, II. 279.

[46] Mayer, *op. cit.*, I. 368.

[47] At least eleven of these may be found in the Gómez Farías Papers, and likewise a letter of Peña y Barragán to Valentín Canalizo, February 27, 1847.

[48] Peña y Barragán to Santa Anna, February 28, 1847. Gómez Farías Papers.

[49] J. M. de Olaguibel to Gómez Farías, March 1, 1847. Gómez Farías Papers.

In the meantime, a report of the disturbances in the capital had reached the army. Santa Anna insisted that this was the cause of his defeat, saying that, had this news not come, his soldiers would undoubtedly have followed up their early successes to victory.[50] Be that as it may, and unkind persons have not hesitated to call this an *ex-post-facto* alibi, he turned his face to the capital, where the contest was dragging on. On March 9, he wrote that he was going to the capital to use firmness and energy in putting down the revolt and that he would immediately retire from power by going to his home or wherever his country needed him.[51] As he approached the city, both sides sent delegations in an effort to secure his endorsement and approval.[52] The rebels had not planned for a protracted and spirited resistance on the part of the government and were inclined to falter long before Santa Anna's arrival.[53] Another person stepped in, fostered the revolt, and kept the men to their guns. "He was Moses Y. Beach, agent of the American State Department and adviser to the Mexican hierarchy. Permission had been given him to bring about peace if he could; and, unable to do this, he seized the opportunity to help Scott" by overthrowing the government.[54] A scheme of his, presumably directed to the same end and demanding more skilful preparation, was his application, on February 6, 1847, for a charter for a

[50] Santa Anna, *op. cit.,* pp. 61-66.

[51] Santa Anna to Gómez Farías, March 9, 1847. Gómez Farías Papers.

[52] Zamacois, XII. 641-643.

[53] A. C. Ramsey, *The Other Side,* p. 163.

[54] Smith, *War with Mexico,* II. 13.

national bank. The capital stock was to be six million pounds sterling, of which the government was to own one half. The stockholders were to select the governing board, and all government funds were to be handled gratis. Other details were worked out,[55] but are not pertinent here, since the application, signed by Beach himself, was never acted upon, probably because of lack of time.

When Santa Anna reached the city, he took immediate charge of affairs. On March 31, after a vigorous debate, by a vote of thirty-eight to thirty-five, the Vice-President was repudiated, and Santa Anna, as actual President, was authorized also to lead the army in person. The office of vice-president was abolished, and a president substitute, to be named by the congress, was to take his place. The date for the regular election of president was set for May 15.[56] For the intervening period, General Pedro María Anaya was nominated and elected by the congress as president substitute, entering upon his duties on April 2, 1847.[57]

Santa Anna set off for Vera Cruz immediately. General Scott had disembarked just south of the city on March 7 and had started at once his advance into the country. It would seem that the advice given through Atocha was being most accurately followed.[58]

---

[55] Application of Moses Y. Beach, dated February 6, 1847. Gómez Farías Papers.

[56] Mayer, op. cit., I. 369.

[57] Ramsey, op. cit., pp. 229-230.

[58] Incidentally, President Polk confided to his diary on January 14, 1847, that Atocha was once more in Washington with letters from Santa Anna and Almonte. (II. 325-326.) On February 11, 1847, Julio F. Uhink, son-in-law of Gómez Farías, reported from Vera Cruz that Atocha had arrived there a day or so before. Gómez Farías Papers.

Would Santa Anna do his part? Scott's advance was steady. By May 15, he was at Puebla; by August, before the City of Mexico.

With the war thus carried into the heart of the country, strenuous efforts were made to raise funds. The forced loan on the clergy, provided by the laws of January 11 and February 4, 1847, was dropped after the governmental overturn in March, on the offer of two millions of real money.[59]   Nearly every issue of the *Boletín Oficial* for the months of May and June, has a list of from five to twenty names of persons who had given cash in sums up to twenty *pesos* each, or supplies for the cause.[60]   On June 27, it was announced that all who would pay arrears on certain taxes would get rebates of from a third to two thirds of the sums due.[61]   The government was forced to fall back upon the Church once more.[62]   Protests were strong, but the needs were so dire and at the same time so obvious that there was no serious danger of an overturn in the government as the result.   While steps were taken to prevent ruthless injury to the Church,[63] and while the demands were heavy, it was generally felt that they were not confiscatory in any serious degree.[64]   In four loans from the clergy, only about three millions of *pesos* were secured.   Negotiations savoring of gambling ventures secured a few hundred thousand

[59] Smith, *War with Mexico*, II. 15, 254.

[60] *Boletín Oficial*, May-June, 1847.

[61] *Ibid.*, No. 18, June 27, 1847.

[62] *Reflexiones sobre la ley de 17 de Mayo*, pp. 5, 25-26.

[63] Zamacois, XIII. 73.

[64] *Reflexiones sobre la ley de 17 de Mayo*, p. 18.

from British and other foreign interests,[65] but these sums, after all, were negligible.

The repudiation of the liberal, Valentín Gómez Farías, was not so general as to cause him to lose his influence among his old constituents.[66] In fact, he was at once, April 15, asked to represent the department of Jalisco in the congress.[67] In August, another letter was sent to him asking if he would accept the position of deputy for Jalisco for the ensuing term and stating that, if he would not, Fermín would be chosen.[68]

The United States army, having entered the capital on September 16, 1847, Santa Anna, in the village of Guadalupe, resigned the presidency. According to the law, Manuel de la Peña y Peña, chief justice of the supreme court, took over the executive office.[69] Nicholas P. Trist, United States representative sent by President Polk to negotiate a treaty, reported that Santa Anna had intended to make a treaty with the United States [presumably along the lines indicated by Atocha], but that the heavy pressure brought to bear by the so-called *Puros* ("die-hards") caused him to hesitate till it was too late.[70] The country as a whole

[65] Smith, *War with Mexico,* II. 254-255.

[66] Santa Anna, on the other hand, was none too fully endorsed, if the report of Nicholas P. Trist can be relied upon. He stated that on June 2, Santa Anna, who had previously offered his resignation as president, hastily withdrew it on hearing that the congress was preparing to accept it. *Sen. Ex. Docs.* (509), 30 Cong., 1 sess., VII. No. 52, p. 181.

[67] Official notification to Gómez Farías, signed by Cosme Torres and Mar°. Talavera, dated April 15, 1847. Gómez Farías Papers.

[68] Jesús Camarena to Gómez Farías, August 28, 1847. Transcript in Gómez Farías Papers.

[69] Arrangoiz, II. 286.

[70] N. P. Trist to James Buchanan, October 25, 1847. *Sen. Ex. Docs.* (509), 30 Cong., 1 sess., VII. No. 52, p. 212.

was in chaos, anarchy, and misery,[71] while foreigners held the capital and were busy dictating a peace treaty. All eyes turned to the congress that was to meet in November in Querétaro. The moderates hoped to secure control, conclude the treaty, and, if possible, secure for themselves the national government. The irreconcilables, of whom an outstanding leader was Gómez Farías, wished to continue the war to the bitter end, forcing the United States troops to leave the country through a ceaseless guerrilla warfare.[72] While the congress was organizing, there was a week of acrimonious struggle. Finally, the moderates won, electing as the temporary president P. M. Anaya. He kept Peña y Peña in the cabinet and carried on the peace negotiations.[73]

The attitude of the clergy toward the invaders is worthy of note. Where the priests and people had been in contact with the Anglo-Saxon menace for some time, in other words, in the northern part of the country, the bitterness resulting from interracial and religious contests of long standing caused them vigorously to denounce the invaders. Epidemics were attributed to them.[74] The clergy of San Luís Potosí addressed the people of the community in an official letter in which the United States troops were referred to as "these Vandals, vomited from hell to scourge

[71] Manuel González Cosío to Gómez Farías, November 26, 1847. Gómez Farías Papers.

[72] Manuel González Cosío to Gómez Farías, December, 1847. Gómez Farías to his wife, November 10, 1847, and Manuel González Cosío to Gómez Farías, October 15, 1847. Gómez Farías Papers.

[73] Rives, op. cit., II. 592.

[74] S. Compton Smith, Chile Con Carne, pp. 77, 195-196.

the nations", who "worship no god but gold, and aspire to no happiness but the gratification of their brutal passions".[75]

Further southward the care exercised by Washington in avoiding the religious issue seems to have been more appreciated. From the early days of the war, it was realized that the clergy of Mexico must be reassured as to the attitude of the northern republic toward them and their property.[76] To this end, the coöperation of Roman Catholic bishops in the United States was secured, and a number of priests were delegated to accompany the army.[77] They were "not chaplains, . . . there was no law authorizing the appointment of chaplains for the army, but . . . they were employees, such as armies often require, . . ."[78] After the capture of Mexico City, the clergy closed all the churches till they were informed that if the buildings were not opened forthwith the United States flags would be removed from them to indicate the withdrawal of military protection. "No further hint was necessary, . . . and soon the relations between army and Church became entirely satisfactory".[79] On November 23, 1847, the sale of Church property without the approval of United States officials was prohibited.[80] Large numbers of the clergy, however, appreciated a firm administration and realized that their property was being protected

[75] *Niles' Register,* LXXII. 251 (June 19, 1847).
[76] J. R. Poinsett in *De Bow's Review,* II. 32 (July, 1846).
[77] *Diary of James K. Polk,* I. 408-411.
[78] *Ibid.,* II. 188-189.
[79] Smith, *War with Mexico,* II. 227.
[80] Zamacois, XIII. 74-75.

and that the United States offered real religious liberty of a type that made forced loans and confiscations, such as they had been subjected to under Mexican rule, out of the question.[81]   Some, such as the Bishop of Puebla, were so outspoken in their approval that their patriotism was seriously called in question.[82]

Another phase of the religious question during the war was caused by the large number of deserters from the United States army.[83]   Some of them took service under the Mexican flag.   The "Company of San Patricio" was composed of Irish Catholics who had deserted because of the religious appeals made to them.[84] Quite an elaborate scheme to foster desertions was worked out by one Murray together with Nicholas Sinnot.   The scheme, as approved by the colonization bureau and Rejón, minister of foreign relations, provided liberal land grants for Sinnot [Murray had withdrawn] and for the soldiers according to their rank.[85]

[81] Trist to Buchanan, October 25, 1847. *Sen. Ex. Docs.* (509), 30 Cong., 1 sess., VII. No. 52, pp. 209-210.

[82] Ramsey, *op. cit.*, p. 224.

[83] Smith states that 6750 men deserted out of 90,000 serving in the army. *War with Mexico*, II. 318-319.

[84] Smith, *Chile Con Carne*, pp. 247-248; Ramsey, *op. cit.*, 114, note; Zamacois, XII. 695-697; *Niles' Register*, March 13, 1847.

[85] The amount of land that was to be given to deserters according to the plan approved was:

Private	200 acres, with	100 extra per year of service
Corporal	300 acres, with	150 extra per year of service
Sergeant, 2nd class	400 acres, with	200 extra per year of service
Sergeant, 1st class	500 acres, with	250 extra per year of service
Second Lieutenant	750 acres, with	375 extra per year of service
First Lieutenant	1200 acres, with	600 extra per year of service
Captain	2000 acres, with	1000 extra per year of service
Major	3000 acres, with	1500 extra per year of service
Lieutenant Colonel	5000 acres, with	2500 extra per year of service
Colonel	8000 acres, with	4000 extra per year of service

Gómez Farías Papers.

On the other hand, some Mexicans deserted and fought steadily for the United States. A group under one Domínguez alleged that the guerrillas on the Vera Cruz road "had broken up, or rather monopolized, their trade, which was highway robbing. To make therefore, another honest living in another honest way, they changed from robbers to traitors. This information is not derived from a third person, but from Domínguez himself and his men".[86]   Such conduct can be the more readily understood when one realizes that Mexicans freely admit that large numbers of the country people had not been injured by United States troops as much as by the civil wars to which they had been subjected constantly for years.   Furthermore, Scott's policy of paying well for their products and services really made it a fact that the poorer classes were "in a better situation under the Americans than under Mexican Governors".[87]

No sooner had Scott led his troops to victory, than the sentiments of President Polk reached a point where further confidence in either Scott or Trist was out of the question.[88]   This situation culminated in an order for the court martial of General Scott and the recall of Trist.   For a victorious general with his army, three thousand miles away from Washington, to obey such an order was considered by Mexicans to be a manifestation of the finest spirit of democracy.[89]

With the negotiation of a treaty of peace, including the surrender of Texas and California to the United

[86] Ramsey, *op. cit.*, p. 299, note.
[87] Arrangoiz, II. 291.
[88] *Diary of James K. Polk,* II. 412-413; III. 312, 357-358.
[89] Zamacois, XIII. 131; Ramsey, *op. cit.,* pp. 421-422.

States for a money consideration and as an indemnity, party feeling at once blazed forth.[90] The majority party was that of the *Moderados,* followers of Herrera, Anaya, Cuevas, and Peña. They were opposed to Santa Anna and wanted a steady and reliable government to follow peace with the United States.[91] On the whole, the clergy was inclined to support them.[92] Probably the next largest party was that of the *Puros.* They stood for a continuation of the war to the bitter end, Gómez Farías, Ocampo, and Degollado being their chief spokesmen.[93] Some there were, also called *Puros,* who desired to continue the war, not for the purpose of securing a more favorable treaty for Mexico, but so that the United States would be forced to occupy and annex the whole country.[94] Olaguibel was a leader of this small faction.[95] Other minor parties were the *Santanistas,* who opposed peace, thinking that, through a continuation of the war, they might be able to restore their old leader to power, and the *Monarquistas.*[96] The latter had as their chief exponent, Paredes y Arrillaga.[97] They hated Santa Anna, but stood for the same principles as those on which the Church and army systems were based. They had few

[90] For full details of the negotiations see *Sen. Ex. Docs.* (509), 30 Cong., 1 sess., VII. No. 52; Smith, *War with Mexico,* II. 233 ff.

[91] Rives, II. 590-591; Trist to Buchanan, October 25, 1847. *Sen. Ex. Docs.* (509), 30 Cong., 1 sess., VII. No. 52, p. 208.

[92] Ramsey, *op. cit.,* pp. 150-151.

[93] Gómez Farías to his son Casimiro, December 13, 1847. Gómez Farías Papers; Bulnes, *op. cit.,* p. 163. See also J. Fred Rippy in his new book, *The United States and Mexico,* p. 38.

[94] Rives, II. 590-591, 643; Trist to Buchanan, December 6. 1847. *Sen. Ex. Docs.* (509), 30 Cong., 1 sess., VII. No. 52, p. 238.

[95] Mayer, *op. cit.,* I. 405.

[96] Rives, *op. cit.,* II. 590-591.

[97] Mayer, *op. cit.,* I. 405.

avowed adherents, though their potential power was such that a general movement in their direction by the masses would not have been at all surprising.

With the organization of the new congress in January, 1848, by the *Moderados*,[98] there was real danger of a *Puro-Santanista* alliance which might give trouble. When matters came to a vote, however, it was seen that the coalition controlled only one third of the votes of the deputies.[99] On the treaty of Guadalupe Hidalgo itself, the vote in the Chamber of Deputies was fifty-one to thirty-five and in the Senate, thirty-three to four, the votes in the two bodies being taken on May 19 and 25 respectively.[100] The *Puros* took their defeat hard. For example, Benito Gómez Farías wrote to his brother:

> The treaty was approved in the Chamber and by now will have been [approved] in the Senate. I believe that this result will surprise no thinking person; it is the first step of legal and [officially] sanctioned infamy which we present to the world in the name of the nation, and it is to be hoped that the famous Congress of '48 will not stop now till it has completed its work. And we cannot hope that the nation will awake, or that revolutions will save us; the nation will continue sleeping and *pronunciamentos* will only be the miserable efforts of individual aspiration. We will continue, then, without hesitation toward the abyss, and Mexico will drag out her last years of existence through muck, misery, and crime.[101]

[98] Trist to Buchanan, January 25, 1848. *Sen. Ex. Docs.* (509), 30 Cong., 1 sess., VII. No. 52, pp. 287-288.

[99] Trist to Buchanan, November 7, 1847. *Sen. Ex. Docs.* (509) 30 Cong., 1 sess., VII. No. 52, pp. 226-227.

[100] Zamacois, XIII. 144-145.

[101] Benito Gómez Farías to his brother Fermín, May 25, 1848. Gómez Farías Papers.

CHAPTER IX

THE CLIMAX OF CENTRALISM

Now that the war was over, and United States troops were leaving the country, Mexico was once more free to return to internal contests. The struggle was still between the groups with *fueros* and those standing for democratic principles in fact as well as in theory. In the election for president held on May 30, 1848, Herrera secured eleven out of the sixteen votes cast. He refused the honor offered, but the next day the deputies, by a vote of eighty-one to six, rejected his declination. A second refusal met with a second rejection by the deputies, so, on June 3, he took office as president to try to reconstruct a nation torn to pieces by civil wars for thirty years or more and by the recent foreign invasion.[1] The new President was supported by most of the liberals, but this only guaranteed him trouble from the conservatives. Within two weeks after his inauguration Paredes y Arrillaga was in revolt.[2] Others followed suit, till the President was forced to drop most of his constructive program in order to maintain his position as head of the government. It is for this reason that he is frequently said to have accomplished little.[3]

[1] Zamacois, XIII. 159-160.

[2] *Ibid.,* XII. 181-182. After his rebellion was crushed, Paredes y Arrillaga went into hiding in a convent in Mexico City. There he died in September, 1849. With his defeat and death, there was a temporary lull in the activities of the royalists. Zamacois, XIII. 261-262.

[3] Arrangoiz, II. 294.

The repeated revolutions in Yucatán had degenerated into one of the most brutal of all the Indian wars of Mexican history. On a petition of the inhabitants, three hundred and fifty United States troops remained in the Island of Carmen for a time after the war was over so as to protect the country and give the local government time to get control of the situation.[4] As time went on, the war became more and more brutal, till the governor of Yucatán was selling his prisoners to Cuba and the State of Vera Cruz. He said this was the only way to save their lives. The federal government stopped the practice, but the war continued unabated.[5]

The English in Belize were blamed for supplying arms and munitions to the Indians.[6] Possibly this British assistance is explicable, in view of the fact that the United States was attempting to secure control of the proposed Tehuantepec canal route. A treaty of June 23, 1830, had provided that United States citizens were to be hospitably received in Yucatán. This provision was denounced as the thin edge of the wedge of later expansion and as the beginning of a new Texas question.[7] The chief rival of the United States for the route was the Manning-Mackintosh Company, of England, which, in truth, was finally successful in blocking the United States plans. The attitude of the English in general, and of this company in particular, was expressed by J. D. Powles, director of the company, when he wrote in 1846:

[4] Zamacois, XIII. 194.
[5] *Ibid.*, XIII. 278-282.
[6] *Ibid.*, XIII. 339-340.
[7] *Ibid.*, XIII. 382.

I believe that both the British and the French governments are so disgusted with the arrogance, the dishonesty and the rapacity of the United States, that they wod encounter some risk for the protection of Mexico, if they felt that they could *depend upon Mexico herself*. M. Guizot said, in the early part of the present year, in the French Chamber, that "France wod no more tolerate a universal Republic in America than she would a universal monarchy in Europe."[8]

The Indians of the north were also up in arms. During the war they had naturally been allowed far more license than would otherwise have been the case. The depths of brutality to which the war descended became obvious, when guerrilla bands were authorized to prey upon the Indians. They were to be given a bounty of two hundred *pesos* for all Indians taken, whether dead or alive.[9] It has been said, and with a fair degree of plausibility, that these Indian raids were indirectly fostered by the United States mule-traders, who were taking at good prices all the mules offered by the Comanche and Apache Indians. These tribes raised few or no mules, but secured them by raids to the southward.[10] The public-land situation in Texas contributed to this situation, for, whereas that state retained control of its public lands, the Indians were the wards of the federal government. As the settlers advanced, the Indians were pushed out, with no land appropriations made in their favor. Consequently, they resorted more and more to plunder as a means of liveli-

[8] J. D. Powles to E. E. Mackintosh, manager of Manning-Mackintosh Company in Mexico, August 29, 1846. Manning-Mackintosh Papers. Garcia Collection.

[9] Zamacois, XIII. 284-290.

[10] *Ibid.*, XIII. 386-387.

hood.[11] On the other hand, Mexico complicated the situation by disarming the settlers of the northern provinces and leaving them defenseless until the autumn of 1853, since the military colonies provided for by the decree of July 19, 1848, amounted to comparatively little until 1851.[12] The claim that the United States government fostered these raids is absurd, for, in 1852, of the eleven thousand men in its army nearly eight thousand were trying to pacify the newly acquired territory.[13]

In the face of so many serious disorders, Herrera deserves all the more credit for the reduction of the size of the Mexican army. In 1848, the commissioned officers were cut down to 273 in number, including forty-six generals and brigadier-generals—the year before, there were four hundred and twenty commissioned officers, not including either generals or brigadier-generals. The number of men was also reduced to 9999, of whom only 5211 were actually in service.[14] This action of Herrera shows an earnest desire to work for the good of the nation. It is true these numbers increased slightly in 1850, but there was no reversal of policy.[15]

In such a time, the condition of the treasury was of tremendous importance, but unfortunately no Alexander Hamilton arose to reorganize the finances and stabilize the currency, even though such reforms might have been greatly facilitated by the payments from

[11] P. N. Garber, *The Gadsden Treaty*, pp. 33-34.
[12] *Ibid.*, pp. 32-33. See also Rippy, *op. cit.*, chapter IV.
[13] *Ibid.*, pp. 27-32; Sierra, *op. cit.*, I. 235.
[14] Mayer, *op. cit.*, II. 125-126.
[15] *De Bow's Review*, XIII. 351-352 (October, 1852).

the United States, made in accordance with the treaty. Between August, 1848, and June, 1851, the treasury department had no fewer than twelve ministers.[16] No one man had time in which to become acquainted with his work before he gave place to another. On January 2, 1849, the minister, Piña y Cuevas, reported to the chamber a budget for the coming year as follows:

Secretary of Domestic & Foreign Affairs..	922,103 *pesos*
Secretary of Justice & Ecclesiastical Affairs	421,180 *pesos*
Secretary of Treasury (debts, legislature, etc.)	7,551,503 *pesos* 6 *rs.*
Secretary of War and Navy	7,685,733 *pesos* 6 *rs.*
	16,580,520 *pesos* 4 *rs.*
Estimated income	9,838,240 *pesos*
Estimated deficit	6,742,280 *pesos*[17]

It was hoped the deficit would be reduced to four million *pesos* by the rigid economy advocated. Some economies were at once introduced, beginning with reductions of from twenty-five to thirty-three and one third per cent. in salaries of officials.[18]

Probably one of the heaviest burdens faced by the treasury department was the public debt. With accrued interest, this amounted to nearly 150,000,000 *pesos*. At six per cent. interest, it was piling up charges

[16] Piña y Cuevas, *Esposición* . . . [*del*] *Secretario de Hacienda,* 1851, Num. 1; Garber, *op. cit.,* pp. 7-8.

[17] *Esposición* [*del*] . . . *Ministro de Hacienda* . . ., 1849, pp. 5, 8.

[18] Arrangoiz, II. 299.

at the rate of about 9,000,000 *pesos* per year.[19]   In other words, the interest on the debts of the nation amounted to nearly all the estimated revenue for 1849. By an arrangement with the British bondholders, it was agreed that they should cancel over 7,680,000 *pesos* of interest and reduce the interest rate on another 51,200,000 *pesos* to three per cent.[20]   Such concessions were not altogether liberal, in view of the prices at which most of these bonds had originally been bought.   On December 1, 1849, bond sales were reported from a London house for £70,000 of Mexican bonds at from twenty-five and three fourths to twenty-seven and one eighth per cent. of their face value.   In other words, bonds nominally worth £70,-000 had brought in only £18,662 10*s*.   Three per cent. interest on the face value would really mean well over eleven per cent. on the actual amount of the money invested.[21]

In 1850 Minister Manuel Payno attempted to meet the debt situation with a broad policy.   He planned to use part of the payment from the United States to secure a surrender of special privileges by foreign and domestic bondholders.   All local debts were to be refunded at three per cent.; and this new sum, as well as the foreign debts, was to be paid off by setting apart a certain proportion of the customs revenue for that purpose. At the same time, it was understood that in the future all legislative acts were to have

[19] Mayer, *op. cit.*, II. 109-111.

[20] Payno, *Mexico and Her Financial Questions*, pp. 23-25; Arrangoiz, II. 307.

[21] Report of bond sales for Mexican Government, dated December 1, 1849.   Manning-Mackintosh Papers.

general and not special application to debts. This was
the beginning of an excellent scheme, had it not contained some serious oversights. In the first place, the
minister lacked both immediate cash with which to
start it, and sufficient funds to give him a permanent
control of affairs. Also, he miscalculated the internal
debts and was unable to create a single classification
that would eliminate all the older privileged ones. As
his promises fell due, they could not be met. The result of his efforts was to leave the finances in a more
confused condition than they had been in before.[22]
In order to bolster up the proposal, therefore, it was
suggested that the Church guarantee the needed loan.
This, the clergy refused to do, fearing that it might be
the beginning of later trouble. Similarly, in 1853, hy-
pothecation of Church property was suggested, but
this suggestion was also successfully opposed by the
clergy.[23] To the nation at large these repeated failures to meet national debts promptly had never been
considered serious, but to the stability of any given
administration, such a policy was necessarily fatal
sooner or later.[24]

It was encouraging to note in the Minister's
report for 1851 that the net national income had increased to over 16,765,000 *pesos*.[25] However, this
sum was still insufficient to meet expenses, and the de-

[22] Sierra, *op. cit.*, II. 368.

[23] Haro y Tamariz, *Informe . . . al Presidente . . . por el
Ministro de Hacienda*, 1853, p. 9; *Harper's Monthly Magazine*, III. 697
(October, 1851); Bancroft, V. 565-566, 634.

[24] Adorno, J. Nepomuceno, *Análisis de los Males de México*, pp. 12-
13, 71.

[25] *Esposición* [*del Ministro de Hac*]*ienda á la Camara de Diputados*,
1851, table No. 7.

partment of justice, among others, reported that it could not perform its duties and run the judicial system of the country because of the absolute lack of funds.[26]

In addition to financial complications, the old issues of religious toleration, and even of religious freedom, once more made their appearance. This was to be expected as an aftermath of a war in which so many readjustments had been necessary. Two papers, *El Arco-Iris* and *El Eco del Comercio,* started the agitation in 1848.[27] Rocafuerte's old arguments were once more brought out, showing that Protestant countries had progressed and developed. Melchor Ocampo asked, somewhat pertinently, what a man was to do if he did not obey his own conscience in religious matters; for, if he followed the instructions of another, he would have to change his religion with each country he visited and become a Catholic, Protestant, Jew, or Mohammedan as occasion demanded.[28] The answer as given was, that the worship of God is not a "right" but an "obligation"; that the Church is right in its views, and, if a man's reasoning is correct, he will agree with the Church, and there will be no variation or disagreement.[29] In 1849 the congress was expected to take up the subject, but it refused to have much to do with it. In fact, the political movements in Italy against the Pope had so aroused Mexican feeling that he was voted twenty-five thousand *pesos* by the con-

[26] *Memoria del Ministro de Justicia y Negocios Eclesiásticos,* 1852, p. 21.

[27] Zamacois, XIII. 254-255.

[28] Melchor Ocampo, *Respuesta Primera . . . al Señor Autor de Una Impugnación,* pp. 9-10.

[29] *Segunda Impugnación a la Representación del Señor Ocampo,* p. 4; *Carta de un Amigo á Otro,* p. 26.

gress, and the president offered the Sovereign Pontiff an asylum in Mexico.[30] These acts, for the time being, helped to counteract the efforts of the advocates of toleration.

As part of the same spirit of reaction, Querétaro passed through its legislature a law for the reëstablishment of the Jesuits and the return to them of certain confiscated properties. Trouble then arose over the issuance of the order, for neither the governor nor the deputy governor would do it. Finally, after much delay, the law was promulgated by a minor official.[31] Chihuahua, about the same time, because of the Indian situation, decreed the reëstablishment of Jesuit missions.[32] Churchmen, moreover, were overjoyed at the arrival of a regular papal Nuncio. Unfortunately for the bishops, the Nuncio insisted that they make certain reports to him as to the property they held in trust.[33] The resulting strife among the clergymen threatened to do more harm than the arrival of the Nuncio had done good.

The Church had suffered a minimum in the way of waste and expense during the war, and now it was rapidly regaining its former position of power. The value of its property in the early years of the fifties seems to have been about three hundred million *pesos,* or slightly less.[34] Controlling such an amount of property and with a steady income of cash from fees, voluntary tithes, and other offerings, it had entered upon

[30] Bancroft, V. 590-591.
[31] Arrangoiz, II. 315-316.
[32] *Ibid.,* II. 296.
[33] Wilson, *Mexico, Its Peasants and its Priests,* p. 325.
[34] Mendieta y Núñez, *op. cit.,* pp. 75-77.

the business of money-lending on a larger scale than ever. It was increasingly difficult for anyone to oppose the archbishop, that Church lord who "carried in his hands the treasures of heaven and in his money-bags the material that moves[d] the world".[35]

With the increasing efficiency of the Church organization, there was long and bitter controversy over the assessment and collection of fees. The liberals claimed that large numbers of them emanated in reality from the civil power and hence were subject to its jurisdiction.[36] They assiduously studied the rules laid down by the Council of Trent and announced that the civil power was there recognized as having the right to levy fees of various kinds on behalf of the Church.[37] The clergy responded that the bishops were given power to control the Church and hence to regulate fees also.[38] Regardless of the origin of the charges, the fact remained that for laborers to be forced to pay twenty *pesos* for a marriage fee, when they only earned about fifty *pesos* a year, was a direct invitation to most of them to ignore the ceremony entirely. The clergy answered that a man could well afford to wait till he earned the sum, or, if in a particular hurry, he could borrow from his master. If the master made severe terms, it was not the fault of the Church.[39] In other communities, a laborer was required to pay a weekly sum to the Church of one half a *real,* or about three and a quarter *pesos* per year. This

[35] Wilson, *op. cit.,* p. 324.
[36] Melchor Ocampo, *Respuesta Quinta* . . ., pp. 8-9.
[37] *Ibid.,* pp. 20-21.
[38] *Tercera Impugnación* . . ., p. 6.
[39] *Ibid.,* pp. 23-24.

also was a serious drain on his meager earnings and was unjustly levied, since assessments varied on the same class of workers in different communities.[40] The response was made that heavy financial demands fostered a spirit of giving and charity; hence that the Church was fully justified.[41]

When the question arose of "rendering unto Caesar the things that are Caesar's", the Church acknowledged that it had a responsibility. The trouble lay in the fact that it insisted on being the judge as to what belonged to Caesar. Having reached a conclusion as to what should be given, it then made a donation and considered its responsibility ended, absolutely refusing to pay taxes.[42]

Other troubles of an economic nature, which created more feeling than their importance justified, were those arising out of the small amount of property confiscated in accordance with the law of January 11, 1847. As late as June 29, 1849, one Jesús Camerena was still complaining that he could not get a clear title to a certain piece of this property, even though he had complied with all of the regulations. He said that the executive had given the proper instructions, but that minor officials, dominated by their religious scruples, had delayed and held matters up.[43]

[40] Melchor Ocampo, *Respuesta Primera* . . ., p. 4; *Mexico, the Country, History, and People*, pp. 199-200.

[41] *Segunda Impugnación*, pp. 26-27. The case for the opponents of the Church is well summarized in sixteen questions asked by Melchor Ocampo in his *Respuesta Segunda*, dated May 21, 1851, pp. 9-10.

[42] José María Besares, *Inmunidad de la Iglesia*, p. 9.

[43] Jesús Camarena to Gómez Farías, June 29, 1849. Gómez Farías Papers.

In spite of the pro-Church reaction, however, the liberals could not claim that Mexico had a disproportionate number of clergymen for the nation. As a matter of fact, by including all the clergy, the aged and infirm as well as the administrative officers, in 1850, there was only about one for each eighteen hundred inhabitants.[44] The real complaint was, that the city districts, where living conditions were good, were fairly well supplied, while country and frontier districts were practically without ecclesiastics of any kind. Some parishes were seventy-five miles in length and contained children of twelve years of age who had never been baptized; yet, according to the Church, baptism was a prerequisite of salvation.[45]

During the reaction in favor of the clergy, their intolerance became extreme. On the death of Gómez Pedraza, though he had been a friend of the Church during his lifetime and had been attended by priests on his deathbed, burial in consecrated ground was denied for his remains, since he had failed to confess before expiring. He was held in such high esteem, however, that the congress had a special mausoleum built for him.[46]

If the Church felt strong enough thus to oppose public sentiment, it could also be expected to make a vigorous set of answers to the attacks of the liberals. There was no hesitation in claiming that the three essentials of a nation were the Roman Catholic religion, then independence, and, finally, liberty.[47] The

[44] Zamacois, XIII. 368-369.
[45] Y. O., *La Reforma Social de Méjico*, p. 15.
[46] Bancroft, V. 129.
[47] *Los Seudo-Liberales ó la Muerte de la República Mexicana*, p. 29.

right of censorship was unhesitatingly claimed for all
books;[48] deism was denounced as an approach to ma-
terialism and atheism,[49] but real liberty and equality
were true Catholic principles, since "the black and the
white, the slave and the master, the noble and the
plebian kneel before the same altar."[50]   If the Church
was intolerant, it claimed not to persecute anyone;
it simply demanded that the country should close its
doors to Protestants, as a father would close the doors
of his house to those who would injure his children,
or as a city would exclude persons with contagious di-
seases.[51]   It was the duty of the government also to
suppress all teachers of false doctrines and to punish
them, "if not as heterodox, at least as disturbers of the
peace".[52]   To those who advocated civil marriage, the
Church pointed out the situation in France, where civil
marriages seemed to have had a tendency to increase
the number of promiscuous unions.[53] In regard to the
large possessions of the clergy, it was maintained that
wealth was needed to lend dignity as well as to insure
the continuity of any program undertaken. Also, without ample resources, the Church could not gain or hold
the respect of the leaders of the land, themselves rich
men.[54]

These arguments were, for the time being, very
effective throughout the coutry.   Large numbers of

[48] Agustín Flores Alatorre, *Contestación dada al Supremo Gobierno*
., p. 19.
[49] *Los Seudo-Liberales,* p. 31.
[50] *Ibid.,* pp. 13-14.
[51] *Carta de un Amigo a Otro,* pp. 12-13.
[52] *Ibid.,* p. 16.
[53] *Colección de Documentos Relativos a Matrimonios Civiles,* pp.
10-11, 20.
[54] Balmes, *op. cit.,* pp. 17, 37.

petitions were sent to the congress against the taking of any rash steps. The citizens of Ixtlam went so far as to assert that the war for independence was fought for the sake of the Church.[55] From Aguas Calientes, a petition with some five hundred signatures protested against freedom of religion,[56] while, from Guadalajara, a petition containing about 1380 names asked for complete protection of the Roman Catholic faith and its transmission unimpaired to future generations.[57]

During this period of controversy and reconstruction, the economic conditions of the country were improving somewhat. The telegraph was being introduced, and on April 25, 1852, a line was completed from Vera Cruz to Orizaba, partly by government aid. The official opening of the line took place May 4.[58] The three savings banks of the country all showed very satisfactory balances of from 2684.50 *pesos* to 152,041.31 *pesos*. It is true that one bank in Aguas Calientes had closed in 1853, but two years later another was opened there.[59] The mining industry was steadily improving, as may be seen from a report of the Rosario mine. In 1851, it produced 169,422 *pesos* of silver at a profit of 80,063 *pesos;* in 1853, the output was 863,365 *pesos,* with a profit of 388,110 *pesos;* and in 1855 the figures reached 1,298,783 and 563,779 *pesos* respectively.[60]

[55] *Representación de los Vecinos de Ixtlám* . . . *contra tolerancia,* p. 3.

[56] *Representación de los Vecinos de Aguascalientes,* pp. 1-8.

[57] *Representación de los Vecinos de Guadalajara.*

[58] Zamacois, XIII. 491, 532.

[59] Lerdo de Tejada, *op. cit.,* pp. 53-54.

[60] *London Quarterly Review,* CXV. 186 (April, 1864). The chief backset to this prosperity was the cholera epidemic of 1850. Zamacois, XIII. 375-378.

Increase in the population had been steady though slow. The great emigrant nations of Europe of the earlier nineteenth century were those which preferred the Anglo-Saxon to the Spanish type of civilization, and the stable government of the United States to one subject to as many vicissitudes as that of Mexico. In 1846 Mexico may have had eight million inhabitants.[61] By 1854 there is little doubt that the population had attained that figure. The number of foreigners in the country, though small, was increasing. In 1854 Mexico had 1213 more immigrants than emigrants. The number of persons actually registered as foreigners was over nine thousand, of whom one thousand or twelve hundred had come from England and the United States. Including those not registered, there were probably twenty-five thousand,[62] who directly or indirectly were busy introducing new ideas and customs.

Regardless of the increasing number of foreigners, education was necessarily a slow process, especially when at least three fourths of the people were said to be illiterate. The conditions were probably at their best in Mexico City, where, it is said, a little over four per cent. of the total population attended school.[63] Of the 122 schools there, with 7636 pupils, the government maintained four, with 488 pupils; convents supported two, with 150 pupils, while the other 116 schools, with nearly 7000 pupils, were maintained by private initi-

[61] Rives, *op. cit.*, II. 101, note.
[62] Lerdo de Tejada, *op. cit.*, pp. 29-30; García y Cubas, *op. cit.*, p. 15.
[63] *De Bow's Review*, XIII. 345 (October, 1852).

ative with some government aid. Two years later, the government opened a school of agriculture also.[64]

As to the condition of the press, it may be said that in 1848 penalties of from six months to two years in solitary confinement for libel or for denunciation of public officers seriously curtailed its liberty because of the broadness with which the laws were interpreted.[65] Conservatives still claimed that freedom of the press meant the wholesale spreading of immorality, anarchy, and ruin,[66] while very little in the way of education and progress would result.[67] This situation was not without its bearing on politics.

For a man to vote, he had to be enrolled in the National Guard, a provision which took the franchise from large numbers.[68] At the elections in 1848, there was considerable danger of trouble in Guadalajara, for example, when the officials imprisoned and intimidated members of the opposition.[69] *El Universal* injected the idea of monarchy. *El Monitor Republicano* promptly took up the gauntlet for the liberals, but the silence of most of the papers of the nation was ominous.[70] No distinct lines of party cleavage could be drawn;[71] the stand of prominent men was generally known, but that of minor individuals was seldom to

[64] Sierra, *op. cit.,* I. 509-511.
[65] Zamacois, XIII. 213.
[66] *Los Seudo-Liberales,* p. 10.
[67] *Ibid.,* p. 9.
[68] Jesús Camarena to Gómez Farías, August 17, 1849. Gómez Farías Papers.
[69] *Ibid.,* September 3, 1849.
[70] Zamacois, XIII. 295-298.
[71] Martínez, *op. cit.,* pp. 158-159.

be predicted with accuracy.[72]   In December, 1850, the elections resulted in the choice of Mariano Arista, minister of war and a liberal, as the executive to follow Herrera, a man who had been inclined to the *Moderados.* On January 15, 1851, the new President took office, and Herrera retired "with the reputation of being a lover of peace and an honest man. He was the first President of Mexico who peacefully and legally transferred the chief magistracy to another's hand."[73]

Arista's career, prior to his administration, was that of an opportunist who had been an extreme liberal in 1828 and 1833, though still earlier he had been a royalist. He was banished to the United States and returned, as he said, "a moderate republican".[74]   His record in the army during the war with the United States had been none too good. In short, he was a typical guerrilla chieftain, who was intensely ambitious and full of energy, but with the shortcomings of his kind.[75]

Discontent appeared in many sections of the country. The government was said to be letting favorable contracts to newspapers in order to subsidize them and gain their support.[76]   Governor Melchor Ocampo of Michoacán brought matters to a head in that department by the unwise introduction of extensive religious reforms coincident with heavy increases in taxation.[77]

[72] Cf. Pomposa Verdugo to Gómez Farías, October 6, 1849. Gómez Farías Papers.

[73] W. S. Robertson, *History of the Latin American Nations,* p. 485.

[74] Arrangoiz, II. 316-317.

[75] Priestley, *Mexican Nation,* p. 319.

[76] Zamacois, XIII. 519-520.

[77] Bulnes, *op. cit.,* p. 95; Zamacois, XIII. 566-568; Arrangoiz, II. 336.

The result was trouble that spread rapidly to much of the rest of the nation, for the clergy did not need urging to join a movement in opposition to the liberals.[78] Credit for the initiation of the *Plan de Hospicio,* the formal enunciation of principles by the rebels, is usually given to Guadalajara. Trouble arose also in Orizaba, whence it was reported that the capital was in turmoil. In fact, no one appears to have had faith in the stability of the government.[79] The administration, on its part, laid restrictions with a heavy hand, foreigners being treated with particular severity. If a man, Mexican or foreigner, was ill at the time of a political arrest, that made little difference. One newspaper calmly remarked, "Those illnesses are now a threadbare excuse."[80] The revolution was engineered and carried through by the conservatives, who were steadily gaining in power and prestige.[81] This meant that the congress, which met in January, 1852, was already largely repudiated by the country, because the deputies supported Arista and the liberals.[82]

The President soon realized that his cause was hopeless. Even abroad, as early as October, 1851, it was thought that the country was ripe for a general revolution.[83] The troops were in favor of any outstanding military leader, preferably Santa Anna. Knowing the circumstances, he resigned in January, 1853.

[78] Arrangoiz, II. 324-327.

[79] Ángel to Casimiro Gómez Farías, July 20, 1852. Gómez Farías Papers.

[80] Zamacois, XIII. 573-575.

[81] *El Partido Conservador en México,* pp. 7-9.

[82] Arrangoiz, II. 323.

[83] Benito Gómez Farías to his brother Casimiro, October 30, 1851. Gómez Farías Papers.

Juan Bautista Cevallos, chief justice of the supreme court, was chosen by sixteen of the twenty-one votes cast to act as president *ad interim.* This office he held for a month and a day.[84] The Guadalajara rebels did not lay down their arms, so he attempted to secure control of their movement by having himself chosen as its leader. On the failure of this scheme and his disagreement with the congress, the army stepped in and took charge of affairs, turning the power over to General Manuel de Lombardini with the equivalent of dictatorial power, but with the understanding that he would bring Santa Anna back to Mexico.

One of the leaders and the spokesman of the conservatives was Lúcas Alamán, the historian.[85] On March 3, 1853, he had written to Santa Anna, stating plainly and clearly the position of his party with respect to the Church and other political issues. Among the principles laid down as fundamental were: the preservation of the Roman Catholic faith; a central government sufficiently strong to be effective; a reorganization of the government, abolishing the representative federal system; the redistribution of units of administration so that old state lines would be entirely abolished, thus making less likely a return to the federal system; an army sufficiently strong to suppress robbery and Indian incursions, and the organization of the central government by Santa Anna and a few councilors without the intervention of a congress.[86] Though Santa Anna had frequently changed his policy, if not

[84] Zamacois, XIII. 606-616.

[85] Antonio de la Peña y Reyes, *Lúcas Alamán,* p. v.

[86] *El Partido Conservador en México,* p. 41; *Historia de la Orden Mexicana de Nuestra Señora de Guadalupe;* Arrangoiz, II. 337-338.

his principles, the conservatives thought that his personal popularity plus their own strength would mean
almost certain victory. The prize once secured, they
hoped to be able to control him through their own
strength.

On March 17 the votes for president were counted.
Of the twenty-three votes cast, eighteen were for
Santa Anna.[87] Three days later he reached Mexico
from Jamaica and at once entered upon the discharge
of his duties. In the selection of his ministry, it was
a foregone conclusion that the portfolio of foreign relations would go to Lúcas Alamán. Haro y Tamariz
and J. M. Tornel, both prominent men and *Santanistas*
but more or less contaminated by liberal ideas, were
placed in charge of the treasury and war departments
respectively.[88] These three men pleased the nation
more than they did the President; but he was not to be
hindered by them for long. Alamán died in June,
Tornel followed him in September, and Haro y Tamariz resigned in August, after Santa Anna had refused to allow him to float a loan guaranteed by Church
property.[89] As the places became vacant, they were
filled with men after the President's own heart.[90]

The Jesuit order was reëstablished in the land by a
decree dated May 1,[91] though this did not mean that
Santa Anna intended to give the Church and the
clergy a controlling hand in affairs. If anyone had

[87] Zamacois, XIII. 624.
[88] *El Partido Conservador en México*, p. 12.
[89] Sierra, *op. cit.*, I. 236.
[90] Anselmo de la Portilla, *Historia de la Revolución contra la Dictadura de Santa Ana*, p. 8.
[91] Noll, *op. cit.*, p. 174.

this impression, they had a chance to see their mistake on September 5, when he issued a decree declaring that in crimes of conspiracy no *fuero* was to be effective. If any doubt still remained, it was shortly dispelled by the execution of Manuel Gómez, curate of Cacalotenango, who was guilty of aiding a guerrilla leader.[92] On the other hand, a number of prominent Masons were banished, including Juárez, Degollado, and Alatriste,[93] though this was probably because they were liberals rather than because they were Masons.

Santa Anna rapidly concentrated power in his own hands. A report from Mexico in July noted that this was obvious to all.[94] Town officials heretofore elected were now appointed, and public employees were refused the right to take any part in the discussion of public questions. Needless to say, the freedom of the press was curtailed, if not abolished.[95] The attitude of the President toward his subordinates was well expressed in a communication sent to the Commanding General of Vera Cruz, which contained this gem: "A public functionary *ought to close his ears,* and to work without any thought [on his own part]."[96]

Probably the popularity of the President was at its height in the last months of 1853. On all sides could be heard such flattery as:

Today Divine Providence has placed the destinies of our native land in the hands of the good citizen, the intrepid warrior, the immortal Don Antonio López de Santa Anna; may

[92] Portilla, *Historia de la Revolución,* p. 123.

[93] Mateos, *op. cit.,* pp. 130-131.

[94] *Harper's Monthly Magazine,* VII. 549 (September, 1853).

[95] Zamacois, XIII. 653; Noll, p. 174.

[96] Portilla, *Historia de la Revolución,* p. 12.

this be a beginning, a certain indication that the hour of its restoration has arrived.[97]

His inordinate love of pomp and ceremony led to the reëstablishment of the Order of Guadalupe, which had been originated by the ill-fated Iturbide.[98] This order had about it all the elements of an incipient nobility and certainly conduced to aristocracy. Castañeda, a supreme court justice, refused an invitation to become a member, saying that he could not afford to do so. Juan Bautista Cevallos, the chief justice, rejected the honor, saying that it was one not suitable in a republic, whereupon the President deposed him from the bench as unsuitable for office.[99] Even the University of Mexico felt the effects of this craze for ceremony. The Dictator interfered quite frequently with the courses offered and caused many honorary degrees to be conferred upon non-students.[100] On December 16, 1853, moreover, the President declared himself Perpetual Dictator, having already assumed the title of "Most Serene Highness".

In his relations with the United States Santa Anna has been the object of much blame and of very little praise in his native land. There was still a great deal of agitation in the northern republic to press the claims of the Tehuantepec Railroad Company of New Orleans, while newspapers, such as *De Bow's Review,*

[97] Mariano de Camino, *Discurso Cívico,* pp. 10-11.

[98] It is interesting to note that the national hymn of Mexico was first sung, September 11, 1854. Pérez Verdía, *op. cit.,* p. 427.

[99] Portilla, *Historia de la Revolución,* appendix No. II.

[100] H. I. Priestley, *The Old University of Mexico. University of California Chronicles,* XXI. No. 4, p. 19.

carefully watched the trend of trade between the countries and devoted exhaustive articles to the subject.[101]
The grant to a United States syndicate to develop in-
teroceanic communication in the Tehuantepec region
was so large and was being pushed with such energy
in the United States that Mexican officials became
quite alarmed.[102]   In addition, with the inauguration
of President Pierce, in 1853, a vigorous foreign policy
was adopted that was not impeded by "any timid fore-
bodings of evil from expansion".[103]

Santa Anna, meanwhile, was badly in need of
funds with which to carry on his expensive government.   The desire in the United States for a Pacific
railroad provided him with an opportunity to secure
them; for the route desired by the United States
advocates of the road passed through Mexican territory for a short distance, owing to engineering difficulties further north. Gadsden, the United States Minister, was authorized to negotiate for the desired strip
of territory.   Without undue difficulty, the treaty was
drawn up, and the Mesilla region, also known as the
Gadsden Purchase, was surrendered for fifteen million
dollars and the assumption by the United States government of all the claims of its citizens against Mexico.
The opponents of the Dictator said that this alienation
of Mexican soil was a direct violation of the oath of
office taken by him, when he swore "to defend the in-

---

[101] *De Bow's Review,* XIII. 49 (July, 1852) ; XV. 198 (August, 1853).
For a review of the Tehuantepec claims see J. J. Williams, *The Isthmus
of Tehuantepec.*

[102] Garber, *op. cit.,* p. 49.

[103] *Ibid.,* pp. 68-69.

dependence and integrity of the Mexican territory".[104]
His apologists answered that "The sale of the Mesilla
was not voluntary [and] was not an undertaking of
the government", but was a part of the policy of the
United States to which Santa Anna had no force to
oppose; that if he had not sold a small district the
United States would have taken a much larger one.[105]
Some justification for this assertion arose from the
action of delegates to such gatherings as the commercial convention of the southern and western states held
in Charleston, South Carolina, in 1854.[106]

The peculiar Raousset de Boulbon episode was also
connected with the same border region. This erratic
character entered Sonora from the north in September,
1852, with two hundred and fifty armed men. He
stated that his sole purpose was to provide police protection for some mines. After brief negotiations, he
withdrew his men from the country, and the next year
was received at Mexico City as a friend by Santa
Anna. The two worthies soon disagreed, whereupon
Raousset returned to California and organized an expedition with which he announced he would conquer
for himself a republic in Sinaloa, Sonora, Chihuahua,
and Durango. He was captured with three hundred
and twelve men (forty-eight of whom were killed)
and was executed August 12.[107] In spite of the fact
that the whole expedition was a fiasco, it was a clear

---

[104] Portilla, *Historia de la Revolución,* p. 16.

[105] Bulnes, *op. cit.,* pp. 118-122.

[106] *Journal of the Proceedings of the Commercial Convention of the
Southern and Western States,* 1854, appendix XVII.

[107] Zamacois, XII. 540-543, 576-582, 589-591, 665, 735, 789-798. For
further information on filibuster raids see Rippy, *op. cit.,* chapter V.

indication that serious dissatisfaction prevailed in the country when such a handful of men dared to flout a military dictator.

The tide had begun to turn, in spite of the vain attempts to encourage colonization[108] and build up the country on the one hand and to dazzle the people with pomp and magnificence on the other. These latter displays, especially, had little influence on the regions at a distance from the capital, where the people were being subjected to Indian attacks, the ravages of cholera, and consequent hard times.[109] The change in the sentiment of the Mexicans as a whole was most accurately reflected by the attitude of Benito Gómez Farías, who was in London, in 1854, attached to the Mexican legation there. On April 7, he wrote that word had just come of the rebellion of Álvarez in the south and added: "I think there is no one who expects any good from a man like Álvarez!" But, on April 30, he was disturbed by the dictatorial policy of Santa Anna. May 18, he reported that he had just heard of the defeat of Álvarez (a false report based on Santa Anna's campaign), who threatened the country with worse evils than those which would result from a continuation of the existing régime. June 30, he still did not expect Álvarez to succeed, since his principles were not constructive enough, but he now admitted that probably another man would start a similar movement that would sweep the country.[110]

---

[108] Mendieta y Núñez, op. cit., p. 72.

[109] Zamacois, XIII. 707-708, 811.

[110] Benito Gómez Farías to his brother Casimiro, April 7, 1854; to his father, May 18, 1854; to his father, June 30, 1854, and to his father, April 30, 1854. Gómez Farías Papers.

Whatever the amount of political unrest, the income of the nation appeared to be improving steadily after 1850, to judge from the reports of the ministers of the treasury department.[111]   In fact, the estimates for the year 1855 showed a balanced budget with over 785,000 *pesos* for extraordinary expenses that might arise after the other obligations of the nation had been met.[112]   If this was the true situation, it is exceedingly difficult to account for the surrender of cotton-exporting permits to the house of García, Despons and Kern worth 323,767 *pesos* for 50,000 *pesos* cash and 67,376.70 *pesos* in government bonds.[113]   The conclusions to be drawn are: either that the budget was "doctored" or that there had been rank favoritism—or worse—in the matter of the cotton permits, even though the actual value of the bonds involved may have been underestimated.   The only alternative to these conclusions is, that both the government and the firm concerned thought a change in administration to be imminent, with the result that the value of the permits was substantially reduced in the minds of all concerned.

That Santa Anna realized the possibility of a serious revolt would appear from his negotiations for three regiments of Swiss troops as soon as the Mesilla treaty was completed.[114]   Though a denial of such negotiations was made, it appeared to carry little

[111] G. Prieto, *Informe* [*a la*] . . . *Cámara de Diputados por el Ministro de Hacienda*, 1852, pp. 5-6; Manuel Olasagarre, *Informe presenta*[*da*] *al Supremo Gobierno,* 1855, *appendix,* pp. 1-7.

[112] Olasagarre, *op. cit.,* pp. 34-36.

[113] Zarco, I. 593-595.

[114] Portilla, *Historia de la Revolución,* p. 10, note.

weight. Quite possibly the reason the troops were not secured was, that the temper of public opinion would have made such an enlistment of foreign troops productive of more harm than good. The opposition in the south centered around Juan Álvarez, the old chieftain and a full-blooded Indian of Guerrero. For a number of years he had been in collusion with Ignacio Comonfort, a local leader of considerable importance, and in regular correspondence with him. The latter had, on June 10, 1853, been named customs collector at Acapulco with a salary of six thousand *pesos*,[115] but he was still in touch with the discontented elements.

Álvarez was the first to break with the administration and actually start a revolution. This happened in February, 1854. On March 1, Colonel Florencio Villareal, who had been dismissed by Santa Anna, issued the Plan of Ayutla.[116] A man with few principles, he later deserted the liberal cause, which he was now proclaiming at the head of four hundred *pintos* (half castes).[117] The chief demands of the rebels were: (1) the overthrow of Santa Anna and all others who opposed the new plan; (2) after the adoption of the Plan by a majority of the nation, the general-in-chief to summon a representative from each department and territory to select a president *ad interim* and to act with the others as his council; (3) reorganization of the local governments to conform to the Plan;

---

[115] Commission issued to Comonfort and signed by Santa Anna, dated June 10, 1853. Comonfort Papers. García Collection.

[116] A. Rivera, *La Reforma y el Segundo Imperio*, p. 7; García Granados, *op. cit.*, p. 11; Arrangoiz, II. 343, 346.

[117] *Ibid.* These "pintos" lived in the southern portion of the country. The name was given to them because of the dark spots on their skins. They were of mixed Indian and Negro blood.

(4) the calling by the president *ad interim,* two weeks after taking office, of a convention to approve his acts and draw up a constitution; (5) due provision for the army and the readjustment of customs duties as soon as possible; (6) the annullment of certain laws and decrees of Santa Anna, and (7) General Nicolás Bravo to ask Juan Álvarez and Tomás Moreno to join the movement and lead it.[118]

Santa Anna knew the situation in the south and shifted Comonfort to another post,[119] but this did not remove the danger. In fact, the rebels authorized Comonfort to go to the United States and secure five hundred thousand dollars with which to carry on the war.[120] He proceeded at once to San Francisco, but could not secure satisfactory terms. Thereupon, he went across the continent, but he could get little encouragement in the east till Gregorio de Ajuria, a Mexican liberal then living in New York, volunteered private funds of his own.[121] Meanwhile, Gadsden, the United States minister in Mexico, actively sympathized with the rebels and urged Pierce to break off all relations with Santa Anna and to send an army to aid the liberals.[122]

---

[118] *La Nacionalidad,* June 12, 1856, gives the "Plan" in full.

[119] Zamacois, XIII. 723.

[120] The manuscript of Comonfort's "full powers" is available in the Comonfort Papers. It is signed by Ygnacio Pérez Vargas as a notary public of Acapulco, and countersigned, as being correct, by U. S. Consul, Chas. L. Denman and Juan de Alzuyeta, Consul of Ecuador. It also bears the signature of Juan Álvarez and other liberal leaders.

[121] Portilla, *Historia de la Revolución,* pp. 150-159.

[122] Garber, *op. cit.,* p. 153.

The warfare was conducted in an extremely brutal manner. The rebels were to be hanged when captured, their houses and villages burned, and their crops, live stock, and all other means of subsistence destroyed.[123] Santa Anna himself took charge of the army for the campaign against Álvarez. He personally interviewed General Bravo, then quite feeble, and secured a letter from him urging the revolutionists to lay down their arms. Strangely enough, a few days later both the General and his wife died. Many thought they were disposed of by Santa Anna, who was said to have used pressure to secure the letter.[124] In the campaign, little actual fighting occurred, though a minor victory was secured by Álvarez, and Santa Anna returned to Mexico City to order a magnificent celebration in honor of the victory of the national troops. This deceived very few, and the time-servers forthwith began to calculate the strength of their positions and the advisability of trimming their sails.[125]

Seeing that his personal prestige was waning, Santa Anna commissioned Gutiérrez Estrada to try to secure an European sovereign for Mexico. Estrada's

[123] Portilla, *Historia de la Revolución*, p. 188.

[124] *Ibid.*, pp. 102-103.

[125] L. G. de A. (Luís García de Arellano is suggested by Garcia) to Gómez Farías, May 25, 1854. Gómez Farías Papers; *Harper's Monthly Magazine*, IX. 251 (July, 1854). An interesting side light on the people of the country is the use made of signs and omens by both parties. While Santa Anna was on his campaign against the rebels, it was advertised that a splendid eagle (called the imperial) after circling over the troops, lighted near Santa Anna and allowed him and him alone to touch it. On the other hand, when Santa Anna returned to the city, he enjoyed a splendid triumph during which he passed through a triumphal arch. Two days later a violent storm destroyed the arch and caused many headshakings and comments to pass around, albeit with much circumspection. Portilla, *op. cit.*, pp. 68, 105-106.

commission read: "I confer upon him by these Presents the plenary powers necessary to enter into arrangements, and make proper offers, at the Courts of London, Paris, Madrid and Vienna, to obtain from them or any one of them, the establishment of a monarchy derived from any of the royal races of those Powers." The entire support of the clergy was given to this idea.[126] In order to secure much needed funds, the Dictator then approached Gadsden on July 18, 1855, and tried to sell more territory to the United States. Gadsden, however, was very lukewarm to the proposal, owing to his extreme dislike of Santa Anna.[127]

A last desperate effort to bolster up the popularity of the administration had been resorted to in December of the preceding year. At that time, a plebiscite was held to decide whether Santa Anna should continue to rule. Those who voted in the affirmative were to write their names in one book, while those voting in the negative were to use another. The opponents of the government thought that this was simply a trick by which to secure their names, so few of them dared to take part in the process. In Mexico City, for instance, the vote was 112,452 to 1, while other districts sent in similar reports.[128] Again, few people were deceived, and during the first half of 1855 the well-wishers of the administration became few and far between.

In August, 1855, Santa Anna went to Vera Cruz and there resigned. It is a more accurate statement to say that he fell from office after throwing away popu-

[126] C. Edwards Lester, *The Mexican Republic*, p. 32.
[127] Garber, *op. cit.*, p. 167.
[128] Zamacois, XIII. 825, 829.

lar support, rather than to say that he was overthrown. The clergy, while they feared the liberals, were not yet willing to be dominated by Santa Anna. The creoles, having lost their power and now comparatively unimportant, joined the *mestizos* as moderates, for the *mestizos* were becoming directly opposed to a dictatorship.[129]

In spite of his many and serious shortcomings, all of Santa Anna's work had not been bad. Brigandage was checked; education, at least among the upper classes, was supported, and the Jesuits were reintroduced to help the poorer classes; closer relations with the Vatican were secured, thus strengthening the international position of Mexico; and internal improvements, many of them spectacular but others of permanent value, were fostered.[130]

With this final leave-taking of Santa Anna, a period of Mexican history closed.[131] A man of strength, possessed of a magnetic personality had gone. He had taken part in the launching of eight *pronunciamentos,* five put forth by himself and three made on his behalf. Twice he was made president by the federalists and three times by the centralists. Twice he was banished, only to be recalled to the highest office in the land. Twice he was captured by his enemies, and each time grave fears were entertained by his friends for his life. Primarily a soldier, he contributed in no small degree to the betterment of the

[129] Molina Enríquez, *op. cit.,* pp. 52-53; *La Sociedad,* December 1, 1855.

[130] Bancroft, V. 633.

[131] Sierra, *op. cit.,* I. p. 240.

judicial system of the nation.[132]   Denounced as a "demon of ambition and discord" who, like Attila, was "the Scourge of God", he was cursed by all classes and conditions of people.   On his leaving the country, a broadside had this to say: "In the woods and in the valleys, in the cities and in the country, the echo repeats these words: cursed be Santa Anna; cursed be the assassin of his country."[133]   Yet, with his peculiar idealism and self-deception, he thought that he had acted constantly for the good of his country.   Nineteen years later, writing his *Historia Militar y Política*, at the outset of the concluding chapter, he wrote:

Mithradates in exile breathed vengeance . . .
I breathe pardon, forgetfulness, good for my country . . .[134]

His life was fraught with ambitions, contradictions, successes, and failures; he was one of the most remarkable characters Mexico has ever produced.

[132] Wilson, *op. cit.,* p. 121.
[133] Broadside entitled *Apóstrofe a Santa Anna.*   García Collection.
[134] Santa Anna, *op. cit.,* p. 184.

CHAPTER X

THE LIBERALS TAKE CHARGE

The opposition to Santa Anna had been composed of such varied elements that permanent coöperation among them was out of the question. The Mexican people were definitely through with the military Dictator who had been a prominent figure for so long, but, further than that, they scarcely knew what they wanted. The question now to be faced was whether the conservatives, who had opposed Santa Anna from Puebla, or the liberals under the leadership of Álvarez would dominate the scene.[1] The position of Vidaurri, who had issued a manifesto in Monterey, was another uncertain element, no one knowing just where he stood. Later he became an imperialist, but at this time he was associated with the liberals.[2]

On the resignation of Santa Anna, the *Junta Patriótica,* as provided for by the Plan of Ayutla, was called together by General Díaz de la Vega, who at the moment was in command of the troops in Mexico City. That body chose Mariano Riva Palacio as its presiding officer[3] and then proceeded to select Martín Carrera as president *ad interim.* Carrera had a good record, but he had not been an outstanding leader of

[1] Arrangoiz, II. 346.

[2] Fermin Gómez Farías to his Father, October 6, 1855. Gómez Farías Papers.

[3] An attempt was made to secure the support of Valentín Gómez Farías by offering to make him vice-president of the *Junta.* Luís Moncada to Valentín Gómez Farías, August 27, 1855. Gómez Farías Papers.

the revolution. Recognition of his right to act was at once refused by Comonfort, Álvarez, Haro y Tamariz, and others, on the ground that Díaz de la Vega was not authorized to summon the *Junta* in the first place. The conservatives in Puebla likewise refused recognition to Carrera, but the main army of the liberals steadily approached the capital. Its leaders, Álvarez and Comonfort, rapidly gained adherents and appointed men to office as the opportunity offered.[4]

Seeing that his efforts to consolidate the various factions among the liberals were failing, Carrera resigned from the executive office. The logical step of consolidation under the leadership of Álvarez was then taken, he being the successful commander-in-chief who had really fought the war through to its successful conclusion.[5] As he approached the capital with his army, Gómez Farías kept him informed as to conditions in the city.[6] In accordance with the Plan of Ayutla, Álvarez proceeded to select the representatives of the various districts who were to act as the members of the new *Junta Patriótica*. On October 4 they met at Cuernavaca, presided over by Gómez Farías, to elect the president *ad interim* of the republic. Many thought that Comonfort would be the selection of the *Junta* and were quite surprised at the choice of Álvarez, even though they were ready to support the

[4] Ignacio Comonfort to Fermín Gómez Farías, August 29, 1855. Gómez Farías Papers.

[5] Ignacio Comonfort to Valentín Gómez Farías, September 18, 1855. Gómez Farías Papers.

[6] Juan Ávarez to Valentín Gómez Farías, September 18, 1855; Valentín Gómez Farías to Comonfort and to Alvarez, both dated September 19, 1855. Gómez Farías Papers.

latter when chosen.[7]   The vote stood: Álvarez, thirteen; Ocampo, three; Comonfort, three, and Vidaurri,
one. Comonfort asked his friends to vote for Álvarez.
On the other hand, Álvarez's son voted for Comonfort, and the father asked that he be left in charge of
the army while others administered public affairs.[8]

The President at once appointed his ministers. The
new minister of .war, Ignacio Comonfort, was his
right-hand man, and Melchor Ocampo, Guillermo
Prieto, Benito Juárez, and Lerdo de Tejada were
placed respectively in the departments of state, treasury, justice and ecclesiastical affairs, and public works
(*fomento*). These men, with the possible exception of
Comonfort, were pronounced liberals and were known
as opponents of the Church on former occasions.
Juárez and Álvarez were Indians,[9] a clear indication
that a new class was beginning to arise. Now it was
no longer creoles and a few *mestizos,* but *mestizos* and
Indians, together with a few creoles, who were in
charge. The Masonic element was also strong in the
cabinet. In the *Rito Nacional* Juárez was an ardent
worker, having obtained the highest rank in the
order.[10] Comonfort was a member of the *Escoceses*
and had taken the thirty-third degree.[11] Both Ocampo

[7] Fermín Gómez Farías to "Mi mui queridós Papá Mamá y her-
manos", September 24, 1855. Gómez Farías Papers; *La Nacionalidad,*
October 11, 1855.

[8] Comonfort to Valentín Gómez Farías, October 2, 1855. Gómez
Farías Papers; *La Nacionalidad,* October 14, 1855; Ocampo, *Mis Quince
Días de Ministro,* in *Obras Completas,* II. 96.

[9] Priestley, *Mexican Nation,* p. 322.

[10] Molina Enríquez, *op. cit.,* p. 259.

[11] Certificates of the various Masonic degrees taken by Ignacio Comonfort may be found in the Comonfort Papers.

and the President himself were Masons.[12] From the appointment of such a group, the clergy could derive little comfort, except for the fact that they had a "friend at court" in the person of the Minister of War. His relations with the Archbishop were cordial,[13] and, Mason though he was, in the formation of the council he protested that the clergy should have two representatives. The liberals answered that the council, according to the original plan, was to represent departments "as political entities" and not classes of the people.[14] The populace as yet knew little of the disagreement in the cabinet. Even had it known, it would have been slow in rising to support the Church, so long as Álvarez had his victorious troops, many of whom were Indians and *pintos,* at his back.[15]

This was the first rift, more significant than serious it is true, in the fair prospects of the new government. Vidaurri, who had secured the personal support of many liberals,[16] sent word that he fully recognized the new administration and that his whole-hearted support could be relied upon.[17] In spite of this assurance, within six or seven weeks reports began to come in questioning his loyalty.[18] Another more serious disagreement arose over the army. Ocampo and Juárez, as true liberals, wished to do away with a

[12] Mateos, *op. cit.,* p. 135.

[13] *La Nacionalidad,* October 25, 1855.

[14] Ocampo, *Obras Completas,* II. 100.

[15] Wilson, *op. cit.,* p. 400.

[16] Fermín Gómez Farías to his Father, October 6, 1855. Gómez Farías Papers.

[17] *La Nacionalidad,* November 11, 1855.

[18] *Ibid.,* December 30, 1855.

standing army, or at least to reduce it to an absolute minimum, but again Comonfort was found to be strongly opposed to the idea. Feeling ran so high that Ocampo resigned—the first ominous break in the ranks.[19]

Conditions in the cabinet rapidly went from bad to worse. Comonfort, one of the outstanding leaders, and, it would appear, sincerely attached to Álvarez, found himself less and less in harmony with his chief.[20] Reports of the renewed friction were not slow in getting out, and in a short time the whole country was disturbed, each section favoring this, that, or the other man or policy.[21] The conservatives, supported by the closely organized Church machine, quickly took advantage of the discord in the ranks of their opponents.[22] Unfortunately for the administration, funds began to run low; so the salaries of all public employees were cut fifty per cent. As *La Nacionalidad* expressed it, it might have been better to reduce the number of employees, for half paid and hungry workers were not good servants unless they were heroes, and heroes were rare.[23]

It was left for Juárez, minister of justice and ecclesiastical affairs, to fire the first official gun in the new campaign that was to tear open the whole Church question and rack the ship of state from stem to stern. On November 23, 1855, the law, generally known as

[19] Bulnes, *op. cit.*, p. 242.

[20] M. Siliceo to Manuel Dablado, November 14, 1855, November 17, 1855; García, ed., *Los Gobiernos de Alvarez y Comonfort*, pp. 36, 41-42.

[21] L. M. de Ceballos to Manuel Doblado, November 10, 1855. *Ibid.*, p. 27; *La Sociedad*, December 4, 1855.

[22] *La Nacionalidad*, December 6, 1855.

[23] *Ibid.*, November 18, 1855.

the *Ley Juárez,* was announced to the nation by the President.[24] Nearly all parties recognized the danger of bringing the religious issue to a crisis,[25] and diplomacy would have dictated a most careful period of preparation before any drastic step was taken. But the extreme liberals, such as Degollado, would not wait and had forced the issue to the front.[26] Article forty-two of the law suppressed all special tribunals except those of the Church and the army. In the future, the jurisdiction of military courts was strictly limited to cases arising from military crimes. Furthermore, it was clearly indicated that Church courts would very soon cease to have any civil power whatsoever. Article forty-four, indeed, provided that the ecclesiastical *fuero* could be renounced.[27]

Forthwith, the country was in a furor. From the earliest days of Mexican history, the privileged classes had enjoyed their *fueros.* The clergy rushed into the contest with all of their mental ability and financial resources. It was maintained that Article forty-four defeated justice by placing the court at the disposition of the criminal and not the criminal at the disposition of the court, since by renouncing his *fuero* or not an accused ecclesiastic could choose a civil or ecclesiastical court at will. Furthermore, the application of canon law was no longer guaranteed, for this law was only applied by Church courts.[28] The dignity of the Church

[24] Bulnes, *op. cit.,* p. 122.

[25] *El Partido Conservador en México,* p. 38.

[26] *La Nacionalidad,* October 18, 1855.

[27] Zarco, I. 148, note; Bancroft, V. 670-671; *La Sociedad,* December 1, 1855.

[28] *La Sociedad,* December 3, 1855 (Seventh pastoral letter of the Bishop of Michoacán).

and the maintenance of a respected priesthood was said to demand separate trials, so that clerical disgrace would not become public scandal.[29]   On pain of drastic ecclesiastical penalties, the clergy were ordered not to renounce their *fueros*.[30]   When the news reached Rome, on December 15, the Pope pronounced an anathema against Juárez.[31]   On the other hand, the liberals maintained that the ecclesiastical *fuero* had been a privilege, not a right, and that as a privilege it could be revoked by the power that conferred it.[32]   They also claimed that the clergy had excited the people, not by emphasizing the real question of *fueros*, but by so associating it with the fundamentals of religion as to secure fanatical support for a weak cause.[33]

Since the same law struck at the privileges of the army, a coalition of the Church and army was invited against the government at the very time when the latter would have done well, if possible, to keep them apart.   Again the cry of *Religión y Fueros* (Religion and Privileges) was heard on all sides.   The ecclesiastics carefully fostered this coöperation and popular support.   An outstanding Church paper, *La Cruz,* wrote:

> The army is the greatest obstacle to the progress of socialism . . . when one succeeds in popularizing the idea that the army ought not to mix in political affairs under any pretext, but that it should respect the people, then one will be able to get along without it and even though opposed to it.[34]

[29] *La Sociedad,* December 3, 1855.
[30] *Ibid.*
[31] *Manifestación [de]* . . . *los Illmos. Sres. Arzobispo de México y Obispos* . . ., 1859, p. 39.
[32] *El Libertador,* March 10, 1856.
[33] Garza y Garza, *Cuestión del día sobre el Fuero Eclesiástico,* p. 27.
[34] *La Cruz,* III. 268 (October 2, 1856).

The Mexicans were told that they despised tyranny of any kind, including that which the Álvarez group was now exercising.[35] The first demand to be expected was that Comonfort should be placed in the position of Álvarez.[36] By the end of November, it was generally known that the two were not in harmony, so the resignation of Álvarez, disappointed as an executive and already an old man, was the more confidently awaited.[37] His resignation, or retirement as it should be called, in favor of Comonfort took effect December 11, 1855.[38]

During his term of office, Álvarez followed the plans of the *Puros,* the direct successors of the liberals of 1833 both in spirit and in fact. The support of this group was vigorous but not widespread and hardly calculated to restore confidence in a disordered country.[39] It was said to be composed of enthusiastic but inexperienced young men, individuals who openly showed their evil ways, together with a few reliable and responsible characters.[40]

The new executive, Comonfort, faced a peculiarly difficult situation. The people were so accustomed to considering their leaders as rascals that little loyalty

[35] *La Sociedad,* December 1, 1855.

[36] *La Política del General Comonfort,* pp. 25-29.

[37] M. Siliceo to Manuel Doblado, November 28, 1855. García, ed., *Los Gobiernos de Álvarez y Comonfort,* p. 62; *Harper's Monthly Magazine,* XII. 405 (February 1856).

[38] *La Nacionalidad,* December 20, 1855; Portilla, *Historia de la Revolución,* p. 251. The congress approved the transfer of power from Álvarez to Comonfort by a vote of seventy-two to seven, thus enabling the latter to appear before the nation with its hearty endorsement. Bancroft, V. 682.

[39] Portilla, *Méjico en 1856 y 1857,* p. vi.

[40] *La Nacionalidad,* December 30, 1855.

could be relied upon. For a man to remain in office, he needed either to be popular with the masses as a result of giving them something, or else with the classes for the same reason. With either kind of a following, reforms were next to impossible. An example of the fickleness of even the educated classes may be seen in an utterance of *La Sociedad*. On December 10, it fully supported Comonfort, yet six days later it said:

Sr. Comonfort was, in a word, the man of [our] hope.

What has happened? These hopes have fled away like smoke, since they have been changed to bitter doubts, and little is lacking for their place to be taken by desperation.[41]

Why the change? Simply because *La Sociedad* did not approve of the new cabinet, though its personnel should have been quite accurately foreseen by anyone who was acquainted with the events of the day.

However, Comonfort's semiconservative policy did not leave him without supporters. On December 6, Manuel Doblado, governor of Guanajuato, had issued a *pronunciamento* against Álvarez. Two days later, Comonfort sent him word that the latter was resigning because of a "bad state of health".[42] On the eighteenth of the month, Doblado responded with a statement to the effect that he had feared Álvarez meant to introduce Protestantism, but that he would gladly aid Comonfort.[43] For his cabinet, Comonfort chose men of only moderately liberal ideas, and not one

[41] *La Sociedad,* December 10, 1855; December 16, 1855.

[42] Telegram from Comonfort to Manuel Doblado, December 8, 1855. García, ed., *Los Gobiernos de Alvarez y Comonfort,* p. 109.

[43] *La Nacionalidad,* December 23, 1855.

of them was a Mason.[44]   This of course pleased the
clergy; and the Bishop of Potosí wrote to Doblado that
Comonfort and he (Doblado) would make a combination entirely satisfactory to the Church.[45]

Unfortunately it could also be said:

Sr. Comonfort, a man of generous and noble sentiments,
honorable by all tests, adorned with great virtues, full of be-
nevolence and humanitarian sentiments, did not measure up to
the gigantic stature which leaders of the people ought to have
when it is necessary to impel them along the paths of
progress.[46]

At once, Comonfort found himself in the midst of a
host of difficulties, both major and minor.   Forbes and
Barron, consuls of the United States and England,
respectively, were accused of stirring up revolt in the
country.   This question was settled only after due
apologies and an indemnity was paid to England.[47]

Other relations with the United States were also
creating trouble.   Runaway slaves had been given
their freedom on escaping into Mexico from Texas and
other southern states.   This policy created friction.[48]
Raids, such as that of Captain J. H. Callahan in October, 1855,[49] were taking place on both sides of the
Rio Grande.   A more threatening situation in the
eyes of many Mexicans was that created by the fili-
bustering expeditions of William Walker into Nicara-

[44] Mateos, op. cit., pp. 137, 140.

[45] Pedro, Obispo del Potosí, to Manuel Doblado, December 13, 1855.
García, ed., Los Gobiernos de Álvarez y Comonfort, p. 137.

[46] Parra, op. cit., p. 9.

[47] Zarco, II. 920-988; Portilla, Méjico en 1856 y 1857, pp. 92-97, 124,
227.

[48] Garber, op. cit., pp. 159-160.

[49] Ibid., pp. 161-162.

gua. They could not appreciate such gratuituous advice as the following when they knew that the United States wanted to control a route to the Pacific through Central America:

> Walker is on a mission of civilization, he is placed in front of a revolution which will not retrograde.
>
> The victories of Walker will be of service to you [Mexico] ; the consequent movement of civilization will light the torch of intellect on your Southern border. Deal honestly with him and with his people, and they will make you valuable neighbors. . . . Have no war of religion with them. Men who are truly religious never fight about it.[50]

Another thing was the old Tehuantepec Isthmus question, which would not down. In December, 1856, a commercial convention met in Savannah with five hundred and sixty-two delegates present from ten southern and western states. The committee on resolutions reported favorably on the following:

> Resolved, that this Convention regards interoceanic communication across the Isthmus of Tehuantepec as important to Southern interests, and that the enterprise undertaken at

[50] *De Bow's Review,* XXI, 356, 360 (October, 1856). For the Mexican view see: *La Sociedad,* June 14, 1856. The following is a typical example of the articles so frequently found. It is taken from *La Nacionalidad,* October 21, 1855, which in turn had copied it from *La Revolución:*

"VERY IMPORTANT.—We have just seen a letter, written in the United States by a person worthy of all credit, whose contents we vigorously call to the attention of the supreme government and of all patriotic republicans. The letter says:

'Washington, September 29.—Sr. D.N.—In this country it is thought that the supreme moment has arrived for the annexation of Mexico, taking advantage of the disorder and anarchy which divides it.' With such an object the American press insolently predicts the conquest ; the disgraceful *(inmundo)* newspaper the *Picayune* [of New Orleans] being the leading *filibuster* that proclaims it . . ."

New Orleans, by virtue of the contract with Mexico, mentioned in the eighth article of the Gadsden Treaty, deserves encouragement.

It was then recommended that the United States government let mail contracts to those in charge of the enterprise concerned.[51] That the War for Southern Independence would block this, the Mexicans could not foresee.

To the great joy of the administration, a treaty of friendship, navigation, and commerce with Prussia was signed in 1855, though it was not published till June of the following year.[52] With France, affairs were not on such a good footing, because of pending claims and earlier misunderstandings. The sentiment of the people was indicated by the fact that the French Minister was entertained with a charivari. This Zarco, in his paper *El Siglo XIX,* wrote up with a great deal of gusto. The Minister promptly asked for Zarco's trial and conviction on the charges of libel and slander. The congress, then in session, derived much amusement out of the affair and unanimously agreed that there was no case against Zarco, who was one of its most popular members.[53]

With Spain, relations were even more critical. Large numbers of claims were pending which the Spanish Minister, backed by warships, presented for settlement.[54] Comonfort, glad of the opportunity to increase the army, prepared for an attack at Vera Cruz and urged Riva Palacio to keep the army recruited

[51] *De Bow's Review,* XXII. 196 (February, 1857).
[52] *La Nacionalidad,* June 22, 26, 1856.
[53] Zarco, II. 246-255.
[54] Payno, *Mexico and Her Financial Questions,* pp. 143-153.

up to its maximum, "since if there should not be war with Spain, these measures will always please the State".[55]   In accordance with the Mexican demands, the Spanish fleet was withdrawn, whereupon a treaty was signed by the ministers.   Unfortunately, this treaty was rejected by Spain, so that once more a dangerous anti-Spanish sentiment began to appear.[56]

Another minor question that created unrest arose from the old issue of the liberty of the press. This desideratum was thought to have been attained by the accession of Álvarez, and the limitations on importation of books into Vera Cruz was lifted October 10, 1855.[57] By December 31, however, *La Sociedad* was saying: "Perhaps for the last time we are making use of a right which we thought secured for all time by the revolution begun in Ayutla. Perhaps for the last time we are saying what we think, . . ."[58] By January 12, 1856, *El Omnibus* had suffered a two hundred *pesos* fine, and other papers had received various warnings.[59]

But, overshadowing all these questions in seriousness and vital importance, was that one, seemingly ever present, of what was to be done with the Church. The government could make three possible answers: that of the liberals, to make itself superior to the Church; that of the moderates, to accept those ecclesiastical demands which were good, postponing others;

[55] Comonfort to Mariano Riva Palacio, June 5, 1857. Riva Palacio Papers. García Collection.

[56] Arrangoiz, II. 349.

[57] *La Nacionalidad,* November 4, 1855.

[58] *La Sociedad,* December 31, 1855.

[59] *Ibid.,* January 12, 1856.

and that of the conservatives, to accept the Church demands, protesting if they were harmful. In these three cases, respectively, the clergy considered that they should oppose the government as a father would a wayward son; remonstrate with it, as a father would with a wilful son; or accommodate it, as a father would a good son.[60]

An issue was made over the suppression of the convent of San Francisco and the treatment of the city of Puebla. Among the various plots hatched for the overthrow of the government, one developed in the convent mentioned. The date set for the *pronunciamento* was September 16, 1856, but the administration received warning of the danger, and, on the night of the fifteenth, the conspirators were captured. Among them were certain Franciscans. Comonfort declared that the property, with the exception of the church building, the chapel, and the holy vessels, should be confiscated for the use of the nation.[61] At once there was a tremendous outcry that the President was destroying the Church and that this was the beginning of a program which would ultimately destroy all Church property. In February of the following year, an executive decree restored to the Franciscans the right to reëstablish their monastery in a part of the building to be designated by the minister of public works.[62] A similar situation developed in Puebla in the latter part of March, 1856. The inhabitants of the town had always supported the Church

[60] Agustín de la Rosa, *Juramento de la Constitución*, p. 15.

[61] Mateos, *op. cit.*, pp. 150-151.

[62] *La Cruz*, IV. 321 (February 25, 1857).

most consistently, and from it had issued a large proportion of the most vigorous conservative propaganda. Hence it is not surprising, after an armed insurrection had threatened Comonfort from Puebla, that he should issue orders to confiscate sufficient Church property to reimburse the government for the expenses incurred in quelling the uprising.[63]

By the middle of the year, 1856, matters were coming to a climax in many ways. The President's apologists have insisted that he was still dominated by the *Puros* and by the effects of his association with Álvarez.[64] This was possibly the case. At all events, on June 5, orders were issued for the suppression of the Jesuits and allowing those who had taken religious vows to foreswear them.[65] Next, a severe cut in the size of the army was ordered. Whereas Santa Anna had had an army of forty thousand, this number was reduced to 9,603 by the act of April 29, 1856.[66] On various pretexts, Comonfort was able to minimize the effects of the law; but, in spite of all he could do, the actual army was reduced to about two thousand officers and fewer than twelve thousand men.[67]

On the twenty-fifth of the following month, the government promulgated the famous *Ley Lerdo,* a decree named from its author, Lerdo de Tejada. It abolished the right of civil and ecclesiastical corporations to hold real property, except that which was directly used for the purposes of worship. The price

[63] Bulnes, *op. cit.,* pp. 202-204; *Harper's Monthly Magazine,* XIII. 118 (June, 1856).

[64] Arrangoiz, II. 348.

[65] Bulnes, *op. cit.,* pp. 202-204.

[66] *Ibid.*

[67] Lerdo de Tejada, *op. cit.,* pp. 77-78.

of the property, when sold, was to be the sum which at six per cent. would yield the rent actually being charged.   If any given property was not being rented, it should be sold at auction in the presence of a government official.[68] Careful preparation was made for the enforcement of the law. Minister Siliceo, for instance, wrote to Manuel Doblado:

> The law will go forward to you by the next mail; but first I have wished to notify you in order that you may make your preparations, so as to preserve quiet in that religious folk *(gente de bonete)* and so that you may know that the Minister of the Treasury will be able to appropriate six or eight hundred *pesos,* in order that two young fellows, like Ayala and Gasco or some others, should write, together with yourself, popularizing the law and sustaining it for three or four months. That will be the time necessary for putting it in force.[69]

The law did not mean that Church property was to be confiscated for the use of the nation. Even the *ejidos* (property held in common by Indian villages), were shortly after included in its general scope.[70] It was an attempt to force all large property holders to disgorge and sell their enormous holdings,[71] so as to get the land into the hands of the middle and poorer classes and give them that incentive which comes from private ownership—an incentive which they had never felt.[72] It was also hoped and expected that property would become more mobile when broken up into smaller

[68] McBride, *op. cit.,* p. 69.

[69] M. Siliceo to Manuel Doblado, June 25, 1856.   García, ed., *Los Gobiernos de Alvarez y Comonfort,* pp. 210-211.

[70] For other plans in the congress see those of Castillo Velasco and Ponciano Arriaga. Zarco, I. 516-517, 568-569; *La Sociedad,* June 28, 1856.

[71] McBride, *op. cit.,* p. 92.

[72] *Ibid.,* p. 133.

pieces, and that its productivity, value, and service to the nation would be greater with the abolition once and for all of the evils of absentee landlordism and poor supervision.[73]   But the law affected the clergy so vitally and the rest of the country so little in proportion, that again the issue was essentially one between the Church and the state.

Printing presses worked overtime to turn out broadsides and pamphlets by the score.   Each author felt in duty bound to make an elaborate estimate of the Church property that would be affected, then to hazard a guess, supported with such reasoning as he was capable of, as to whether the country would be saved or ruined by the process of sale that was to be enforced.   The Church positively refused to allow its books and records to be examined, with the result that precise data were not available.   In Mexico City alone, the property holdings were enormous, probably including half of the houses.[74]   After a detailed study of the various sources of income, not only of the clergy but of the entire nation, Sr. Lerdo de Tejada, in a splendid statistical report, estimated the total value of the real property, rural and urban, at 1,355,000,-000 *pesos*.[75]   Of this, a portion worth from 250,000,-000 to 300,000,000 *pesos* was owned by the clergy, making due allowance for the fact that the Church property might have decreased somewhat in value of recent years.[76]   Through loans, the clergy also con-

---

[73] *El Constituyente*, editorials, July 6, 10, 1856; *La Sociedad*, July 8, 1856; *La Nacionalidad*, August 10, 1856.

[74] Lerdo de Tejada, *op. cit.*, pp. 82-83.

[75] *Ibid.*, p. 43.

[76] *Ibid.*, pp. 82-83; García Granados, *op. cit.*, pp. 69, 100-101.

trolled large amounts of property that they did not own.[77]

The reception accorded to the law was that which might have been expected. On June 28, three days after its announcement, a group of twenty-eight congressmen, led by Zarco, asked that the rules of procedure be suspended and that the congress approve the decree at once. By a vote of fifty-eight to twenty-seven, this was done, so that preliminary readings and the reference to a committee were avoided. All attempts to postpone discussion on the bill were blocked, and, after a short debate, the decree was approved by a vote of seventy-eight to fifteen.[78] The town council of Morelia officially thanked Lerdo de Tejada for the law, saying that it was most popular in that community.[79] By September word came from Vera Cruz that fourteen estates had been sold and that tenants of others had made application for the right to acquire the lands on which they lived.[80]

The argument that this law was for the good of the whole nation and hence should be supported by the Church was even heard in Church circles; some clergymen took advantage of it and secured property for themselves.[81] Other churchmen agreed not to oppose the execution of the law.[82] Among the latter was the Bishop of Guadalajara, who was said to be convinced that the law was just and right.[83] Archbishop Garza

[77] Parra, *op. cit.*, p. 72.
[78] Zarco, I. 596-615.
[79] *La Nacionalidad*, July 27, 1856.
[80] *Ibid.*, September 7, 1856.
[81] *Ibid.*, August 10, 1856; December 4, 1856.
[82] *Ibid.*, June 22, 1856; September 21, 1856.
[83] *Ibid.*, September 11, 1856; October 2, 1856.

was in a most difficult position. As head of the Church in Mexico, he was forced to lead the fight in its behalf, though personally he was said to be none too enthusiastic about the contest.[84] He stated that he would defend the position of the Church till the Holy See sent its approval of the laws, then he would willingly consent also.[85] On the other hand, he had no patience whatever with those clergymen who were acquiring property that was being sold in accordance with the law in question, and he suspended the dean and two canons of the metropolitan church because they had bought the houses in which they lived.[86]

Bishop Labastida, of Puebla, had been having serious trouble with the government because of the revolt that had centered in Puebla and which most certainly had been indirectly, if not directly, fostered by the clergy. The confiscation of Church property, following the revolt, was carried out somewhat harshly[87] and led to further recriminations.[88] The Bishop had always been a monarchist at heart—another item which counted against him in a contest with the government;[89] and his previous record included an incident in 1852, when, it would appear, he incited students in a seminary under his control to a revolt.[90]

[84] Bancroft, V. 691-692.

[85] J. Trinidad Basurto, El Arzobispado de México, pp. 135-136.

[86] Portilla, Méjico en 1856 y 1857, p. 106. The Archbishop was a good man, intensely idealistic, who knew little of the practical side of life. He was austere, highly respected by all both as an official and as a man, and had a compelling force about him that usually secured results. M. Payno y Flores, Memoria Sobre la Revolución de Diciembre de 1857 y Enero de 1858, pp. 36-37.

[87] S. Bordonova, Conducta del Obispo de Puebla, p. 35.

[88] Sierra, op. cit., I. 243-244.

[89] Basurto, op. cit., p. 139.

[90] El Constituyente, May 29, 1856.

His episcopal circulars, moreover, were questionable. in their loyalty, and one of his addresses contained this sentence: "Catholic priests ought to shed their blood to the last drop to conserve intact the treasure of the faith." This statement was scattered broadcast with the obvious interpretation that "treasure of the faith" meant "Church property".[91] It was also said that certain clergymen of his diocese had actively encouraged the revolutionists.[92] The Bishop claimed that he was innocent of the charges made[93] and that the only funds he had given to Haro, the rebel, were bestowed after the latter actually became governor of Puebla and not while he could be classed as a rebel.[94] His friends asserted that they were not allowed a chance to defend him in the press[95] and that the government, needing a victim, chose the Bishop as the most suitable because of his effective protests against confiscation of Church property.[96] It is really more probable that the government of Comonfort decided to make an example of him, hoping that it would also serve as a warning to those clergymen of lower ranks who were verging toward sedition.[97] Whatever was the real motive actuating the government, there is no doubt that the Bishop was exiled.

[91] Basurto, p. 143.

[92] Bordonova, *op. cit.*, p. 50; *La Sociedad*, April 26, 1856 (Reply of Lafragua to the Bishop of Puebla).

[93] *Representación del Illmo. Obispo de Puebla*, in *El Constituyente*, May 4, 1856, supplement.

[94] Bordonova, p. 63.

[95] *La Sociedad*, April 3, 1856.

[96] Mateos, *op. cit.*, p. 148.

[97] Bordonova, pp. 8, 16, 33-34, 84.

As he was leaving the country, word reached him of the law of June 25. Forthwith, he decreed as to the diocese of Puebla; first, that all sales or changing of hands of Church property as a result of the said law, he held and would hold void; second, that any person acquiring such property should return it to the Church and would be excommunicated till the final transfer was completed; third, that all subsequent owners were to be included in this excommunication; and fourth, that officials who enforced the said law were specifically excommunicated.[98]

The liberals admitted that some unavoidable evils might creep in during the transfer of so much property, but insisted that the greatest good of the whole nation was being sought[99] and that that which was for the good of society was in harmony with God's will and purpose.[100] The Church responded that such a hectic circulation of property would be abnormal and would indicate ill health in the body politic.[101] The acquisition of its property by the Church being legal, confiscation could only be justified on the basis of the public good.[102] This, the Church most vigorously maintained, was being served so long as its houses were occupied with contented citizens and its farms regularly cultivated by satisfied tenants.[103] To take property from the clergy would cause it to fall into

---

[98] Bordonova, op. cit., pp. 75-76.

[99] Contestaciones habidas entre el Illmo. Arzobispo de México . . y . . . Montes, p. 7.

[100] La Nacionalidad, July 24, 1856.

[101] Balmes, op. cit., p. 63.

[102] Letter of "Un Suscritor Católico" in La Sociedad, July 6, 1856.

[103] Representación del . . . Cabildo Metropolitano al Soberano Congreso, p. 11; La Cruz, IV. 470 (April 2, 1857).

the hands of speculators and a few rich men. The whole agricultural system would be disturbed, and no good could possibly be accomplished.[104] Furthermore, if Church property, together with that of civil corporations, were legally destroyed at this time, no property in the future could feel safe from a similar ruthless attack.[105]

In answer to the statement that such huge properties gave abnormal incomes to a few men, it was stated that this was not true, since the Church did an enormous amount of charity work. As an example, in Guadalajara, out of a total of 26,045 baptisms, 5421 marriage ceremonies, and 21,607 burials, there were 1528 baptisms, 317 marriage ceremonies, and 17,441 burials for which no fees were received, and 4259 baptisms, 1225 wedding ceremonies, and 1253 burials for which only partial fees were collected.[106]

So far as the passage of the law was concerned, it cannot be said that it was unexpected. In fact, numerous laws based more or less upon the same principles had already been put in effect by the different departments. As late as May 11, 1856, Durango had proposed a reduction of fifty per cent. in the rents of lands held in mortmain in areas that had suffered from Indian raids and the hard times resulting therefrom.[107] But, in spite of such acts, it must be admitted that the Mexican people were not ready to use the property the *Ley Lerdo* would have given them. For the Indian,

---

[104] *La Sociedad*, May 26, 1856; *La Cruz*, IV. 135 (January 22, 1857).

[105] Garza y Ballesteros, *Cuarta Carta Pastoral*, p. 11.

[106] *La Cruz*, V. 225 (June 25, 1857).

[107] *El Constituyente*, May 11, 1856.

the destruction of his communal holdings[108] meant, in all too many cases, that his last chance for independence had gone and that he would now fall back into more complete serfdom or peonage than ever before, since he would be entirely dependent upon some master.   In other words, so far as the *ejidos* were concerned, the law hastened their absorption into the neighboring holdings, for the Indian could or would not keep that which was offered to him.[109]

As the law actually worked out, tenants on a large estate seldom dared to make the required application so that they could acquire the piece of land to which they were entitled under the law.   One reason for this was the opposition of the clergy and their power over the people.   Consequently, those who "denounced" property were usually wealthy men or speculators who were willing to take a chance,[110] whereas, the Indians and most of the *mestizos* remained as innocent of private land ownership as before.[111]   The actual number of landholders increased very little, if at all,[112] though the sale of property started off briskly enough.   By the end of August about two million *pesos* worth of property had changed hands,[113] while in the next month the amount was raised to about thirteen mil-

[108] McBride, *op. cit.*, pp. 129-130; Ross, *op. cit.*, p. 81.

[109] McBride, *op. cit.*, pp. 90-91.

[110] Mendieta y Núñez, *op. cit.*, pp. 84-85; Antonio Aguado to Manuel Doblado, July 7, 1856; García, ed., *Los Gobiernos de Álvarez y Comonfort*, p. 257.

[111] McBride, *op. cit.*, p. 155.

[112] Portilla, *Méjico en 1856 y 1857*, pp. 70-71; F. J. Miranda, pamphlet dated Puebla, July 13, 1859, no title, p. 14.

[113] *El Constituyente*, supplement, August 24, 1856; *La Nacionalidad*, August 31, 1856.

lion *pesos*.[114] Following this, came a decline in the sales, and the total amount transferred in 1856 was just a little over 23,019,000 *pesos*.[115]

As a Mexican historian of note has said, if the Church had had a statesmanlike pope and Mexico an archbishop of like ability, instead of good men who were not statesmen, the situation might have been met by the acceptance of the *Ley Lerdo*. This would have given the Church good commercial paper, guaranteed by real estate in such a way that it would have appreciated in value as time passed. Thus the Church would not have suffered anything like the loss that was inflicted upon it as a result of its stubborn resistance, and a long and bitter war might have been avoided.[116]

Before this contest had been settled, another began in January, 1857, due to the new provision for registration of statistics of "birth, marriage, adoption or arrogation, priesthood, and the profession of a religious vow, whether provisional or perpetual, and death".[117] At the same time, control of cemeteries was taken from the Church and turned over to civil officers. The effect of such wholesale restrictions placed upon the power of the clergy may well be imagined.

Still another law, known as the *Ley Iglesias* (the Church Law), of April 11, 1857, required the clergy to perform their duties for charity in case the persons who desired or needed their services were not earning a

---

[114] *La Democracia*, October 9, 1856.
[115] Bancroft, V. 694, note; Bulnes, *op. cit.*, p. 394.
[116] Sierra, *op. cit.*, I. 246, 248.
[117] Bancroft, V. 708, note.

living wage. When collections were made by force or
undue pressure, the person guilty was to pay a fine of
triple the amount collected, one half to go to the authorities and the other to the victim. Civil officials,
when they saw fit, were empowered to initiate cases
without first receiving complaint from the injured
person. For refusal to perform the ceremonies of
baptism and marriage, the penalty was to vary from a
fine of ten to one hundred *pesos* to banishment from
the district of from fifteen to sixty days. Appeals on
the part of the clergy were to go to the governor of
the department in which the incident occurred, and,
in case any curate by this law was left without a reasonable income, the government was to take care of
him.[118] This last provision was a chief point of attack, for it was said that the parish priest would not
get enough to live on if he had to depend on voluntary
contributions only. In other words, he was being
required to render highly specialized services without
due recompense and was placed in a position where
it was next to impossible for him to secure justice.[119]

It should not be supposed that all this discussion
was strictly confined to the laws here referred to in
the order of their passage. The whole question of
religious freedom was considered, though in nearly
all cases the greatest respect was professed for the
Roman Catholic clergy as such.[120] At times, it is true,
the most disgusting charges of immorality, filth, and

---

[118] *La Democracia,* July 23 and 26, 1857; *El Constituyente,* July 13,
1856.

[119] Narciso Bassols, *Leyes de Reforma que Afectan al Clero,* pp.
23-26; *Opúsculo en Defensa del Clero . . .,* pp. 30-31.

[120] *La Voz de Iturbide,* March 1, 1857.

general degradation were brought against certain communities of the regular clergy.[121] These, however, were the exception, and most of the liberal papers went out of their way to brand as a lie any reference to their editors being personally opposed to the Church, or even tinctured with ideas of Protestantism.[122] When the stage took up the question and presented the drama of Gil y Zarate entitled, *Carlos II el Hechizado,* in which the fanaticism and immorality of the clergy were stressed, *La Sociedad* was so stirred up that it devoted one fourth of an entire issue to a scathing denunciation in the form of a review of the performance.[123] On the other hand, those who wanted toleration asked why Rome had it and Mexico did not;[124] why keep the Church in Mexico as a hot-house plant, with special protection, when religious freedom made stronger and hence better Catholics[125] and when it was a well known fact that the Church was making most satisfactory progress in the United States?[126]

The Church was only too glad to have these other questions introduced, for they enabled it to call attention to the ultra-radical tendencies of the opposition.[127] The division of opinion among Protestants was an ever fruitful subject of discussion.[128] If these dissidents were allowed in the country, marriages would natur-

---

[121] *La Nacionalidad,* October 9, 1856.

[122] For an example of this see *El Constituyente,* September 4, 1856.

[123] *La Sociedad,* May 27, 1856.

[124] *Ibid.,* April 19, 1856.

[125] *El Constituyente,* July 31, 1856.

[126] "Un Parroco Jalisciense", *Caso de Consciencia sobre el Juramento Constitucional,* p. 17.

[127] Bancroft, V. 690.

[128] *La Cruz,* III. 138-139 (September 4, 1856); Martínez, *op. cit.,* p. xvii.

ally take place, and how could it be expected that a girl of twelve would stand against the ideas of her husband?[129]   When the Church granted liberty for right living and right thinking—as it judged such matters—what more could be desired?[130]

During these times of pamphlet warfare and political agitation, some real progress was made in the general welfare of the country.   A minor reform of the new administration grew out of its friendship for the laboring classes.   A decree of Santa Anna, dated July 30, 1853, prohibited tenants living on an estate from forming a *pueblo* to handle their local affairs without the consent of the master.   Thus their last chance for organization in order to secure redress was swept away.   On May 19, 1856, the congressional committee of government advised that the decree be revoked.   Four days later, the report of the committee was accepted by a vote of seventy-three to eleven.[131]

[129] *La Sociedad,* April 22, 1856.

[130] *El Libertador,* March 27, 1856; *La Cruz,* III. 324 (October 16, 1856).

[131] Zarco, I. 258-259, 286-287. A somewhat flattering picture of conditions on the sugar plantations is found in *La Sociedad* December 23, 1855. The daily wage of the laborers was given at from two to nine *reales* (.25 to 1.12 *pesos*); house-rent free for a building 13' x 19', together with a shed and corral for livestock; one or two animals [usually burros] were fed by the owner of the estate; likewise pigs and chickens. Cash payment of wages was made weekly. The laborer was to buy his stores at the estate commissary or elsewhere [?]. By payment of one half *real* per week the laborer was freed of parochial dues, while the estate agreed to pay the marriage fee of the laborer, as well as burial fees for him, his wife, unmarried daughters and young sons. Hours of labor were from sunrise to sunset, with thirty minutes rest for breakfast and one hour for lunch. If the laborer wished to rent land to raise corn for his own use he was allowed to do so. A final statement was to the effect that Negroes did most of the work, since Indians were not suited to the conditions.

The immigration question was also considered, since the population of the country showed an annual increase of only 144,000, or less than two per cent. Of the total population, about twenty per cent. was assumed to be of pure European stock; twenty-seven per cent., Indian, and the remaining fifty-three per cent., mixed.[132] It is obvious from the above figures that there was still little immigration. As before, responsible settlers with wives and families dependent upon them would not go to a disorderly community when they could enter the United States. Even Catholics preferred safety with religious toleration to serious disorder accompanied by religious conformity.[133] Nor was Comonfort able to do much during his term of office to encourage immigration, though, by way of internal improvements, he developed the use of gas lights in Mexico and supported the building of railroads, to say nothing of a series of engineering works, which helped to free the capital from the periodic danger of floods.[134]

Under the administration of the liberals more interest than before was shown in public instruction. In December, 1855, four primary schools were established by the local government of Guanajuato in towns where no schools had previously existed.[135] The college of Guanajuato was also reorganized January 1, 1857, with very fair salaries to be paid to its officers. The chaplain received three hundred and sixty *pesos;*

[132] García y Cubas, *op. cit.,* pp. 14-15; *Boletín de la Sociedad Mexicana de Geografía y Estadística,* VII. 158.
[133] *La Sociedad,* December 12, 1855.
[134] Portilla, *Méjico en 1856 y 1857,* pp. 266-274.
[135] *La Nacionalidad,* December 2, 1855.

seven professors, six hundred each; eight, one thous-
and each; one (of drawing and painting), one thous-
and four hundred; and the rector, two thousand.[136]
The National College of Agriculture for boys from
thirteen to twenty years of age also was given active
support. Between 1856 and 1857 its salary budget
was increased from fourteen thousand *pesos* to twenty-
seven thousand four hundred for the addition of
new courses and instructors.[137] The University of
Mexico, on the other hand, could expect little mercy.
The liberals had attacked it in 1833, only to have
Santa Anna restore it the next year. In 1854 it came
still more completely under his control. Now, in
1857, it was again closed, on the grounds that it was
a source of pernicious doctrines and a centre of Church
propaganda.[138]

Communications were improving slowly but surely. *Pronunciamentos* necessarily injured the efficiency of the post office,[139] but expenses were being
reduced, while efficiency was increased.[140] Letters began to carry adhesive stamps instead of requiring the
payment in money on the delivery of each letter.[141]
New postal rates were introduced,[142] and the post office

[136] *La Voz de Iturbide,* January 7, 1857.

[137] *Reglamento de la Escuela Nacional de Agricultura,* 1856, 1857.
See Articles 13 and 60-63 for each year.

[138] Priestley, *The Old University of Mexico,* p. 19.

[139] *Informe de la Administración de Correos,* January 4, 1857, p. 5.

[140] *Ibid.,* p. 21 ff.

[141] The first postage stamp noticed on private correspondence was on
a letter from Agustín Frude [?] Villa to Fermín Gómez Farias and was
dated October 21, 1856. After this date the stamps became increasingly
numerous.

[142] *Informe de la Administración de Correos,* 1857, pp. 38-40; *La
Democracia,* January 11, 1857; *La Voz de Iturbide,* December 31, 1856.
The decree of Comonfort provided the following rates:

rapidly ceased to be a sort of institution that inspired
an individual to write to the Director, sending him several letters, and stating that since he did not have the
correct addresses he would appreciate it if the Director
would look them up and send the letters on their
ways.[143] The telegraph also became increasingly effective. By the end of 1856, there were three lines in
operation from the capital to Vera Cruz, León, and
Toluca, being about three hundred and fifty, three
hundred and twenty, and fifty miles in length, respectively.[144] The rates were quite reasonable, varying
from four *reales* (half a *peso*) up to a *peso* and a half
for a ten word message, the rate of course depending
upon the distance.[145]

	Up to 16 leagues	Over 16 leagues
A simple letter	1 *real*	2 *reales*
A letter of ½ oz.	2 *reales*	3 *reales*
A letter of ¾ oz.	3 *reales*	4 *reales*
Package of 1 oz.	4 *reales*	5 *reales*
Package of 2 oz.	8 *reales*	9 *reales*
Package of 3 oz.	12 *reales*	13 *reales*
Package of 4 oz.	16 *reales*	17 *reales*
Package of 6 oz.	24 *reales*	25 *reales*
Package of 8 oz.	32 *reales*	33 *reales*
Package of 10 oz.	40 *reales*	41 *reales*

Over 10 ounces the rate was ½ *real* for each ¼ ounce.

[143] This was actually done by General Diego Álvarez in a letter to
Valentín Gómez Farías, Director of the post office, dated November 26,
1855. Gómez Farías Papers.

Aside from revolutions, the most serious hindrance faced by the
postal system was the difficulty experienced in securing efficient men to
handle the mail on salaries that were inadequate and frequently non-
existent. *Informe de la Administración de Correos*, 1857, p. 17.

[144] Lerdo de Tejada, *op. cit.*, pp. 66-67.

[145] Marcos Arróniz, *op. cit.*, p. 54. Meanwhile the opera was not being
slighted. One notice referred to the following operas which were to
be sung in the second series of the season: *Hernani, Semiramis, Attila,
Tancredo, Lucía, Favorita* and *El Trovador. La Sociedad*, December
4, 1855; *Ibid.*, January 4, 1856; *La Voz de Iturbide*, March 4, 1857.

Coinage of gold and silver during 1845 amounted to nearly seventeen million six hundred thousand *pesos*,[146] but the record of exports shows that this sum and more was being sent abroad. The total value of the exports of the country was about twenty-eight million *pesos,* and the imports about twenty-six million. However, this was not so satisfactory as it appeared, for the gold and silver exported amounted to twenty-two million five hundred thousand or more and meant that the splendid agricultural regions in Mexico were still doing little or nothing in the way of increasing foreign trade.[147] The government estimates of revenue and expense for 1855-56 and 1856-57 admitted a probable deficit of two millions and a quarter annually.[148]

On the whole, with the support of a liberal Congress, Comonfort appeared to be handling the situation in a fairly satisfactory manner. The revolt of the conservatives in Puebla had been quelled and redounded to his credit, the leader Haro y Tamariz having fled the country for the time being.[149] Later movements of the same group were also checked by the vigilance of the government.[150] Added prestige had been secured through the voluntary retirement of the loyal Juan Álvarez.[151] His reiterated insistence on his resignation in May and June of 1856, in spite of the votes of the congress to the contrary, gave still more strength

[146] García y Cubas, *op. cit.,* p. 7.

[147] *Ibid.,* pp. 17-18; Lerdo de Tejada, *op. cit.,* pp. 55-56.

[148] Sierra, *op. cit.,* II. 371; Lemprière, *op. cit.,* p. 235, note.

[149] *La Nacionalidad,* January 17, 1856.

[150] Comonfort to Manuel Doblado, April 26, 1856. García, ed., *Los Gobiernos de Alvarez y Comonfort,* p. 178.

[151] *La Nacionalidad,* January 31, 1856.

to the liberals.[152]   On the other hand, the revolt of
Vidaurri in the north failed to secure aid from the
United States and was suppressed.[153]   One result of
these successes was, that they made possible the reduction in the size of the standing army.[154]   While, as has
been stated, Comonfort was opposed to drastic reductions, they were in line, nevertheless, with the policies
advocated by the party of which he was the official
leader.   So far as most of the people were concerned,
he was the government, and to him, in the public mind,
went the praise or blame for official acts.

[152] A record of the attempted resignation of Alvarez may be found in
Zarco, I. On June 24, 1856 he bowed to the will of the congress in not
receiving his resignation, though he did not again serve as President.
[153] *Harper's Monthly Magazine*, XIII. 840 (November, 1856); *Ibid.*,
XIII. 553, 693 (September, October, 1856).
[154] Lerdo de Tejada, *op. cit.*, pp. 77-78; Bulnes, *op. cit.*, p. 203.

CHAPTER XI

THE CONSTITUTIONAL CONVENTION

As soon as Álvarez had assumed the office of president, the call was issued for the selection of the members of the constituent congress provided for by the Plan of Ayutla. This congress was to act in the double capacity of a legislature and a constitutional convention. The delegates were chosen by an indirect system. The primary electors were selected December 16, 1856, on the basis of one delegate for each five hundred inhabitants or major fraction thereof. A majority of the votes of the adult males of a community was to elect. In case of a tie, the presiding officer of the local board of election was to cast the deciding vote.[1]

December 23, one week later, these delegates, chosen by the *juntas primarias,* met in the secondary conventions (*juntas secundarias*) to select representatives for the department, district, or territorial *juntas.* At these gatherings one representative was to be chosen for every twenty delegates or major fraction thereof, provided each convention had at least one delegate. To sit in a department, district, or territorial convention, an elector had to be a resident of one year's standing of the district represented and had to be at least twenty-five years of age and a full citizen, though no office-holder was eligible for election.[2]

[1] Zarco, I. 20-23.
[2] *Ibid.,* I. 23-24.

The department or, according to the liberals, state conventions met on January 6, 1856. Here a two-thirds vote of those present was required to elect. The number of delegates for the constituent congress was to be based on one representative for each fifty thousand inhabitants or major fraction thereof. The acting President of the republic was not eligible for election, and no delegate could represent more than one department, territory, or district.[3] No ecclesiastic was allowed to vote or be voted for in any of the conventions.[4] Through this indirect system and the restrictions so carefully prescribed, the liberals secured complete control of the congress when it assembled.

On February 14, seven and a half weeks after their selection, the national deputies met in the capital.[5] On the first day there were thirty-eight delegates present.[6] On the two following days fifty-six and sixty-three respectively reported, while on the seventeenth a quorum of seventy-eight had arrived. The election of officers took place, and the congress was formally opened on the eighteenth.[7] The sentiment of the body may be seen by the men selected to act as its

[3] There was no conflict in these provisions, for a man could be a citizen of several states at the same time by virtue of property qualifications. In fact Ceballos, Yáñez, Olvera, Ramírez, V. Gómez Farías, López and La Rosa were chosen by two states each, while Arriaga was elected by eight. Zarco, I. 25-27.

[4] Ibid.; Bancroft, V. 668.

[5] The delegates were allowed traveling expenses at the rate of two pesos for three miles. Their salaries were at the rate of two hundred and fifty pesos per month, but were to be paid by the state, district or territory represented. Zarco, I. 29.

[6] The congress had been scheduled to meet in Dolores Hidalgo, but for the sake of convenience it was changed to Mexico City by a presidential decree of December 26, 1855. Ibid., I. 27-28.

[7] Ibid., I. 36-42.

first officers. They were: Ponciano Arriaga, president, with Isidoro Olvera and Francisco Zarco as secretaries, all of them Masons and the last named the well-known liberal editor of *El Siglo XIX*.[8] It is to him that the thanks of all Mexicans are due for his careful history of the congress, even though the exuberance of the partisan overwhelmed the detachment of the recorder on such occasions as the approval of the *Ley Juárez*:

> No more fueros! No more privileges! . . . equality for all citizens! complete sovereignty of the temporal power! justice for all! The country ought to congratulate itself on this result, and the assembly has taken a great step which will enliven those hopes which inspire the friends of true democracy.[9]

The great conservative leaders of the day were not present.[10] Had there been a few churchmen in the convention, little would have been added to the strength of the conservative cause; but some of the sting would have been removed from a situation that chafed the sensibilities of many good people. Due to the steady opposition of the Church to the Plan of Ayutla and all it stood for, however, the course taken by the liberals was to be expected.[11] The *Moderados* were represented by a few of the delegates who spoke from time to time and by Ezequiel Montes, Luís de la Rosa, and José M. Lafragua from the President's cabinet.[12] A majority of those present did not represent commercial or industrial life or even the laboring

[8] Mateos, *op. cit.*, pp. 137, 140.
[9] Zarco, I. 182.
[10] *La Nacionalidad*, February 24, 1856.
[11] Bulnes, *op. cit.*, p. 214.
[12] Parra, *op. cit.*, pp. 13-15.

classes. They were interested in the more theoretical of the political interests of the day rather than in economic matters. In fact, the phrase "political theorists" describes them most aptly.[13] "In the one hundred and fifty-four [five] representatives, there were one hundred and eight lawyers, the rest being military men and public employees of the nation or of the States." The opponents of the congress insisted that these lawyers were either very young or very old, the former as yet having no clients and the latter being beyond the age of work.[14] In view of the actual accomplishments of the congress, this statement would seem extravagant.

The predominance of liberals was shown in connection with Benito Gómez Farías. He had been accused of libel against Barron, Forbes and Company because of the charges he had made against them in *La Pata de Cabra* in connection with the revolt in Tepic. As a result of the suit, he was sentenced to pay a fine of three hundred *pesos* and costs and to imprisonment for six months. This had happened after he was elected as a deputy but before he had taken his seat in the congress.[15] On his application for admission, he was received unanimously and later served one term as vice-president of the body. This cannot be cited as a blow struck at the conservatives, for anti-foreign sentiment was doubtless a considerable factor in the vote, but it did show the great popularity of the outstanding liberals.[16] The same feeling

[13] Bulnes, *op. cit.*, p. 215.

[14] *Ibid.*, p. 214.

[15] *Documentos Relativos al Juicio de Imprenta Promovido por E. Barron contra B. Gómez Farías.*

[16] *Ibid.*

was exhibited in connection with the father, Valentín Gómez Farías. He was a man of seventy-four and in very poor health. He was not able to attend the early sessions, but on the day that he first appeared "he had scarcely reached the door . . . when all the representatives by a sudden and spontaneous movement greeted him with enthusiastic applause, giving this sign of sympathy to the worthy citizen who with extraordinary self-abnegation had consecrated his entire life to the defense of liberty."[17] During the month of August he was ill, so a committee was appointed to visit him and to ask the government to make a special appropriation for his use.[18]

An interesting question arose when Lafragua reported plans for a religious function to ask the aid of Providence for the congress in its work. For fear of questions of etiquette as to precedence between the president of the republic and the president of the congress and similar details, the proposition was rejected.[19]

Unfortunately, from the beginning of the sessions, the balconies were open to the public. This meant that, as was the case in France during the Revolution, the people had no hesitation in interrupting the discussion of questions of national import with their *vivas* or *mueras,* showing their approval or dislike of the speaker or of what he was saying. Such a system also contributed greatly to excitement throughout the nation, for with open galleries any simpleton could be present for part of a speech and

[17] Zarco, I. 376-377.
[18] *Ibid.,* II. 151.
[19] *Ibid.,* I. 46-47.

then go out and start all kinds of absurd rumors. At
times during the proceedings, disorder became so
serious that business had to be suspended.

The congress early went on record showing its
attitude toward the dictatorship of Santa Anna. Reports on the acts and decrees of his government were
made once each week. Some of them were referred to
committees for investigation, and others were acted upon at once. Even such decrees as had already been revoked by Álvarez were not free from attack. When a
committee reported that one such act was a dead letter
and could conveniently be ignored, a violent debate
ensued, which showed a mixture of hatred for Santa
Anna and a jealousy of the acts of the existing provisional government. The result was that the report
of the committee was rejected by a vote of seventy-
nine to three.[20] On June 26 a bill was introduced repu-
diating the decree of Santa Anna of December 16,
1853, which had prolonged his dictatorship indefinitely. This measure was debated briefly on July 3, but
was then postponed for a little over two weeks because
of the introduction of a draft of the new constitution.
After a second discussion on the nineteenth, the bill
was approved unanimously by the eighty-one delegates
present. Thus the last portion of Santa Anna's administration was formally nullified.[21]

The question of states rights was early an issue before the congress. The country had suffered seriously
from overcentralization, so a natural reaction caused
many to go to the opposite extreme, while many one-
time centralists now admitted:

[20] *Ibid.*, I. 430-434.
[21] *Ibid.*, I. 114 ff., 130 ff., 592-593, II. 154.

On specifying, then, in the future constitution the powers which the supreme federal government ought to have as an undisputed fact *(como un axioma)*, to it and it alone belongs the right to issue those laws, approve those governmental acts and decide those judicial contests which directly affect the general interests of the nation, or those common to the various States . . .

Thus it is seen that the central powers control foreign and domestic commerce, and that at the same time each State is free to establish the local mercantile code which seems best to it, "as well as to handle all other questions of purely local interest".[22]

By the small states it was declared that representation in the congress was based upon population and that consequently such departments as Mexico, Puebla, Jalisco, and Morelia decided all the laws, and that the rest of the nation had to obey them.[23]   Olvera was one of the leaders of the states-rights group. In fact, in the discussion on Article 15 of the plan for the constitution, he even opposed the idea of national legislation on the question of religious liberty, saying that this too should be left to state option.[24]   On the same grounds, he opposed section four of Article 24, which had reference to the right of trial by jury, claiming that some districts were not ready for this reform and that a general law would consequently be injudicious, though some states were ready for it.[25]   Olvera also desired a bicameral legislature, so as to have a senate to act as the guardian of the small states.[26]   Inciden-

---

[22] *La Nacionalidad,* May 11, 1856.
[23] Y. O., *La Reforma Social de Méjico,* p. 24.
[24] Zarco, I. 495.
[25] *Ibid.,* I. 495-499.
[26] *Ibid.,* I. 500-507.

tally, this was obviously a matter of real principle with him, for while he was elected by both Guerrero and Mexico, he was actually representing the latter, a large state. Consequently, his stand would certainly not increase his personal popularity. While the small states lost many of their demands, the general idea of states rights was secured in Article 48 of the draft (which became Article 117 of the finished document) reading:

The powers which are not expressly granted by this Constitution to federal officials, are intended to be reserved to the States.[27]

This article was approved by a vote of eighty to one. The opposition pointed out the difficulties which might arise from variation in laws from one place to another, but this argument appeared to have little effect.[28]

Somewhat allied to the states-rights question, was that which arose from the demands of the various states and territories for modifications of their boundaries or for recognition as states. On July 10, 1856, it was decided to have a special committee composed of one deputy from each territorial division represented, this committee to examine and make recommendations on the large number of applications that had been filed.[29]

A trouble, petty but nevertheless serious, that faced the congress was that of maintaining a quorum with which to do business.[30] Although only a bare ma-

[27] Ibid., I. 473.

[28] Y. O., La Reforma Social de Méjico, pp. 27-28.

[29] Zarco, I. 683. J. M. Lafragua to Manuel Doblado, June 3, 1856. García, ed., Los Gobiernos de Álvarez y Comonfort, p. 197.

[30] Priestley, Mexican Nation, p. 328.

jority of the deputies was necessary, for forty-eight days scattered through the session everything' was at a standstill, because half of the delegates were not at their posts. At other times the sessions, already begun, had to be suspended because a quorum was no longer in the hall.[31]   Probably one contributing factor to this lack of interest was the fact that for a number of years congresses had occupied a very subordinate place in the Mexican scheme of government.   This apathy was evidently feared from the beginning, and on March 1, 1856, Ocampo sponsored a measure to have the roll called at the opening and close of each session and for the publication of resulting records in the newspapers.   After nearly a whole day spent in discussion, the bill passed by a vote of fifty-two to thirty.[32]   Accordingly, it was possible to check from day to day in the columns of *La Sociedad* and other papers the names of the delegates present and of those absent with or without permission.[33]

On the whole, the sessions were orderly, but in the heat of argument there were occasional "reversions to type".   Two physical encounters were settled privately, but a third case was actually brought before the congress for settlement.[34]   At times, general disorder became serious, as on July 1, 1856, when the presiding officer attempted to cut short a long discussion. The result was turmoil, in which all the deputies appear to have tried to make themselves heard and seen at once, the galleries freely and vociferously lending

[31] Zarco, *passim.*
[32] *Ibid.,* I. 66-71.
[33] *La Sociedad* regularly published these lists.
[34] Zarco, II. 415.

their aid. Enough of the deputies left the hall to break the quorum, and so the session came to an ignominious and riotous end. The remainder of the delegates then went into "executive session", with the galleries cleared.[35]

As has been intimated, from the opening of its deliberations, a delicate situation existed in the relations between the provisional government and the congress. The call for the election of deputies had been made by Álvarez, and most of the delegates chosen were liberals. Now that the body was in session, it found Comonfort acting as the executive with a cabinet composed in large measure of *Moderados*. True, the first important act of the congress had been equivalent to a vote of confidence in Comonfort, when, on February 21, it approved of the change in the executive by a vote of seventy-two to seven. While this looked like harmony, it actually postponed the contest, and both groups knew it. On April 12, it was proposed that Álvarez' nomination of Comonfort as a *General de División* be approved, but three days later the measure was defeated "almost unanimously".[36] The congress approved of Comonfort as president, but had no intention of giving him so much power that he could make a dictator of himself, as Santa Anna had done.

By May feeling had become acute, and trouble was threatened over the appointment of his council by Comonfort.[37] This was barely smoothed over, when,

[35] Antonio Aguado to Manuel Doblado, July 2, 1856. García, ed., *Los Gobiernos de Álvarez y Comonfort*, pp. 222-223; Zarco, I. 630-631.

[36] Zarco, I. 135, 137.

[37] An unsigned letter to Manuel Doblado, May 24, 1856. García, ed., *Los Gobiernos de Álvarez y Comonfort*, pp. 194-196.

in June, the fundamental question arose for which all had been preparing. This was: did the executive have the right to veto an act of congress? It was a natural question, in view of the double function being discharged by the legislative body. As a legislature, all precedent in Mexican affairs demanded that at least a veto over its acts be given to the executive. On the other hand, this same congress was drafting a constitution, which was to be the fundamental law of the country. Furthermore, by the Plan of Ayutla, the congress had been given the right to review the acts of the executive.[38] On these matters a special committee presented a report that read as follows:

> First, It does not pertain to the powers of the government to make objections or observations on the decrees and resolutions which the sovereign extraordinary constituent congress promulgate in accordance with the powers which article five of the Plan of Ayutla, modified in Acapulco, confers upon it.
>
> Second, This agreement will be communicated to the government for its information.

The report was given its first reading June 25, its second, two days later. On July 1, after a warm debate, the opposition being vigorously led by Siliceo of the Comonfort cabinet, it was accepted by a vote of sixty-five to twenty-seven.[39]

Fortunately, this did not bring about a rupture between the two branches of the government. In fact, on July 22, a vote of confidence was passed by a heavy majority.[40] Again, on the morning of October

---

[38] Zarco, I. 419, 420, 425.

[39] *Ibid.*, I. 575.

[40] Antonio Aguado to Manuel Doblado, July 22, 1856. García. ed., *Los Gobiernos de Alvarez y Comonfort*, p. 240.

20, when word came of the new conservative *pronunciamento* in Puebla against the government, in secret session the congress gave the government a unanimous vote of confidence.[41]   Later, when the danger had passed and Comonfort had granted liberal terms to the rebels, it denounced the administration, declaring that the latter had surrendered as much as the rebels.[42]

In the meantime, Comonfort published, May 15, a temporary plan of government known as the *Estatuto Orgánico,* which was to be in effect till the new constitution was promulgated.[43]   The *Estatuto Orgánico* placed definite limits on the power of the executive and indicated good faith on his part in so far as the Plan of Ayutla was concerned.[44]   The plan provided for centralization in governmental power more effective than any temporary reorganization of the old federal system could have been.[45]   Free private instruction was permitted.   Provisions were made for a bill of rights guaranteeing the writ of *habeas corpus;* for public criminal trials, except where public morality would be injured; for the prohibition of slavery; for freedom from forced loans, and prohibition of civil and political distinctions based on birth, origin, or race. For only seven crimes, military offenses not included, was capital punishment allowed.   The executive was forbidden to cede, mortgage, or in any way alienate Mexican territory, and no hereditary office or title of

[41] Zarco, II. 469-470.
[42] *Ibid.,* II. 633 ff.
[43] This decree may be found in Zarco, I. 296-326.
[44] Pérez Verdía, *op. cit.,* p. 433.
[45] Zarco, I. 322-326.

nobility was to be granted. Naturalization of foreigners was made extremely easy, but the government would recognize naturalization of Mexican citizens abroad only after its express consent had been secured. On the other hand, the privileges of citizenship were to be lost as a result of certain crimes. For political purposes the clergy were denied citizenship, since no ecclesiastic could vote or be voted for in any popular election,[46] but this did not affect other civil rights.

As required by the Plan of Ayutla, the *Estatuto Orgánico* was sent to the congress for its approval. The federalists at once took very positive exception to the centralized government provided. They said that the friends of a unitary system and the clergy now had a banner around which they could rally in opposing the installation of a "federal, democratic, tolerant, and eminently progressive constitution, such as the spirit of the congress and the majority of the nation promise." The decree was received May 26 and given its first reading June 4. On the seventh of the month the question came to a vote, and the decree was accepted by a vote of forty-five to forty.[47] Many deputies who voted in the affirmative insisted that they did so for the sake of expediency, in order to avoid confusion and trouble in the nation, and not because they approved in principle the central government established by the decree.

More liberal or radical decrees of the President were treated quite differently. The *Ley Juárez* was one of the first of such measures to be acted upon.

[46] Zarco, I. 307-318.
[47] *Ibid.*, I. 372-373.

Some of the deputies were inclined to argue that the law was in effect and that approval was consequently unnecessary. This argument, however, was brushed aside. "There was no orator who attacked the principles contained in the law," though several attacked minor defects in it.[48] When the vote was taken, it stood eighty-two to one.[49] Likewise, when the *Ley Lerdo* was reported, it was accorded a similar reception. The rules were at once suspended by more than the requisite two thirds majority, and the law was approved by a vote of seventy-eight to fifteen.[50]

One other general matter should be referred to before taking up the formation of the new constitution proper; namely, the question of the Jesuits. Their educational work had been missed and badly needed. There could be no doubt that many people were in favor of maintaining their work.[51] However, to have been reëstablished by Santa Anna was scarcely a recommendation so far as the congress was concerned. On June 6, 1856, the majority report of the committee advising revocation of the decree of Santa Anna was accepted by a vote of sixty-eight to fourteen. "This may be called an infringement of the principles of unlimited liberty so much boasted of";[52] but the liberals satisfied themselves by asking the following questions: Was not the purpose in

[48] García Granados, *op. cit.*, pp. 26-27.

[49] Zarco, I. 100, 137-140, 166-182. García Granados gives the vote at eighty-one to one, but the secretary of the Congress, Sr. Zarco, has been followed here. García Granados, *op. cit.*, pp. 26-27.

[50] Zarco, I. 596-615.

[51] *La Sociedad*, May 24, 1856.

[52] Bancroft, V. 687.

founding the Order to support the papacy and counteract the Reformation? Have the Jesuits ever given up their vow of absolute obedience? Are they not still a secret society more dangerous than any other? Are not their educational efforts used as an opportunity for them to plant their ideas in the most effective and dangerous places? The liberals then came to the conclusion that "the expulsion of the Jesuits is not to be regarded as religious persecution, but as a measure of precaution. It is the institution, not certain individuals, who are expelled."[53]

Returning to the question of the instrument of government, it may be said that to a large number of people in Mexico the constitution of 1824 stood as the symbol of liberty and progress. For them it had remained an ideal during the periods of highly centralized government and dictatorship. In view of this, it was not surprising that on February 20 Castañeda moved to readopt the old constitution as amended in 1847.[54] The matter rested there for a time, while the committee was busy drafting the new instrument. After the committee had reported and passions had been aroused over certain articles, another attempt was made by the friends of the constitution of 1824 to substitute it for that proposed by the committtee. The movement was led by Arizcorreta, Aguado, and Fuente, minister of foreign relations in the cabinet. Such a large number of amendments and changes were advocated, however, that a confused and "patched" document was the result, and, aided by a technical de-

---

[53] *El Constituyente*, June 15, 1856; Zarco, I. 376 ff.
[54] Zarco, I. 49 ff.

cision on the part of the chair, the whole movement was squelched.[55] From time to time many other suggestions were made, and one other complete plan of government was introduced into the congress just before the committee was ready to report.[56] Although they do not seem to have been seriously considered, they had some value in providing the ideas of the delegates in an available form for the use of the committee.

Just after the organization of the congress, provisions were made for a committee on the constitution. The leading members of this committee were: José María Romero Díaz, José María Mata, Isidoro Olvera, León Guzmán, and Ponciano Arriaga. José Antonio Gamboa[57] took particular advantage of the announcement, on February 28, that the committee would meet daily in the mornings, to enable those members of congress who desired to do so to attend.[58] After a little more than four months of work, the committee was ready to report. Whether by accident or design, the conservative press inclining to the latter view, the report was made on July 4. It was decided that at first the document as a whole would be discussed, with debate on the individual articles later on. Further it was agreed that for the future the constitution should have the right of way in all regular sessions, while the legislative duties of the body should be re-

[55] Antonio Aguado to Manuel Doblado, July 26, 1856. García, ed., *Los Gobiernos de Álvarez y Comonfort*, p. 247; Zarco, II. 203-204, 266-284. Rabasa, *La Organización Política de México*, pp. 77-79.

[56] Zarco, I. 529-542.

[57] Rabasa, *op. cit.*, pp. 54-55; Antonio Aguado to Manuel Doblado, May 21, 1856. García, ed., *Los Gobiernos de Álvarez y Comonfort*, p. 186.

[58] Zarco, I. 65.

served for Saturdays and for such other special sessions as the presiding officer might designate.[59]

Arriaga presented the document to the congress on behalf of the committee, pointing out some of the difficulties that had been faced and saying frankly that they had largely followed the document of 1824, adapting it to the new conditions faced by the nation.[60] "Two principal sources serve to inspire that political code; for the declaration of the rights of man, the doctrine [is] that of the French Revolution of 1789, and for the political organization of the Republic [it is] the Constitution of the United States."[61]   In the general debate, held on July 4, 7, and 8, the opposition did not delay its attacks.   Olvera specified religious freedom and the lack of a senate as objectionable features; Cortes Esparza opposed all mention of religion and freedom of the press and stated that the country was not yet ready for jury trials; Castañeda wanted the constitution of 1824 as it stood; García Granados feared the diversity of state laws and the lack of centralized municipal control; Ignacio Ramírez wanted a rearrangement of the states and more protection for the laboring classes; Barragán feared the liberal movement was too radical and that the document was too specific; Ampudia said it was too long and too vague; and de la Rosa, also minister of foreign relations for a short time, opposed a life term for supreme court justices and the idea of giving to the states all powers not mentioned specifically as belonging to the federal gov-

[59] Zarco, I. 640-641.

[60] *Ibid.*, I. 441, 443, 457. A most valuable and detailed comparison in parallel columns of the two documents, is given by Zarco, II. 205-219.

[61] Pérez Verdía, p. 436.

ernment.   The defense of the plan was undertaken by Arriaga, Mata, Castillo Velasco, and Gamboa.[62]

The bill of rights, comprising essentially the first thirty-four articles of the draft introduced by the committee and later inserted in the first twenty-nine articles of the constitution itself, was unusually full and explicit.   It included prohibition of slavery (Art. 2); freedom of education (Art. 3); the right of all men to choose their own professions, and no compulsory service (Arts. 4-5); freedom of speech and of the press (Arts. 6-7); right of petition (Art. 8); right to assemble peaceably (Art. 9); right to own and carry arms in self-defense (Art. 10); no passport fees (Art. 11); no titles of nobility or hereditary titles (Art. 12); no *fueros* or special tribunals (Art. 13); no retroactive laws (Art. 14); no extradition of political offenders (Art. 15); no search without proper writ (Art. 16); no imprisonment for civil debts (Art. 17); rights to bail, the writ of *habeas corpus,* fair trial and public defense, and abolition of torture and inhuman penalties (Arts. 18-22); enlargement of prisons to provide for later abolition of the death penalty (Art. 23); no double jeopardy for the same offense (Art. 24); freedom of the mails (Art. 25); no quartering of troops on citizens or compulsory service to be demanded by the military in time of peace (Art. 26); no confiscation of private property except for the public good, and no civil or ecclesiastical corporation to own real estate (Art. 27); no monopolies except those of coining money and the post office, and the regular restrictions under the patent laws (Art. 28).   These

[62] Zarco, I. 644-678.

guarantees were only to be suspended in case of national peril and grave disorder, and then only by the action of the president, when approved by his ministers and congress. In case the latter were not in session, the consent of the special committee of congress, always in the capital for such purposes, was to be obtained (Art. 29).

Needless to say, all of these provisions were not passed without a great deal of effort and much vigorous debate. While Article 2, which prohibited slavery, was approved unanimously, Article 3 got down to the heart of the religious question. Fourteen delegates discussed the matter at length. The newspapers and pamphleteers were likewise much exercised on the subject, since the sessions of the congress were public. It was said that freedom of education simply gave complete license for charlatans to prey upon the public,[63] that it directly opposed the commission of Christ to the priesthood to "go and teach all nations", for this great commission also implied that no others should do the work.[64] In spite of the furor aroused, the article was approved August 11 by a vote of sixty-nine to fifteen. Article 4 met with little opposition.

Article 5 created more trouble. It nullified any contracts for compulsory personal services, even under the cover of a religious vow. It was said that this was not strong enough to protect the poor laborer driven to make harsh contracts with his master by force of cir-

---

[63] A. Zerecero, *Observaciones . . . a la Constitución,* pp. 11-12.

[64] *Manifestación que hacen los Vecinos de Morelia;* Alvires, (*Primeras*) *Reflexiones sobre los decretos . . . que prohiben el Juramento Constitucional . . .,* p. 17; *Interesante Estudio sobre Instrucción Láica Obligatoria.*

cumstances and custom,[65] also that it prevented compulsory military service.[66]   The real fight on the article, however, came as a result of its effect on religious vows.   Again the public was much interested and flocked to the galleries of the congress to hear the debates.   At one time the Secretary recorded that the disorder was such that the voice of the speaker attacking the article was drowned by the hubbub.[67] Churchmen claimed that this article was an attack aimed at the very foundation of the Church, for if religious vows were not supported by the government, the regular clergy of both sexes would leave their institutions and enter into the state of matrimony, thus bringing scandal upon their organizations and undoing much of the work accomplished at so great a cost.[68] José Antonio Gamboa, speaking as a physician, said that he knew the conditions in the nunneries and that many emotional young girls were taken into them, who later wished to leave.   As proof of this, he referred to the law of 1833, under which three women left one convent with which he was acquainted in Oaxaca.   Gamboa went on to say that he would support an act to enforce such vows taken after the applicant had reached the age of twenty-five.[69] Another interesting debate arose on this same article; the question was asked whether it nullified the obedience clause in marriage vows.   If so, it was claimed that it was a

[65] Zerecero, *op. cit.*, pp. 13-14.
[66] Bulnes, *op. cit.*, pp. 232-234.
[67] Zarco, I. 722-723.
[68] Agustín de la Rosa, *op. cit.*, pp. 32-33.
[69] Zarco, I. 727-728.

direct attack on the decrees of the Maker of the Universe.[70]   Precedents were sought and found as to the attitude of European churchmen toward this same question.[71]   The disruption of the home, with all of its attendant consequences, was pictured.   The liberals maintained that woman was not a slave and should not be considered such.[72]   Furthermore, they insisted that the constitution was referring to "civil" liberties and not to "natural" liberties, such as those involved in the family relationship.[73] In spite of a strong opposition, mustering as many as thirty-seven votes at one time, the various clauses of the article were approved.

In regard to articles 6 and 7, on freedom of speech and of the press, there was no serious opposition from the standpoint of underlying principles.   Francisco Zarco, however, made two strong addresses, saying that the exceptions as to "private life, morality and public peace" could be expanded by a hostile administration till the exceptions nullified the law.[74]   The conservatives claimed that, under cover of this freedom of the press, there was an open invitation for unlimited attacks upon the Church.[75]   In spite of the opposition, the clauses of the articles were approved by votes of from sixty to thirty-three, to ninety to two.   Article 8, on the right of petition, was passed

[70] *Opúsculo en Defensa del Clero*, p. 6.
[71] *Colección de Documentos Relativos a Matrimonios Civiles*, pp. 15, 23.
[72] Zarco, I. 733.
[73] Alvires, *(Primeras) Reflexiones*, p. 17; *(Segundas) Reflexiones*, p. 44; *Manifestación que hacen los Vecinos de Morelia*, pp. 5-6.
[74] Zarco, I. Reports for July 25 and 28 give two addresses by the author attacking Article 14.
[75] *La Sociedad*, June 24, 1856.

with a substantial vote and little discussion. Article 9, guaranteeing the right of unarmed citizens to assemble for free discussion, was approved unanimously without debate.

Article 10, granting the right to own and carry arms for protection and self-defense, was mildly criticized because it would place arms in the hands of the lower classes.[76] Article 11, establishing the right to move around in, to enter, and to leave the republic without a passport or safe conduct, together with Article 12, abolishing all titles of nobility and hereditary titles, were passed with no opposition. Article 13 was practically a repetition of the Ley Juárez, which had already been approved by the congress. The same arguments were advanced as before in regard to the ecclesiastical fuero,[77] though there were few or none to support the military fuero in the public debate. The prohibition of retroactive and ex post facto laws (Art. 14) and of extradition for political crimes (Art. 15) passed with a substantial majority, though it was claimed that the second prohibition might encourage slaves in foreign countries to commit crimes and come to Mexico, since it was provided that the rights of man, once conferred, could never be re-

[76] Zerecero, op. cit., pp. 16-17. That the sessions were not entirely without humor is shown by the following report of Zarco:

Art. 6. "Todo hombre tiene derecho de poseer y portar armas para su seguridad y legítima defensa . . ."

"Debemos añadir que en muchos discursos hubo el tecnicismo de las circunstancias, esto es, que se habló de puñales, dagas, espadas, sables, trabucos, tranchetes, verduguillos, rifles, pistolas, escopetas de viento, piedras, reatas, culebrinas, alabardas, tijeras, corta-plumas, navajas, estiles y cuanto ha inventado la industria humana para destruir á los hombres, ó para defenderlos, . . ." I. 710.

[77] For an example see Alvires, (Primeras) Reflexiones, p. 17.

voked.[78]   The prohibition of "writs of assistance",
warrants for indiscriminate search (Art. 16), and
of imprisonment for civil debts (Art. 17), and the
grant of the right to demand the privilege of giving
bond in many cases (Art. 18), and the writ of *habeas
corpus* (Art. 19) were all easily approved, the last
two without any discussion.   Article 20, guaranteeing the right to every person accused to have full rights
of defense, to know and to face his accuser, etc., was
said to encourage loss of time by the courts; nevertheless, it was passed with little opposition.   The abolition of torture and of peculiar and unusual penalties
(Arts. 21-22) likewise met little or no opposition.   As
for the mooted abolition of the death penalty (Art.
23), many thought that the proposal was decidedly
premature, even if the government was authorized to
prepare for its enforcement by enlarging the jails to
take care as soon as possible of the prisoners who
would thus be left on hand.   The immediate abolition
of the death penalty for political offenses was unanimously approved, and capital punishment was permitted only for certain specified crimes, such as treason, highway robbery, incendiarism, patricide, pre-
meditated homicide, and serious military offenses.
Article 24, prohibiting double jeopardy for the same
offense and limiting the number of appeals, passed
by a vote of sixty-four to fifteen.   The inviolability of
the mails (Art. 25) was the subject of a vigorous debate, it being held that the government should have
the right to censor the mails at all times; the opposition was able to secure twenty-five votes on one bal-

[78] Zerecero, *op. cit.,* pp. 17-19.

lot.   Article 26, which prevented the quartering of troops on inhabitants in times of peace, was held to be inexpedient, because the peace and safety of the country at times demanded a retention of this right, but the vote in favor of the article was seventy-one to sixteen.[79]

Article 27 stirred up another hornets' nest in the nation, though the congress was almost unanimous in its approval.   To the first part, which provided that private property should not be confiscated except for the public good and then only after due process of law, there was little objection.   Then came the prohibition of civil and religious corporations from holding or administering real property except those buildings actually used for purposes of worship.   The discussion of this provision brought on a repetition of all the arguments over the *Ley Lerdo*.   A later writer has said that, "If the constitution provided the cause of the Three Years War, it was because it included Article 27, . . . the law of June 25.   The other laws passed up till then would not have caused the war."[80]   The prevention of monopolies, except such as those connected with the coinage, the post office, and patents (Art. 28), met no serious opposition. The suspension of individual liberties by the executive under certain restrictions (Art. 29) was approved by a vote of sixty-eight to twelve.

On the article providing full religious liberty, the discussion opened, July 29, with a strong attack on Protestantism by Castañeda.   Gamboa responded that

[79] *Ibid.,* pp. 20-21.

[80] Molina Enríquez, pp. 71; Alvires, (*Primeras*) *Reflexiones,* p. 18; García Granados, *op. cit.,* p. 41.

he stood for liberty of conscience and wanted either the Inquisition and all it stood for or else complete liberty, that if the Catholics had not overcome the Indian cults in three hundred years something was wrong. Zarco pointed out that the expulsion of the Jews and Moors from Spain had ruined her, while Piedmont with religious liberty was the hope of Italy. The next day the galleries were jammed, many reactionaries being present. It was decided that all who so desired should have the right to speak on the momentous question. Cortes Esparza and Arizcorreta opposed the article, the latter saying that the Church advanced as rapidly as possible but that it had not accepted the recently advocated democracy because it was fundamentally unsound. He said that the article preventing slavery was nullified by this one, which gave religious freedom and hence allowed Mohammedans to enter with their concubines. Here he was interrupted with applause, shouts, and whistles. Prieto and other speakers met with frequent interruptions from the galleries, most of the applause being from the conservatives, till Mata called attention to the fact that no one had yet opposed freedom of conscience. He then made a strong plea for progress. Two days later he spoke again, declaring that, in 1848, thirty thousand German families who wanted to enter Mexico as settlers had been stopped by the lack of religious liberty. On August 5 a ballot was expected, and one hundred and ten deputies were in their places. Montes, minister of justice and ecclesiastical affairs, spoke on behalf of the government, opposing the article as premature and inadvisable. The public session was closed after thirty-seven speeches had been delivered. The only vote taken was a test vote indicating that the deputies were not "ready for the question". This vote stood sixty-five to forty-six. In executive session, the question was referred back to the committee.[81]

Here the matter rested while the nation became duly excited. Petitions began to flood the congress long before debate actually started on the article. In fact, some had come in as early as April and June, before the committee on the constitution made its report.[82] On July 9 and 10, *La Sociedad* printed the names of about one thousand five hundred Mexican women, who petitioned that the sanctity of the Roman Catholic religion be maintained.[83] The next day this was followed by a similar petition with the names of some seven hundred and fifty men attached, and on July 12 a third appeared, signed by about eighty women of a small village, directly protesting against Article 15 of the Plan.[84] The Secretary of the congress reported two petitions as reaching that body on August 14, two on the eighteenth, and one on the twenty-sec-

[81] Zarco, I. 771-876; II. 5-96.

[82] Zarco, I. 136, 370.

[83] This petition of the women aroused much comment. *El Constituyente,* July 17, 1856, had this to say:

"Which is the most virtuous woman? 'She of whom least is said', answered a wise old man of Greece, 'and who speaks least', added a modern [wise man] . . .

. . . Who can say how many weddings planned will not be completed, and how many others which would have been proposed except for this affair [the women's petition], have by it been made impossible? What well-born man can aspire to the hand which writes or signs political petitions, and to the heart of a woman which is opened to the hatred of religious sects which God, the Pope, and the world look at with charity?"

[84] *La Sociedad,* July 9, 1856.

ond, all opposing toleration. On the other hand, petitions came from Vera Cruz and the Island of Carmen in Yucatán for religious freedom.[85]

There had been a steady growth of sentiment in favor of religious freedom,[86] but the question was really feared by the deputies. It was requested that action on the article be postponed till the rest of the constitution had been adopted.[87] As already observed, the matter was thoroughly discussed before it was referred back to the committee, and nothing definite was done till January, 1857. The article was again reported to the congress, but that was all, till January 25. On that day, as the session was nearing its end and the deputies were leaving, Gamboa asked leave on behalf of the committee to withdraw the article permanently. Some claimed that he had deliberately chosen his time so as to secure a "snap" judgment. After a heated argument, it was found that a quorum was not present, so the question rested till the next regular session, when the article was withdrawn without further debate by a vote of fifty-seven to twenty-two.[88] Associated with the article was a provision for the nation to control parochial perquisites (*obvenciones parroquiales*). This provision was rejected by a vote of forty-four to forty-two. Likewise, a provision stating that the nation was not to help collect such perquisites was withdrawn, as being a matter for the minister of justice and ecclesiastical affairs to settle.[89]

[85] Zarco, II. 266, 514. See also: *Ibid.*, II. 147, 153, 192.

[86] *Ibid.*, I. 783-784.

[87] *Ibid.*, I. 708.

[88] *Ibid.*, II. 813-816.

[89] *Ibid.*, I. 817 ff.

Thus the new constitution was drafted with no definite religious items in its bill of rights.[90]   The position of the executive through the whole struggle had been unequivocal.   Three of his cabinet ministers, Luís de la Rosa, José María Lafragua, and Ezequiel Montes, had spoken from the tribune opposing the article, with the result that many began to question the sincerity of the liberal principles of Comonfort.[91]

Articles 30 to 38 dealt with citizenship, its origin, methods of acquisition, duties, and obligations.   The methods of acquiring it included birth of Mexican parents, marriage and having Mexican children, ownership of real estate, and naturalization by taking the requisite oath of allegiance.   The franchise was given to adult males at the age of eighteen if married, or of twenty-one if unmarried, provided the persons concerned had an honest means of livelihood. Some advocated a literacy test, saying: "We believe, then, [that it is] indispensable for the exercise of suffrage to have citizens at least twenty years of age and able to read and write."[92]   The committee on the constitution included this provision in Article 40 of their draft, but when opposition developed, it was withdrawn.   In appointment to a public office, other things being equal, Mexicans were to be given the preference.   With the exception of the provisions for a literacy test, the report of the committee was accepted with slight modifications and little debate.

As to the type of government wanted, there was no doubt at all in the minds of the deputies.   Articles 39-

[90] García Granados, *op. cit.,* p. 34.
[91] Bulnes, *op. cit.,* p. 246.
[92] *La Nacionalidad,* May 15, 1856.

41 definitely stated: "National sovereignty resides essentially and ordinarily in the people. All power emanates from the people and is instituted for their benefit." The will of the Mexican people was to determine the future changes in their government, though it was then said to desire "a representative, democratic, federal Republic, composed of free and sovereign States". The states were to handle their internal affairs, but were not to meddle in national matters. With a few brief comments upon the anomalous condition of the territories, the three articles were adopted by overwhelming majorities, in spite of the centralized government so recently established by Comonfort and the known opposition of the conservatives.

Articles 42-49 fixed the territorial limits of the states and territories. Much scheming and counter scheming took place. As already stated, the wish of each state was to get desirable acquisitions, and the territories desired statehood. Colima and Tlaxcala, in fact, were made into states, and the Federal District, long since entitled to representation as a state so far as population was concerned, was promised this status and was to be known as the Valley State (*Estado del Valle*) as soon as the capital should be moved.

Article 50, providing for the division of the powers of government among legislative, executive, and judicial departments, no two ever to be united in the same person or group, was approved unanimously after slight debate. Article 51 provided that the "Exercise of the supreme legislative power shall be deposited in a single assembly which shall be called the Congress

of the Union."[93]   It was maintained that a senate was
one of those remnants of aristocracy, which caused delay in lawmaking, and that to adopt a bicameral system
would be a servile copying after the United States.[94]
The opposition pointed out the poor record of the uni-
cameral system under Iturbide, in 1836, when it established centralism, and, in 1847, when it allowed Santa
Anna to dominate congress.[95]   This argument, in addition to the pleas of the small states that a senate
was their only means of protection, was of no avail.
After a protracted debate, the article was adopted by
a vote of forty-four to thirty-eight.   Biennial elections (Art. 52) were approved without discussion, as
was the provision for the election of substitute deputies (Art. 54).   Some dispute arose over the size of
the districts, part of the deputies standing out for one
representative for each eighty thousand inhabitants
in spite of a committee recommendation of one for
each thirty thousand.   It was finally agreed that there
should be a deputy for each forty thousand inhabitants
or major fraction thereof, each territory also to be
entitled to at least one representative (Art. 53). After
lengthy discussion, the indirect method of electing representatives was agreed upon (Art. 55), in spite of
the vigorous protests of Francisco Zarco and Ignacio
Ramírez that in this manner public opinion was not
represented and never would be formed on any given
subject.

Article 56, enumerating the qualifications for a
deputy, gave rise to a discussion that lasted almost a

[93] This was changed to a bicameral system in 1874.
[94] *La Nacionalidad,* April 27, 1856.
[95] Zarco, I. 678.

week. The first clause, to the effect that deputies must be Mexican citizens, was approved unanimously. The second required residence in the district represented. About one third of the delegates insisted that leading men of the nation should be chosen, regardless of their residence, especially since certain districts might not have good men available at all times, while others would have an oversupply. Finally, the idea of states rights and the necessity for local representation won, the vote standing fifty-four to twenty-five. The third clause specifically prevented ecclesiastics from serving as deputies. Since Article 35 listed among the prerogatives of citizenship the rights to vote and be voted for, the conservatives claimed that, if the clergy could not act as deputies, they had lost at least a part of their citizenship. Furthermore, the nation, was deprived thus of the services of good men, and the principles of democracy were being violated.[96] In spite of this argument, the fear of the priesthood was such that the prohibition was adopted by a vote of seventy-one to eight. The final clause, providing that residence in a given district should not be lost while filling public office elsewhere, was passed unanimously.

Acceptance of election as a deputy was declared incompatible with the holding of any other public office (Art. 57), and special consent of congress was required before a deputy or substitute deputy should be allowed to receive appointment by the executive to any salaried office after his election or during the term he was then serving. Articles 59-63 were approved

---

[96] *Opúsculo en Defensa del Clero*, pp. 8-9; Ramón Camacho and José Guadalupe Romero, *Contestación a las reflexiones sobre los decretos episcopales que prohiben el Juramento Constitucional*.

without discussion. They provided for the inviolability of deputies for opinions expressed in the discharge of their duties; for control by congress over
the election of its members; that a quorum consist
of a majority of the deputies elected, but that less
than a majority should have the right to compel the
attendance of absentees; that the congress should meet
semi-annually, one of its sessions not being subject to
prorogation by the executive; and for the presentation
of a message by the president at the opening of the congress to show the condition of the republic. Article
64 was unanimously approved after a short discussion; it provided that the congress should be empowered to pass laws and resolutions only (*leyes o acuerdos
económicos*). In this way, the right of issuing ordi-
nances on special subjects was taken from it, in spite
of the protests of a few members.

By a unanimous vote, it was decided that laws
could be initiated by the president, by the deputies to
congress, or by the legislatures of the various states
(Art. 65). Articles 66-71, outlining the procedure
for the passage of laws, were approved without serious objection, though some delegates still wanted a
bicameral system. On the last day of the first session
of the congress in each year, the president was required
to submit his annual report on finances and his estimates for the coming year. These proposals were to
be referred to a committee, which was to report at
the opening of the next session, three and one half
months later. In the second session of each year,
financial matters were to have the right of way. In

case of "extreme urgency", an immediate vote on any given bill could be secured, provided two thirds of the deputies present wished to suspend the rules requiring submission of the measure to a committee, a report by that committee, and then one or two public discussions.

The powers of congress were described in thirty subdivisions of Article 72. On the whole, they reflect the fear of the executive, which had become an integral part of the Mexican political thinking of the day. Congress was granted the power to raise, to maintain, and to regulate a standing army; to control the national guard, even to the point of giving to the president power to move it; as well as to declare war, to issue letters of marque, and to control foreign troops entering or leaving Mexican territory. The control of foreign and interstate commerce, the ratification of treaties, the approval of appointments in the diplomatic service and in the army, and the control of naturalization were turned over to congress, as were all powers in connection with the formation of new states and the regulation of state boundaries. Some of the opponents of the new form of government did not hesitate to say that its most serious defects were to be found in these inclusive powers granted to the legislature, when that body was, according to Article 56, which required residence in the district represented, to be formed of ignorant country fellows without knowledge of public affairs. A dozen or more leaders would be able to lead "like a flock of the most patient sheep" a hundred or more of their associates. Furthermore, there was a danger that the president would control them and become a tyrant, or else not control them and become a mere figure head.[97]

Further fear of the executive was shown in the provisions (Arts. 73-74) for a permanent deputation, to be composed of one representative from each state and territory. This group was to represent congress during its recess, maintaining its integrity against executive encroachment, and having the power to call the body in special session, either with or without the consent of the president.

The executive function was to be entrusted to a president (Art. 75) chosen by an indirect system (Art. 76). The second of these provisions met the same criticism that had been offered to the indirect method of selecting deputies, but was approved nevertheless. Article 77 required a candidate for the office of president to be a resident Mexican citizen, thirty-five years of age and exercising full rights of citizenship at the time of election. No ecclesiastic was eligible. To none of these requirements was there particular opposition. The term of office (Art. 78) was set for four years, beginning the first of the December following the election. In case of death or inability of the president to serve, the chief justice of the supreme court was to take his place with an *ad interim* appointment till the existing executive could resume his duties or till a new election could be held. After such an election, the new incumbent was to serve till the last day of November of the fourth year following his election (Arts. 79-80). Thus it was not necessary for the presidential and congressional elections to be held

[97] Zerecero, *op. cit.*, pp. 38-41.

within the same year. It will also be noted that, by
the elimination of the vice-presidency, there was no
danger of disagreement between the two chief executive officers, such as had been the case at times in the
past. Resignation of the president was to take place
only for grave cause (*causa grave*) and then on approval of congress (Art. 81). On the other hand, if
the executive delayed the election of his successor, or
if for any other reason no candidate had been chosen,
the actual incumbent must retire from office and turn
it over to the chief justice (Art. 82). Article 83 provided the oath of office, while Article 84 required that
the executive remain at the seat of government except for such serious reasons as might be approved by
congress or the permanent deputation.

The powers of the president (Art. 85) included
the naming of diplomatic and army officers, declaration
of war, and the control of the army and national guard,
all with the approval of congress. The carrying on
of foreign affairs was in his hands, except that treaties
had to be ratified by congress. He also exercised the
pardoning power for criminals sentenced by the federal
courts. All presidential acts required the counter signature of the cabinet officer whose department the act
affected. In addition, cabinet members were required
to report directly to congress each year as to affairs
in their departments (Arts. 86-89). Aside from enforcing the laws, naming minor officials, and handling
foreign negotiations, this set of powers looks more
like a set of restrictions. Even the right to pardon
federal prisoners was secured for the president only
after a lively contest, in which those who wished the

power as an attribute of congress were defeated by
the narrowest of margins, the vote being forty-two to
forty-one.

The federal judicial system was to be composed of
a supreme court, together with circuit and district
courts (Art. 90). The supreme court was to have eleven justices and other necessary officers (Art. 91), the
justices to serve for six-year terms after indirect election (Art. 92). A candidate for the post was required
to be a Mexican citizen by birth, thirty-five years of
age, and a trained lawyer (Art. 93). The last provision met considerable opposition but was approved
by a vote of forty-seven to thirty-seven. After once
taking the oath (Art. 94) as a supreme court justice, a
man could resign during his term of office only for
grave cause and with the consent of congress (Art.
95). The organization of the circuit and district
courts was left to future laws (Art. 96). The powers
of the federal courts (Art. 97) were taken over, with
practically no changes, from the Constitution of the
United States. The only point on which serious debate arose was as to whether the federal courts should
have jurisdiction over cases involving representatives
of foreign countries. It was feared that grant of this
jurisdiction would bring about friction with the executive department in its handling of diplomatic affairs.
By Articles 98 and 99, the supreme court was given
original jurisdiction in cases arising between states
and those to which the union was a party, also the right
to settle questions of jurisdiction arising between
courts of different states, between a state court and
a federal court, or between inferior federal courts.

In other cases the supreme court had appellate jurisdiction (Art. 100). The federal courts were also given jurisdiction over all disputes arising from the violation of personal privileges listed in the bill of rights or from federal interference in the states and *vice versa* (Art. 101). Disputes over private rights were also subject to state jurisdiction in many cases. Because of the possibility of conflict here, many delegates opposed the clause, the final vote being forty-six to thirty-six. Article 102 provided the special writ of *amparo* by which any law resulting in an injustice in any particular case could be enjoined or estopped in so far as that case was concerned without the law itself being officially impaired.

Deputies to congress, supreme court justices, cabinet members, and governors of states were to be liable to impeachment for private or public misconduct; but, during his term of office, the president should be exempt from legal process except for treason, violation of the constitution, attacks on electoral liberty, or serious crimes of the common order (Art. 103). In the latter case, congress was to act as a grand jury to determine whether that official should be removed from office and the case turned over to the regular courts (Art. 104). For official misconduct, congress was to sit and determine guilt by a majority vote, whereas the supreme court was to pass sentence (Art. 105). When condemned for official misconduct, the power of pardon could not be invoked (Art. 106), though a man was subject to trial only during his term of office and for one year after its expiration (Art. 107). No official *fuero* could be invoked by a public official in crimes against the "civil order" (Art. 108). There was some trouble in the wording of these provisions, so, after full discussion by the congress, they were withdrawn by the committee and redrafted.

Article 109 provided that the states must adopt a "popular, representative, republican government". They could arrange treaties of limits among themselves, provided such agreements were aways subject to the approval of congress (Art. 110), but they were prevented from making foreign treaties and alliances, except in the case of frontier states coöperating against Indians, and from issuing letters of marque, coining money, and issuing money or stamped paper (Art. 111). Without securing the consent of congress, they could not levy export or import duties, raise a permanent army, own warships, or make war on a foreign power, except in case of actual invasion (Art. 112). Extradition of criminals between the states (Art. 113) and full faith and credit for the acts of one state in another (Art. 115) were also provided for. The governors of the states were required to publish and enforce federal laws (Art. 114), and the national government, on its part, was expected to protect the states from foreign invasion and from internal disturbance on application by the proper authorities (Art. 116). Again, it is apparent that the legislature had reserved to itself the real power. Serious criticism of the right of the legislature to impeach state governors was heard. By a mere majority vote, the congress could thus oust all the state governors, as well as the president, his cabinet, and the supreme court justices.[98]

[98] Bulnes, *op. cit.*, p. 209; García Granados, *op. cit.*, pp. 44-45.

Articles 117-121 were approved without debate. They included reservation to the states of all powers not given to the federal government; prohibition of the holding of two national elective offices by the same person at the same time; prohibition of the disbursement of national funds, except for items included in the regular estimate submitted to congress or provided for by a previous law; a provision that national officials should receive a salary provided by law, the said salary not to be renounced by them or to be increased or decreased during their term of office; a requirement that all public officials take an oath to support the constitution and the laws based upon it. Article 122 made the military distinctly subordinate to the civil authorities in time of peace. To this provision the militarists objected, but they had very little voting strength in the congress. After June 1, 1856, all internal customs duties and sales taxes were to be abolished (Art. 124). The national government was given control of the public buildings necessary for its functions wherever found (Art. 125). Article 126 made the constitution the supreme law of the land.

Article 123 is considered out of its regular order so as to call attention to its provisions more particularly. It gave to the federal government the right to interfere "in matters of religious observance and external discipline" (*materias de culto religioso y disciplina externa*) only as the laws might designate. This article, taken in conection with Article 122, again aligned the Church and the army against the state. Many thought Article 123 to be a rewording of Article 15 of the Plan, which had created such a furor that it had had to be withdrawn.[99]   The qualification of "external discipline" was not defined and hence was held to be subject to interpretation according to the whim or desire of the government.[100]   Taken in connection with the absolute guarantees of freedom of speech, the press, and education, together with the well-known attitude of an executive and congress, who had just promulgated and approved the *Ley Juárez,* the *Ley Lerdo,* and the *Ley Iglesias,* this was understood to amount to religious freedom.

After a lengthy debate, it was decided that the constitution should be subject to amendment by a two-thirds vote of the deputies present in congress whenever recommended by a majority of the state legislatures.   Article 128 reflected the condition of the country; it expressly stated that this constitution was to be a perpetual document, which should never lose its "force and vigor".   In case of overthrow of the government by rebellion, it was, like the phoenix, to arise once more and exist again with the return of peace.[101]

---

[99] Alvires, *(Primeras) Reflexiones,* pp. 19-20.

[100] Agustín de la Rosa, *op. cit.,* pp. 21-26.

[101] The magnitude of the gains made by the cause of democracy in this new constitution is seen by the following list given by Bulnes, *op. cit.,* pp. 227-228:

LIBERTIES

1. Liberty for the private and public expression of ideas in all known ways, with only the limits prescribed in the most liberal nations.
2. Complete liberty of education.
3. Liberty to carry arms.
4. Liberty of personal movement throughout the Republic.

Those other liberties guaranteed by the previous constitutions, such as that of 1824.

GUARANTEES

1. Abolition of the ecclesiastical *"fuero"* and of all special tribunals.
2. Abolition of imprisonment for debt.

The transitory article provided that the constitution should be published and sworn to at once by all public officers; but, with the exception of the laws affecting elections, it was not to go into effect till September 16, 1857. The electoral law passed by the congress provided for the first elections and for the organization of the government. The indirect system was adopted with precincts of five hundred inhabitants each (Art. 2), whose representatives were to go to district conventions (Arts. 1 and 33), each of which represented forty thousand inhabitants. The district delegates were to meet and elect the president, chief justice of the supreme court, and the associate justices (Arts. 43-50). The congress was to count the ballots, and, in case no candidates received a majority, to elect the officers, voting by states. Soldiers were allowed to vote as simple citizens (Art. 13), and no armed forces were allowed near the polls (Art. 61). No person

3. Abolition of judicial costs.

4. Imprisonment to be for crimes deserving physical punishment only.

5. Liberty on bond to be permitted in certain cases.

6. Writ of *habeas corpus* to be used.

7. Free defense in civil and criminal cases. The accused to have the right to face the witnesses and to know the name of his accuser, if there be one. The accused to have all necessary information to aid in his defense.

8. Abolition of death penalty. Prohibition of punishment for political offenses.

9. Prohibition of more than three appeals *(instancias)* in criminal cases.

10. Military not to be able to impress individual services in peace time.

11. Previous indemnity to be paid in case of appropriation of private property for public use.

12. Prohibition of monopolies.

13. Guarantee of the writ of *amparo*.

Other guarantees found in the Constitution of 1824 and previous documents also repeated here.

habitually drunk was to enjoy the franchise (Art. 8).[102]

As their year of labor wore on toward its close, the deputies began to weary of their task and of the obloquy heaped upon them from so many sources. Some of the members of the body itself, moreover, were not above trickery. The presiding officers were elected for one month only. On December 2, 1856, in the election for vice-president, eighteen men received votes on the first ballot. On the second, eighty deputies cast eighty-eight votes, "a prodigy which perplexed the secretariat". On the next ballot only seventy-five votes were cast, less than half the total number of deputies and not enough to elect, even though when the deputies were counted, seventy-nine were in the room. On the next vote, there was still no election, some of the deputies having thrown their votes away. Finally, a fifth attempt secured a decision.[103]

Toward the end of the long session, on January 28, it was decided to meet in continuous session till the work should be completed. That evening several were absent from 6:00 P.M. to 9:30 P.M. A deputation sent to the theatre found seven of the absent members there; of these, two returned to the hall, but the others refused. At 11:30 the meeting recessed till 10:00 A.M. of the next day, but again no quorum was present till 1:30 P.M. No sooner had business started than ten deputies left the hall and were not rounded up till 2:15. At 6:15 an adjournment was taken till 7:00, but it was not till 9:30 that seventy-eight, a bare ma-

[102] For the electoral law, see Zarco, II. 1017 ff.
[103] *Ibid.*, II. 623.

jority, were present.   Debate as to what to do with the
absentees lasted till midnight.   By a vote of seventy-
three to four, the President was authorized to compel
attendance, though a resolution to the effect that the
absentees were unworthy of public confidence failed
by a vote of forty-nine to twenty-one.   The congress
recessed to meet at 10:00 A.M. on the next day, January 30, and by 2:00 P.M. a quorum was actually available.[104]   Such was the spirit of the delegates at the
end of the session.

On January 31 the last election of officers took
place.   The work of the congress was really over, hence
the position of president was merely an honorary one
and carried with it the high privilege of being the first
to sign the completed document that embodied those
liberties for which so much effort, money, and blood
had been spent.   On the first ballot, of the seventy-
nine votes cast, seventy-six went to that veteran hero
of Mexican liberty, Valentín Gómez Farías,[105] who,
though he was officially a delegate to the congress, had
been able to attend the sessions only a few times on
account of his age and feebleness.   In the midst of a
huge concourse, he was literally carried into the chamber by his two sons, Benito and Fermín.   At once the
assembly arose, while, spurred by the excitement of
the hour, "the patriarch of liberty, animated and erect,
took the oath" to support the constitution "in the midst
of a frenzy of enthusiasm".[106]

[104] Zarco, II. 837-889.
[105] *Ibid.*, II. 881-882.
[106] *Ibid.*, II. 910-911; *Diez Civiles Notables de la Historia Patria*, p. 91.

CHAPTER XII

RECEPTION OF THE CONSTITUTION, AND ITS EFFECTS

The nation had been kept only too well informed of the debates in the congress during its work on the constitution. With the formal announcement and publication of the document on February 12, however, it was seen as a whole for the first time.[1] Heretofore, it had been either a promise or a menace, and most of the people who thought at all had come to strong conclusions on individual articles, while they knew practically nothing of the whole instrument. On March 17, 1857, Comonfort sent out a decree requiring all public officers to take an oath to support it.[2] Attention was immediately fixed on the clergy, to see what they would do. From Tabasco came word that they would uphold the document,[3] and the Bishop of Oajaca reported that, while he did not approve all the provisions in the new plan of government, he would have a *Te Deum* sung in the cathedral in honor of the taking of the oaths in its support.[4] As the lines became more distinctly drawn, and most of the Church leaders opposed the measure, some of the inferior ecclesiastics did not hesitate to differ from their superiors, insisting that bishops were not infallible and did not have to be blindly obeyed in all cases, for "as soon as the

[1] Arrangoiz, II. 350.
[2] Rivera, *op. cit.*, p. 20.
[3] *La Democracia*, July 5, 1857.
[4] Bulnes, *op. cit.*, 180.

voice of the bishop does not teach the doctrine of the Church, it has no more force than the reasons upon which it is founded."[5]   Some even admitted that the *fueros* were privileges and not rights.[6]   Advocates of the constitution claimed that public opinion would control the application of the law and that indiscriminate damage would not be done to an institution that was so much respected by the whole country.[7]   Not only that, but, if the bishops were to be allowed to state whether any one law was permissible or not, it was equivalent to turning over to them the entire control of all political issues.[8]

As a whole, the "promulgation of the liberal constitution had rather maddened than paralyzed the clergy."[9]   Absolution was refused to those who took the oath to support it.   This terrible pronouncement caused many to hesitate and even to decline to take the oath.[10]   But the clergy did not merely use their influence as spiritual fathers; they appealed at the same time to the reason of their hearers and readers, saying that it was unfair for churchmen to be excluded from civil offices.   Now that there were no religious qualifications for the members of the executive

[5] "Un Párraco Jalisciense", *Caso de Conciencia sobre el Juramento Constitucional,* p. 5-8; Alvires, *(Primeras) Reflexiones,* p. 4.

[6] "Un Párroco Jalisciense", *op. cit.,* pp. 13-16.

[7] Alvires, *(Segundas) Reflexiones,* pp. 47-48.

[8] Alvires, *(Primeras) Reflexiones,* p. 6.

[9] C. E. Lester, *The Mexican Republic,* p. 34.

[10] J. Noriega to Mariano Riva Palacio, August 14, 1857, Jesús Andrade to Mariano Riva Palacio, May 31, June 2, June 7, 1857, Palacio Papers; *Manifestación que hacen los Vecinos de Morelia.* The contest on this point was acrimonious. The chief arguments of the disputants may be found in Alvires, *(Primeras) Reflexiones,* pp. 13-14, and in Ramón Camacho and José Guadalupe Romero, *op. cit.,* pp. 13-15.

and legislative departments, the Church was entirely without safeguards, and any kind of ruinous and destructive laws might be passed against it.[11] Furthermore, it was claimed that the constitution meant the economic downfall of the nation, because wholesale property confiscations were likely to follow,[12] as well as all those discords of Protestantism[13] which were already leading the United States directly into a horrible civil war based on religion.[14]

The foolishness of certain of the constitutional provisions was repeatedly dwelt upon. It was said to be destructive of the sanctity of the clergy, for now their cases had to be dragged through the publicity and degradation of a public courtroom.[15] Religions were mutually exclusive, and to introduce others into Mexico was deliberately to ask for trouble.[16] The constitutionalists were said to be worse than Protestant Yankees, for the latter had protected the Church property in California, while the former were trying to destroy it in Mexico.[17] From another angle, the position of the Church was quite accurately summed up as follows:

[11] Agustín de la Rosa, *op. cit.*, p. 29.

[12] *Opúsculo en Defensa del Clero*, p. 16.

[13] *La Cruz*, V. 556 (September 3, 1857).

[14] J. H., *El Liberalismo y sus efectos en la República Mexicana*, p. 6. The author of this pamphlet seems to have been ignorant of the fact that at this very time the great Protestant churches of the United States were so far from alignment against each other that they were themselves dividing on the political issues of nullification, secession, and slavery.

[15] Pedro Espinosa, Bishop of Guadalajara, to Minister of Justice and Ecclesiastical Affairs, about February, 1856; Agustín de la Rosa, *op. cit.*, p. 40.

[16] *La Cruz*, V. 556 (September 3, 1857) ; *La Sociedad*, June 26, 1856.

[17] "Un Católico", *Crímenes de la Demagogía*, p. 58.

1. The Church has its own government, independent of all civil power.

2. The government of the Church, by its very constitution, is holy, perfect, unalterable, and perpetual.

3. Temporal governments are, by their nature, profane, imperfect, changeable, and temporary.

4. The Church affects the intrinsic good of the State; no State, however powerful it may be, influences the intrinsic good of the Church.

5. The protection the State gives the Church is rigorously obligatory: the honorary remunerations with which the Church recompenses the State, are merely gratuitous.

6. The protection referred to above does not give, nor is it able to give in any case, the right to intervene in the discipline (whether it be called internal or external), or in the principles of religion.[18]

While the contest was raging over the constitution, the elections were held, which were expected to show the attitude of the people in a definite manner. The liberals controlled their old districts, such as Jalisco, which was even ready to proclaim a new state constitution without the customary phrase, "in the name of God, all powerful, Supreme Author of the Universe and Legislator of its Societies".[19] In Oajaca, much the same condition obtained. In the election for governor, held in the last part of 1857, of the 112,551 votes cast Juárez secured 100,336.[20] The nation as a whole, however, was quite a different matter. The army had to be kept on a war-footing to handle the insurrections that were breaking out. When the votes for president were counted, it was seen that the liberals

[18] *La Cruz*, V. 240-241 (July 2, 1857).

[19] Bulnes, *op. cit.*, p. 334.

[20] *La Democracia*, June 30, 1857.

had won, but by narrow majorities. Comonfort secured an absolute majority of eight thousand only, while no choice was made for the position of chief justice of the supreme court. By the vote of the congress, Juárez, one of the two highest candidates, was chosen.[21] Of the one hundred and fifty-five deputies in the *Congreso Constituyente,* only twenty-one were elected to the first constitutional congress.[22] Liberals secured a majority in the new legislature, but a majority that was not so strong individually or collectively as had been hoped for.[23]

The defeat of Miguel Lerdo de Tejada for the presidency was all the more noticeable because of the first address delivered by Comonfort to the congress, when it assembled. In this address he recommended a number of immediate amendments to the constitution.[24] His cabinet was largely composed of moderates, but the real reason for the recommendation was his dislike of the powers given to the legislature.[25] There can be no question as to the difficulty of his position. To carry out the liberal policies meant not only to give up many of his own prerogatives to the legislature but also to fight out the issue with the Archbishop. If the people had objected to the exile of the Bishop of Puebla, what would they not say if the President acceded to the demands of the liberals and banished the Archbishop, an old man who quite

[21] Bancroft, V. 721.

[22] Bulnes, *op. cit.,* pp. 247-249.

[23] Parra, *op. cit.,* p. 90; "Un Progresista", *Los Moderados y el Estado de México,* p. 5.

[24] Bulnes, *op. cit.,* pp. 256-257.

[25] A. Rivera, *op. cit.,* p. 29; Priestley, *Mexican Nation,* pp. 328-329.

probably would not be able to stand the rigors and excitement of such treatment.[26] Yet, not to face the issue with the Church meant, sooner or later, to break with the liberals and reverse his position on practically all the great questions of the day.

Even the mild conservatives were demanding that the incoming congress continue the dictatorship, postpone for one year the date on which the constitution was to become effective, and call for a new congress to reform the document.[27] Others went about matters more directly, with the result that a number of meetings were held in the president's palace at Tacubaya. Soon the President broke with the liberal Governor of the Federal District, Juan José Baz.[28] Repeated rumors got out that he was planning a *coup d'etat,* even though he continued his close association with Juárez, an undoubted liberal. Comonfort himself wrote:

There were three roads open to me: 1, to leave affairs in the same state in which they were when the Revolution of Ayutla was successful; 2, to throw myself into the arms of the revolutionary principles, and introduce all the innovations demanded by it; 3, prudently to undertake the reforms demanded by public opinion.

The last of these he decided to attempt.[29] To this end, on December 17, the Plan of Tacubaya was announced. Its conservative principles may be seen by the following set of contrasts with provisions of the constitution:

[26] Payno y Flores, *Memoria sobre la Revolución*, pp. 48-49.

[27] Zerecero, *op. cit.*, pp. 42-43.

[28] Payno y Flores, *Memoria sobre la Revolución*, pp. 8-9.

[29] Portilla, *Méjico en 1856 y 1857*, pp. 369-372; Echeagaray, *Apuntaciones para la defensa del General Echeagaray*, p. 8.

PLAN OF TACUBAYA	CONSTITUTION OF 1857
1. Inviolability of Church property and revenues, and reëstablishing of former exactions.	1. A constitutional federal government to be established.
2. Reëstablishment of *fueros*.	2. Freedom and protection to slaves.
3. Roman Catholic religion as sole and exclusive religion of Mexico.	3. Freedom of religion.
4. Censorship of the press.	4. Freedom of the press .
5. Immigrants to come only from Catholic countries.	5. Immigration from all countries encouraged; encouragement for enterprise in industry, especially mining and internal imports [trade].
6. Overthrow of Constitution of 1857 and use of a central dictatorship subservient to Church only.	6. Military under civil powers and no military or ecclesiastical *fueros*.
7. A monarchy to be established if possible; if not an European protectorate.	7. Nationalization of Church property worth $200,000,000, income from which is worth $20,-000,000.
8. High tariff and internal duties *(alcabalas)* and use of monopolies.	8. Commercial treaties of fullest scope to be negotiated, including reciprocity of trade on frontiers.
	9. Lower tariff and no interior duties.[30]

Such a step meant an immediate break with Juárez[31] and other liberals. This was all the more certain, because the Archbishop and the Bishop of Michoacán, "approving the Plan of Tacubaya, removed the ban of excommunication from all who should turn to its support."[32] It would appear that the movement, begun by moderates, had been taken over by the conservatives and was being ardently supported by them.[33] Also, the old bugbear of treachery was brought up, and it was claimed that the President had solicited an alliance with the United States,

[30] Lemprière, *op. cit.,* pp. 37-38. W. Butler, *Mexico in Transition,* quite obviously has used the same table, with certain omissions of his own, pp. 120-126.

[31] Payno y Flores, *Mem. sobre la Rev.,* pp. 69-70.

[32] Bancroft, V. 727.

[33] Payno y Flores, *Mem. sobre la Rev.,* p. 105. See also Payno y Flores, *México y el Señor Embajddor Don Joaquín F. Pacheco,* pp. 73, 78.

by which Mexico would have been made into little
more than a protectorate of the northern republic.[34]

There were three places to be carefully watched
by Comonfort: Vera Cruz, a strong liberal center
and the most frequented port of the country; the interior, or middle west, the liberal centre that was always to be counted upon to give trouble; and the
region in and around the capital, where the national
guard was particularly strong and was aided by other
liberal troops.[35]   There is much truth in the statement that the people as a whole really played a part
in the war that was now beginning.   Many districts
had been truly converted to principles of one kind or
another and were ready to fight for them,[36]—in itself
an encouraging sign.   Families divided on the issue,
but they were at least thinking.[37]   Each party, of
course, accused the other of starting the trouble.
While Comonfort had blamed the liberals, others
blamed the clergy,[38] and still others the moderates,
who, representing much of the wealth of the nation,
by a little effort could have controlled the congress and
might have saved the situation had they acted together
and consistently.[39]   Instead, being weak and fearing
dissolution at the hands of the executive, they dis-
banded, December 16.[40]

[34] Bancroft, V. 707; see also *Harper's Monthly Magazine* XIV. 693
(April, 1857).

[35] Payno y Flores, *Mem. sobre la Rev.*, pp. 25-26.

[36] Arrangoiz, II. 355; Rabasa, pp. 38-39.

[37] Portilla, *Historia de la Revolución*, p. 296.

[38] M. Alvarez, *Historia Documentada de la vida pública del Gral.
José Justo Álvarez*, p. 46.

[39] "Un Progresista", *Los Moderados y el Estado de México*, p. 7.

[40] Lemprière, *op. cit.*, pp. 31-32.

Comonfort hesitated so much when Zuloaga, one of his associates, announced the exceedingly conservative plan of Tacubaya, that after approving the move he then actually defended the palace from attack by the extremists for a time. The situation had in it much of tragedy for this well intentioned but vacillating character.[41] Man after man left him or refused to coöperate with him further. "All are leaving us, Sr. Comonfort said to me. In fact the Palace was empty. *This was the truth, this the denouement.*"[42] Meanwhile, Generals Zuloaga and Miramon, both of them extreme conservatives, adopted even more reactionary principles and attempted to organize the government.[43] Juárez was legally entitled to the acting presidency under the constitution. In fact, he organized a cabinet and, during the ensuing two or three years, fought bravely and consistently for his cause.[44] He was aided by Santos Degollado, the popular leader of the liberals in Michoacán and Zacatecas,[45] and the Masons.[46] The war that ensued was one of the bitterest of the many with which Mexico has been cursed. Plunder and rapine attended the armies in the field; prisoners were slaughtered in cold blood. Physicians attending the wounded were captured and killed; churches were sacked.[47] On the other hand, one of the inspiring

[41] Payno y Flores, *Mem. sobre la Rev.,* p. 33.
[42] *Ibid.,* p. 89.
[43] Decrees of January 28, 1858 and March 1, 1858 provided for the return of much of the Church property. *Boletín Oficial,* April 24, 1858.
[44] Payno y Flores, *Mexico and her Financial Questions,* p. 34.
[45] Alvarez, *op. cit.,* p. vi of prologue; Bulnes, *op. cit.,* p. 284.
[46] Bulnes, *op. cit.,* pp. 339-340.
[47] Sierra, *op. cit.,* I. 261-262; Parra, *op. cit.,* pp. 104-105; "Un Católico", *Crímenes de la Demagogía,* pp. 76-77; Rivera, p. 45; Arrangoiz, II. 361; *Los Asesinatos de Tacubaya,* pp. 10, 22.

things in Mexican history is the bulldog tenacity with which Juárez fought on throughout the war, finally reaching the highest office in the land, but still without financial benefit to himself or his family.[48]

Representatives of foreign nations in Mexico recognized Zuloaga at once. Even the United States Minister, John Forsyth, did the same at first, but was soon instructed to reverse his policy and withdraw the legation from the capital (July, 1858).[49] On April 6, the Senate of the United States ratified the appointment of R. M. McLane as United States minister to the Juárez government. This was a great boon for the liberals.[50] While the McLane-Ocampo treaty was not ratified by the United States Senate, nevertheless all possible aid was given to Juárez by the Buchanan administration.[51] European powers were inclined to look askance at this government, whose headquarters were subject to change without notice. To them, a conservative administration, backed by the property interests and the clergy, was far more attractive than the patriotic proclamations of the liberal reformers.[52] In fact, the Spanish minister doubtless expressed the sentiments of others when he wrote that European intervention was the chief hope of the country.[53]

Slowly but surely the liberals advanced, until they were able to enter the capital and dominate the coun-

[48] Sierra, op. cit., I. p. 258; Sosa, Biografías de Mexicanos Distinguidos, p. 551.

[49] Lemprière, op. cit., pp. 40-42; Harper's Monthly Magazine, XVII. 403, 546 (August and September, 1858).

[50] Zayas Enríquez, op. cit., pp. 90, 125; Bancroft, V. 765.

[51] Bancroft, V. 773-775; Sierra, op. cit., I. p. 263.

[52] London Quarterly Review, CXV. 191-192 (April, 1864). Lemprière, op. cit., p. 193.

[53] Arrangoiz, II. 378-379.

try, December, 1860. The movement that had begun with the expulsion of the Jesuits and the sale of their estates in 1767[54] was now coming to a head. Partly as war measures and partly as a matter of principle, there were promulgated a series of laws in July, 1859, that did much toward completing the work begun in 1833 and carried on by the constitution. On July 12, in a decree of twenty-four articles, it was provided that all property of regular and secular clergy should be confiscated to the nation. At the same time, all religious fraternities and brotherhoods were suppressed, with a further prohibition against all such organizations for the future. Regular clergy, on leaving their monasteries, were to receive five hundred *pesos* cash and, if ill, three thousand *pesos* invested. Convents of nuns were to remain, but no more novices were to be accepted, and those nuns who wished to leave could do so, taking with them the dowry they had brought to the institution or a minimum of five hundred *pesos* cash. The convents were left enough funds to exist on, but all above this was confiscated, as were all manuscripts and books of the religious houses suppressed.[55] What the *Ley Lerdo* had failed to do, this planned to accomplish. It is said that about forty thousand transfers of property took place, and, "the number of landholders must have increased by many thousands, the fruits of the nationalization of Church lands falling mainly into the hands of the *mestizos*."[56] On July 23, 28 and 31, three other laws along the same line

[54] McBride, *op. cit.*, p. 62.

[55] Parra, *op. cit.*, p. 120; McBride, *op. cit.*, p. 70; Luis Cabrera, *The Religious Question in Mexico*, pp. 13-14.

[56] McBride, *op. cit.*, p. 71.

were issued. They made marriage a civil contract, turned over to civil judges the registration of births and deaths and the right to perform marriages, and took from the clergy the right to control cemeteries.[57] Religious toleration was also granted.[58]

August 30, 1862, a further law suppressed all ecclesiastical chapters except that of Guadalajara, which was actively supporting the government. After this date, no priest was allowed to wear clerical or "predetermined" garb outside of church buildings. A still further decree of February 2, 1863, provided for the excloistering of nuns.[59] As was to be expected, a movement as complete as this also included acts against church schools. A number had their property confiscated and its administration assumed by the government.[60]

Of course these acts met with much the same condemnation and support that had been accorded to similar attempts of the earlier period. Charges were made that the property confiscated was squandered recklessly and wantonly,[61] that civil marriage attacked the foundations of the home and of religion,[62] and, in short, that Juárez desired to destroy the Church at all costs.[63] On the other hand, the attacks on the Church had gained in vigor and in boldness, nothing

[57] Parra, op. cit., p. 121.
[58] Noll, op. cit., pp. 217-218.
[59] Zayas Enríquez, op. cit., p. 158.
[60] Sierra, op. cit., I. 514.
[61] García Granados, op. cit., pp. 101-102.
[62] El Matrimonio Religioso . . ., pp. 1-2.
[63] Garza y Ballesteros, Cuarta carta Pastoral, p. 7; Manifestación . . . [de] los Illmos. Sres. Arzobispo de Méx. . . . y Obispos . . ., p. 5.

now being too strong to see the light of print.   An Englishman summed up these charges when he wrote:

The Mexican church, as a church, fills no mission of virtue, no mission of morality, no mission of mercy, no mission of charity.   Virtue cannot exist in its pestiferous atmosphere; the code of morality does not come within its practice; it knows no mercy, and no emotion of charity ever moves the stony heart of that priesthood which, with an avarice that has no limit, filches the last penny from the diseased and dying beggar, plunders the widows and orphans of their substance, as well as their virtue, and casts such a horoscope of horrors around the death-bed of the dying millionaire, that the poor super- stitious wretch is glad to purchase a chance for the safety of his soul by making the church heir to his treasures.[64]

Needless to say, the state of the public finances was wretched.   From January 17, 1858, to November 10 of the same year, the government in Mexico City (conservative) issued bonds worth more than twelve million five hundred thousand *pesos,* for which it had received in cash about four hundred and twenty-five thousand *pesos* and in kind not quite two hundred thousand *pesos.*   The Juárez government was little bet- ter off.   It mortgaged the income of its ports and, by the strictest economy, found itself facing a monthly deficit of four hundred thousand *pesos.*[65]   It would appear that mining was the only prosperous industry, and its prosperity was said to be due to British initia- tive and protection.[66]   Robberies were frequent, the

[64] Lemprière, *op. cit.,* p. 175.

[65] Zayas Enríquez, *op. cit.,* pp. 112-113; J. Nepomuceno Adorno, *Analisis de los Males de Mexico,* p. 59.

[66] F. L., *Études Historiques sur le Méxique,* pp. 78-79.

courts inadequate, and foreign affairs in bad shape.[67] However, these were the natural results of the civil war and should not be charged to the account of the reform itself.

The gains for the cause of democracy were enough to justify enormous efforts to secure them. Some of these were freedom of speech; freedom of education; freedom of the press; abolition of privileged classes; abolition of imprisonment for debt; free defense of those accused of crimes; guarantee of writ of *habeas corpus;* restriction of the power of the military in time of peace; confiscation of property only for national welfare; prohibition of monopolies; and the writ of *amparo* to provide exemption for special cases.[68] And still there remains to be mentioned the series of laws and decrees, beginning with those of Lorenzo de Zavala in the state of Mexico in 1833 and ending with those of President Juárez, which included: (1833-1834), confiscation of the property of the *padres de Filipinas* by the state of Mexico, closing of the University of Mexico, secularization of Church property, removal of civil guarantees for collection of Church dues, and no civil enforcement of monastic vows (most of these were temporary); (1838), Confiscation of property of the Inquisition; (1842), secularization of the Pious Fund of the Californias; (1847), compulsory Church loan; (1855-1859), abolition of *fueros,* confiscation of Church property in Puebla, compulsory sale of Church property throughout the nation, con-

[67] *Ibid.,* pp. 71-75; *Harper's Monthly Magazine,* XVI. 259 (January, 1858).

[68] Bulnes, *op. cit.,* pp. 227-228.

fiscation of Church property throughout the nation, prevention of clerical representation in the government, and abolition of monastic orders.[69]

The story of the struggle for democracy in Mexico from the acquisition of independence to 1857 has been aptly described in the phrases: "misgovernment, discontent, revolution; misgovernment, discontent, revolution". Nevertheless, the author of the phrases points out that these revolutions were not purposeless or the mere grasping for power of ambitious would-be dictators, but were primarily aimed at specific evils.[70] The ambitions of some men did wreck many carefully laid schemes; but just as often as this occurred, other plans were made, and the great movement went on. If the Church had to bear the brunt of the attacks, it was because of its association with those who opposed progress; for the thinking Mexican has always been an essentially religious person and would not have injured this institution had he not felt that drastic measures were absolutely necessary for the future progress and happiness of his nation.[71]

As is often the case, the momentum of the reform, when once fairly started, was so great that some of the later laws announced were harsh, ill-considered, and hasty. However, the real reform was not contained in the laws and decrees, which went into effect after 1857 and which could be revoked by later similar executive decrees or legislative acts, but in the great

---

[69] Martinez, *op. cit.*, pp. 175-177; García Granados, *op. cit.*, pp. 99-100; Rives, *op. cit.*, I. 226. For other minor laws affecting the clergy after 1856, see Bassols, *op. cit.*

[70] Ross, *op. cit.*, p. 33.

[71] Cabrera, *op. cit.*, p. 3.

document which was the fundamental law of the land, the constitution of 1857. The Mexican people, while they were ready to accept the reform in theory, were not yet ready for it so far as that practical experience was concerned which would enable them to put it into real effect. They were suffering from a severe case of political indigestion, and it was now needful for them to be given a rest, so that their education and experience could catch up with their theories. However, a constitution acquired at such a cost and put into effect with such an effort became an ideal which could not be suppressed. While it is true that for a long period the country had virtually autocratic rule, nevertheless, even this showed a great advance over the early dictatorships. If there was a one-man government, there was peace; if large estates accumulated, there was also more general prosperity than ever before; if education was confined largely to the upper classes, this was not exclusively the case, and the *peón* was slowly but surely getting to a position from which he could and would demand and secure his rights; and if there has been another period of revolution and an overthrow of the constitution, which was the fundamental instrument of government for sixty years, this was only to establish a still more democratic constitution. In other words, the constitution of 1857 caught the principles of democracy, which the Mexican people for half a century had been working out, and so expressed and crystallized them in a great legal document that it may properly be said to have closed one era and opened another in the history of the Mexican nation.

BIBLIOGRAPHY

PRIMARY SOURCES

1—MANUSCRIPTS

Comonfort Papers. A collection of letters and papers of Ignacio Comonfort; especially good for the years 1850-1851 and 1860-1863.

Gómez Farías Papers. Some 4,000 letters and papers, official, semi-official, and private, including the letter files of most of the members of the Gómez Farías family; covering the years 1820-1857.

Manning-Mackintosh Papers. Commercial correspondence for the years 1847-1852 to and from the home office in England.

Riva Palacio Papers. Private correspondence with leading politicians of the day. Used especially for the years 1855-1857.

(Note: All of the above documents are to be found in the García Collection in the Library of the University of Texas. They are roughly classified in chronological fashion).

2—PRINTED MATERIALS

CONTEMPORARY ACCOUNTS

ADORNO, JUAN NEPOMUCENO, *Análisis de los Males de México*, México, 1858.

ÁLVAREZ, J. J. and DURAN, R., *Itinerarios y Derroteros de la República Mexicana*, México, 1856.

ARRÓNIZ, MARCOS, *Manual del Viajero en Méjico*, Paris, 1858. A volume of the *Enciclopedia Hispano-Americana*.

BENTON, THOMAS H., *Thirty Years View*, 2 vols., New York, 1889.

BUTLER, W., *Mexico in Transition from the Power of Political Romanism to Civil and Religious Liberty*, New York, 1893.

C[ALDERÓN] DE LA B[ARCA], MADAME, *Life in Mexico* . . ., London, 1843.

Couto, José Bernardo, *Discurso sobre la Constitución de la Iglesia*, México, 1857.

Featherstonhaugh, G. W., *Excursion through the Slave States*, New York, 1844.

F. L., *Le Mexique; Études Historiques au Point de Vue Politique et Social*, Paris, 1859.

Guía de Forasteros. A large number of these are to be found for various years. They provide good descriptive material as well as geographical information.

Humboldt, Alexander von, *Political Essay on the Kingdom of New Spain* . . ., 4 vols., London, 1814.

Lemprière, Charles, *Notes in Mexico in 1861 and 1862: Politically and Socially Considered*, London, 1862.

Lerdo de Tejada, Miguel, *Cuadro Sinóptico de la República Mexicana en 1856*, México, 1856.

Mayer, Brantz, *Mexico, Aztec, Spanish and Republican* . . ., 2 vols., Hartford, 1853.

Los Mexicanos Pintados por sí Mismos. By various authors. México, 1855.

Mexico; the Country, History and People, London, 1863.

Ocampo, Manuel, *Mis Quince Días de Ministro. Obras Completas*, vol. II, México, 1901.

Payno, Manuel, *Mexico and her Financial Questions with England, Spain and France*, Mexico, 1862.

Poinsett, Joel R., *Notes on Mexico, Made in the Autumn of 1822* . . ., London, 1825.

Portilla, Ansemo de la, *Historia de la Revolución de México, contra la Dictadura del General Santa-Anna 1853-1855*, México, 1856.

————, *Méjico en 1856 y 1857; Gobierno del General Comonfort*, Nueva York, 1858.

Rankin, ·Melinda, *Twenty Years among the Mexicans: a Narrative of Missionary Labor*, Cincinnati, 1875.

Santa Anna, Antonio López de, *Mi Historia Militar y Política, 1810-1874, Memorias Inéditas*. Tomo ii *Documentos Inéditos ó muy Raros para la Historia de México publicados por Genaro García y Carlos Pereyra*.

SMITH, S. COMPTON, *Chile con Carne; or, The Camp and the Field*, New York, 1857.

SUÁREZ Y NAVARRO, JUAN, *Historia de México y del General Antonio López de Santa Ana*, 2 vols., México, 1851.

THOMPSON, WADDY, *Recollections of Mexico*, New York and London, 1846.

VALLE, J. N. DEL, *El Viajero en México*, México, 1859.

WILLIAMS, J. J., *The Isthmus of Tehuantepec*, New York, 1852.

WILSON, ROBERT A., *Mexico and its Religion, with Incidents of Travel . . . 1851-1854*, New York, 1855. Second Edition bears title of *Mexico, its Peasants and it Priests . . .*, New York, 1856.

ZARCO, FRANCISCO, *Historia del Congreso Estraordinario Constituyente de 1856 y 1857*, 2 vols., México, 1857. An index to aid in the use of the above is: Pérez Gallardo, Basilio, *Guía para consultar la Historia del Congreso Constituyente de 1857*, México, 1878.

3—CORRESPONDENCE AND DOCUMENTS

BASSOLS, NARCISO, *Leyes de Reforma que Afectan al Clero*, Puebla, 1902.

BORDONOVA, SILVESTRE, *Conducta del Obispo de Puebla, Licenciado Don Pelagio Antonio de Lavastida*, Paris, 1857.

Colección de Aranceles de Obvenciones y Derechos Parroquiales, México, 1857.

Colección de Documentos Relativos a Matrimonio Civil, Guadalajara, 1856.

Correspondencia Autógrafa del Exmo. Sr. Gral. Santa-Anna y el Coronel Manuel María Jiménez. Found in a bound volume in the García Collection.

Documents and Correspondence in regard to the peace treaty with the United States in 1847. *Senate Executive Documents*, 30th Congress, 1st session, VII (509), No. 52.

Exposición que ha presentado al . . . Presidente . . . la Comisión Nombrada por la Reunión de Compradores de Fincas del Clero, México, 1861.

GARCÍA, GENARO, editor, *Los Gobiernos de Álvarez y Comonfort, según el Archivo del General Doblado*, México, 1910.

GARCÍA ICAZBALCETA, JAOQUÍN, *Nueva Colección de Documentos para la Historia de México*, 5 vols., México, 1886-1892.

Iniciativa que la Junta Departamental de Chihuahua dirigió al Soberano Congreso solicitando se deseche la Moción Relativa a que se restablece . . . la Compañia de Jesús, Chihuahua, 1841.

ISTHMUS DE TEHUANTEPEC. *Dictamen de la Comisión Especial de la Cámara de Diputados del Congreso General . . . 1851*, México, 1851.

PACHECO, J. F. Y CÁRDENAS, F. DE, *Colección de Documentos Inéditos Relativos al Descubrimiento, Conquista y Colonización de las Posesiones Españolas en América y Oceanía*, 42 vols., Madrid, 1864-1884.

PENA Y REYES, ANTONIO DE LA, *Don Manuel Eduardo de Gorostiza y la Cuestión de Texas*, México, 1924. In *Archivo Histórico Diplomático Mexicano*, Num. 8.

——————, *Incidente Diplomático con Inglaterra en 1843*. In *Archivo Histórico Diplomático Mexicano*, Num. 3.

——————, *Lucas Alamán, El Reconocimiento de Nuestra Independencia por España y la Unión de los Países Hispano-Americanos*. In *Archivo Histórico Diplomático Mexicano*, Num. 7.

Proclamation. *El C. Miguel Blanco, Gobierno del Distrito de México, á sus Habitantes, sabed*. Dated, February 10, 1861.

Reglamento de la Ley de 25 de Junio de 1856, sobre desamortización de bienes de las corporaciones civiles y eclesiásticas, México, 1856.

Reports of Cabinet Ministers (Precise titles vary):

Justicia y Negocios Eclesiásticos:

1831 by José Ignacio Espinosa.

1832 by José Ignacio Espinosa.

1833 by Miguel Ramos Arispe.

1835 by Joaquín de Iturbide.

1838 by J. Antonio Romero.

1844 by Manuel Baranda.

1845 by Mariano Riva Palacio.

1849 by José María Jiménez.

1851 by José María Aguirre.

1852 by J. Urbana Fonseca.

Relaciones:

1832 by Lucas Alamán.

1844 by José María Bocanegro.

Hacienda:

1849 by Manuel Piña y Cuevas.

1851 by Manuel Piña y Cuevas.

1852 by Guillermo Prieto.

1853 by Antonio de Haro y Tamariz.

1855 by Manuel Olasagarre.

Report of the Director of the Post Office (*Administración General de Correos*), 1857, by Guillermo Prieto.

4—Newspapers and Periodicals

Boletín, 1844-1845. A series of bulletins issued against the Santa Anna rebels by the defenders of Puebla. The title is in obvious contrast to the *Boletín de Notícias,* the organ of Herrera, the Provisional President.

Boletín, [*del*] *Ejército Protector de la Religión y Fueros.* Published in various places and at various times in 1833-1835.

Boletín de la Sociedad Mexicana de Geografía y Estadística, México, 1852—.

Boletín de Notícias, México, 1841 and 1844-1845.

Boletín Oficial, 1847, México 1847.

El Constituyente, see *El Libertador.*

La Cruz, Periódico Esclusivamente Religioso, México, 1855-1858.

De Bow's Review, 1847-1861, New Orleans and Charleston.

La Democracia, see *El Libertador.*

Diversos Periódicos de Méjico, 1820-1900, 3 vols. A number of badly broken files of Mexican newspapers in the Wagner Collection in the Yale University Library.

Harper's Monthly Magazine, New York, 1850-1862.

El Libertador, 1856.   The official newspaper of Juárez, the Governor of Oaxaca.   The name changed in March to *El Constituyente* and in October to *La Democracia.*

El Mosquito Mexicano, México, 1834-1843.

La Nacionalidad, Guanajuato, 1855-1856.

Niles' Register, Baltimore, 1811-1849.

Periódicos Varios.   Badly broken files of scattered newspapers. In the García Collection.

Quarterly Review, London, 1829-1851, followed by the *London Quarterly Review,* New York, 1852-1867.

La Sociedad, México, 1856.   Contains many official documents.

El Telégrafo.   Periódico Oficial del Gobierno de los Estados Unidos Mexicanos, México, 1833-1834.

La Voz de Iturbide (Periódico Oficial de Guanajuato), 1856-1857. Guanajuato, 1856-1857.

Westminster Review, London, 1830-1865.

5—Pamphlets

(Note: The majority of these pamphlets were found in the García Collection.   Others were used in the New York Public Library and the Wagner Collection).

Agras, Jesús, *Reflecciones sobre la Naturaleza y Orîgen de los Males y Trastornos*   .   .   ., Guadalajara, 1864.

Alvires, José Manuel T., *Reflexiones sobre los decretos episcopales que prohiben el Juramento Constitucional .   .   .,* México, 1857.   There are two pamphlets with this title, one dated April 26, 1857 and the other May 20, 1857.   The first received an answer entitled, *Contestación a las Reflexiones,* etc., which was in turn answered by the second of the above pamphlets.

Apuntamientos sobre Derecho Público Eclesiástico, México, 1857.

Los Asesinatos de Tacubaya, México (?), 1859.

Balmes(?), Jaime, *Observaciones Sociales, Políticas y Ecónomicas sobre los Bienes del Clero,* Guadalajara, 1842.

Bassoco, José María conde de, and others, *La Convención Española; contestación a la memoria que sobre ella formó D. Manuel Payno*, México, 1857.

Belaunzarán, José María de Jesús, *Contestación a la Consulta hecha por un Varón Piadoso sobre Ocupación de Bienes Eclesiásticos*, México, 1852.

Bezares, José María, *La Inmunidad de la Iglesia*, Orizaba, 1849.

Bordonova, Silvestre, *Conducta del Obispo de Puebla, Licenciado Don Pelagio Antonio de Lavastida*, Paris, 1857.

Camino, Mariano de, *Discurso Cívico* (Delivered September 11, 1853), Aguascalientes, 1853.

Carta de un Amigo a Otro, contra la introducción de sectas en México, anonymous, 1848.

Caso de Conciencia sobre el Juramento Constitucional. Carta de un Párroco Jalisciense, México, 1857.

Castillo, Florencio, *Exposición que el Gobernador del Obispado de Oaxaca dirije al Supremo Gobierno en Defensa de los Bienes Eclasiásticos*, México, 1834.

Un Católico, *Crímenes de la Demagogía por*, México, 1860.

Un Ciento de Preguntas por ahora sobre Frailes y sobre Rentas Eclesiásticas, México, 1821.

Comonfort, Ignacio, *Política del General Comonfort durante su Gobierno en Méjico*, New York, 1858. Also to be found in Portilla, *México en 1856 y 1857*.

Contestación a las Reflexiones sobre los Decretos Episcopales que Prohiben el Juramento Constitucional, Morelia, 1857.

Defensa de la Manifestación de los Illmos. Sres. Arzobispo y Obispos de la República Mexicana, México, 1860.

Documentos Relativos al Juicio de Imprenta Promovido por E. Barron contra B. Gómez Farías, México, 1856.

Echeagaray, Miguel María, *Apuntaciones para la defensa del General Miguel María Echeagaray*, Guanajuato, 1861. The García Collection apparently has the original manuscript of this pamphlet.

Estrada, Francisco, *Carta Imparcial sobre el Fuero del Clero*, México, 1812.

Es Lícito el Matrimonio á los Clerigos y Frailes, México, 1834.

Espinosa, Pedro, Bishop of Guadalajara, Protest in pamphlet form dated March 21, 1857 to the Minister of Justice and Ecclesiastical Affairs on the acts of the government. No regular title.

Espinosa, Vicente (responsible for publication), *El Matrimonio Religioso establecido por Dios; el matrimonio civil establecido por los incrédulos,* Guadalajara, 1859.

Esposición que el Archicofradia . . . de la Santa Veracruz solicita del Supremo Gobierno la Persistencia de su Panteón, México, 1833.

Flores Alatorre, Augustín, *Contestación dada al Supremo Gobierno,* México, 1850.

Gagern, Carlos de, *Apelación de los Mexicanos a la Europa Bien Informada de la Europa Mal Informada,* México, 1862.

García y Cubas, Antonio, *Noticias Geográficas y Estadísticas de la República Mexicana,* México, 1857.

Garza y Ballesteros, Lázaro de la, Archbishop of México, *Bienes de la Iglesia,* México, 1856.

————, *Cuarta Carta Pastoral,* August 19, 1859, México, 1859.

Garza y Garza, Pedro Dionosio, *Cuestión del Día sobre el Fuero Eclesiástico,* Monterey, 1856.

González, Juan, *Cincuenta y tres Razones . . . que Obligan a Preferir la Religión Católica . . .,* Zacatecas, 1870.

Guerrero, José María, *Dictamen Teológico . . . contra el Ensayo sobre Tolerancia Religiosa de . . . Vicente Rocafuerte . . .,* México, 1831.

Gutiérrez Estrada, J. M., *Carta Dirigida al Escmo. Sr. Presidente de la República . . . y Opiniones del Autor . . .,* México, 1840.

— H. (J), *El Liberalismo y sus Efectos en la República Mexicana,* México, 1858.

Haro y Tamariz, Antonio de, *Exposición . . . sobre la Monarquía Constitucional,* Paris, 1846.

Hon. J. C. Calhoun's Letter to the Hon. W. R. King. Published by Walker and Burke, Charleston, no date.

ICAZA, MARIANO DE; BARREDA; VILLAMIL, JOSÉ L., and others, *Informe Emitido de Orden Suprema por el Presidente y Algunos Capitulares del Ayuntamiento de Esta Ciudad,* México, 1859.

Intento de la Masonería, n.p., n.d.

Journal of the Proceedings of the Commercial Convention of the Southern and Western States, Charleston, 1854.

M. B., *Acción de Gracias del Clero y Puebla Mexicano al Todopoderoso por el Triunfo de la Religión,* Mexico, 1834.

UN MACUILTEPECANO, *Breve Reseña de Algunas Ideas para Establecer en la Nación Mejicana una Forma de Gobierno,* Méjico, 1853.

Manifestación de los Illmos. Sres. Arzobispo de México [y otros] . . . *con ocasión del manifiesto y los decretos espedidos por el Sr. Lic. D. Benito Juárez.* Signed by the Archbishop and the bishops of Michoacán, Linares, Guadalajara, and Potosí, México, 1859.

Manifestación que hacen los Vecinos de Morelia con Motivo del Juramento de la Constitución. Signed by the Ayuntamiento of Morelia and 750 citizens, Morelia, 1857.

MIRANDA, FRANCISCO JANVIER, *Algunas Reflexiones sobre la Cuestión de la Paz,* México, 1860.

——————, Pamphlet with no formal title on "enagenación de los bienes eclesiásticos", Puebla, 1859.

EL MISMO CURA DE MICHOACÁN, *Segunda Impugnación a la Representación del Señor D. Melchor Ocampo,* Morelia, 1851.

——————, *Tercera Impugnación,* etc., Morelia, 1851.

MORALES, JUAN BAUTISTA, *Ecsamen* [sic] *Imparcial de la Ley sobre Administración de Justicia de 21 de Noviembre de 1855, Mandada Publicar por el Escmo. Sr. D. Benito Juárez.* A series of articles in *El Libertador,* February 23, 1856—March 13, 1856.

Morán y Crivelli, Tomás, *Juicio Crítico sobre el Sistema de Hacienda en México*, México, 1865.

Munguía, Clemente de Jesús, *Dos Cartas Pastorales del Obispo de Michoacán*, México, 1860.

Ocampo, Melchor, *Respuesta Primera . . . al Señor Autor de Una Impugnación a la Representación sobre Obvenciones*, Morelia, 1851.

————, *Respuesta Segunda*, etc., Morelia, 1851.

————, *Respuesta Quinta*, etc., Morelia, 1851.

Olasagarre, Manuel, *Cuenta de la Percepción, Distribución, Inversión de los Diez Millones de Pesos, que Produjo el Tratado de Mesilla*, México, 1855.

Opúsculo en Defensa del Clero de la Iglesia Mejicana . . ., Méjico, 1857.

Ortega, Francisco, *Memoria sobre los Medios de Desterrar la Embriaguez . . .,* México, 1847.

El Partido Conservador en México, México, 1855.

Payno y Flores, Manuel, *Memoria sobre la Revolución de Diciembre de 1857 y Enero de 1858*, México, 1860.

————, *México y el Sr. Embajador Don Joaquín Francisco Pacheco*, México, 1862.

————, *Rápida Ojeada sobre la Revolución y el General Comonfort*, Vera Cruz, 1860.

La Política del General Comonfort y La Situación Actual de México, México, 1857.

Privilegios y Gracias Singulares que Goza esta Iglesia Parroquial de S. S. Miguel, Arcángel de México . . ., México, 1844.

Un Progresista, *Los Moderados y el Estado de México*, Toluca, 1861.

Protesta del Illmo. Sr. Obispo y . . . Cabildo de Michoacán contra la lei de 11 de Enero de 1847 sobre Ocupación de Bienes Eclesiásticos, Morelia, 1847.

Protesta del Venerable Cabildo Metropolitano contra el Decreto de Ocupación de los Bienes Eclesiásticos. Signed by Felix Osores, Felix García Serralde, José M. Guzmán and José M. Vázquez, México, 1847.

Reflexiones sobre la ley de 17 de Mayo [*1847*] . . . *que Declara Irredimibles los Capitales Pertenecientes á Corporaciones y Obras Pías,* México, 1847.

Reglamento de la Escuela Nacional de Agricultura, México, 1856.

Reglamento de la Escuela Nacional de Agricultura, México, 1857.

Relación de la Función Cívica que Tuvo Lugar en el Teatro Principal de la Ciudad de Toluca la Noche del 15 de Setiembre de 1853, Toluca.

Representación . . . *contra la Tolerancia de Cultos Religiosos.* . . . Signed by the "Autoridades y Vecinos del Mineral de Jalapa", San Juan, 1849.

Representación de los Vecinos de Aguascalientes al Supremo Gobierno General contra la Tolerancia de cultos, Aguascalientes, 1849.

Representación de los Vecinos de Guadalajara al Supremo Gobierno Federal contra la Introducción de Falsas Religiones en el País, Guadalajara, 1848.

Representación del Illmo. y Venerable Cabildo Metropolitano al Soberano Congreso [sobre los leyes del 11 de Enero y del 4 de Febrero de 1847], México, 1847.

Representación del Illmo. Sr. Obispo de Puebla together with a "Contestación" by LaFragua. In *El Constituyente,* supplement of May 4, 1856.

Representación que Algunos Proprietarios Agrícolas del Estado de Aguascalientes elevan al Soberano Congreso, Aguascalientes, 1861.

Representación que los Vecinos de Ixtiam dirigen al Supremo Gobierno Federal contra la Tolerancia de Cultos en la Nación, Guadalajara, 1848.

ROCAFUERTE, VICENTE, *Ensayo sobre Tolerancia Religiosa,* México, 1831.

ROSA, AGUSTÍN DE LA, *Juramento de la Constitución,* n.p., n.d.

ROSA, LUÍS DE LA, *Observaciones sobre Varios Puntos Concernientes á la Administración Pública del Estado de Zacatecas,* Baltimore, 1851.

Segunda Protesta del Venerable Cabildo Metropolitano sobre . . . Ocupación de Bienes Eclesiásticos, México, 1847.

Los Seudo-Liberales, ó la Muerte de la República Mexicana, México, 1851.

VÁZQUEZ, FRANCISCO PABLO, *Carta Pastoral del Obispo de Puebla de los Ángeles,* dated December 16, 1838, Puebla, 1838.

VIENNET, *Disertación sobre los Bienes Eclesiásticos,* translated by Juan José Baz, México, 1856.

VILLASENOR CERVANTES, IGNACIO, *Algo de Mazones ó sea Diálogo entre un Filósofo y una Maestra de Amiga,* México, 1861.

Y. O., *La Reforma Social de Méjico Deducida del Aspecto Político que el Presenta, y Fundada en la Esperiencia de Cuarenta y Cinco Años,* México, 1855.

ZERECERO, ANASTASIO, *Observaciones del Ciudadano Anastasio Zerecero á la Constitución,* México, 1857.

ZERMÁN, JUAN NAPOLEON, *Manifestación que Hace á Todos las Naciones con Especialidad á la República Mexicana . . . en Defensa de su Honor,* México, 1858.

SECONDARY WORKS

ALAMÁN, LUCAS, *Historia de Méjico.* . . . 5 vols. México, 1849-1852.

ALTAMIRA Y CREVEA, RAFAEL, *Historia de España y de la Civilización Española,* 4 vols., Barcelona, 1914.

ÁLVAREZ, MELCHOR, *Historia Documentada de la Vida Pública del Gral. José Justo Álvarez . . . de la Guerra de Reforma,* México, 1905.

Apuntes Cronológicos, tanto de los Gobernantes que ha habido desde la Conquista hasta nuestros días, como de los personas que han sido Secretarios de Estado, después de Consumada la Independencia. In *Bol. de Soc. Mex. de Geog. y Estad.,* vol. viii, p. 185 ff.

ARRANGOIZ, FRANCISCO DE PAULA DE, *Méjico desde 1808 hasta 1867. Relación de los Principales Acontecimientos Políticos.* . . . 4 vols., Madrid, 1871-1872.

ARRIAGA, PONCIANO, *Oración Funebre Pronunciada en la Alameda de Méjico el 30 de Setiembre de 1851*, México, 1851.

ARRÓNIZ, MARCOS, *Manual de Biografía Mejicana. . . ,* Paris, 1857.

Artículo sobre la Población de la República. In *Bol. de la Soc. Mex. de Geog. y Estad.*, vol. vii, 137 ff.

BANCROFT, HUBERT HOWE, *History of the Pacific States of North America*, vols. iv-ix being *Mexico, 1516-1887*, San Francisco, 1883-1888.

BASURTO, J. TRINIDAD, *El Arzobispado de México*, México, 1901.

BUENROSTRO, FELIPE, *Historia del Primero y Segundo Congresos Constitucionales de la República Mexicana.* 9 vols., México, 1874-1886[?].

BULNES, FRANCISCO, *Juárez, el Verdadero, y la Verdad sobre la Intervención y el Imperio*, Paris, 1904.

———, *Juárez y las Revoluciones de Ayutla y de Reforma*, México, 1905.

CABRERA, LUÍS, *The Religious Question in Mexico*, 1915 (?)

CHAPMAN, CHARLES E., *A History of Spain*, New York, 1918.

Diez Civiles Notables de la Historia Patria, México, 1914.

GALLO, EDUARDO L., *Hombres Ilustres Mexicanos*, 4 vols., México, 1873-1874.

GARBER, PAUL NEFF, *The Gadsden Treaty*, Philadelphia, 1924.

GARCÍA DE ARRELLANO, LUÍS, *Poesias Cívicas y Corona Poética a los Heroes de la Independencia*, México, 1868.

GARCÍA GRANADOS, RICARDO, *La Constitución de 1857 y las Leyes de Reforma en México*, México, 1906.

Historia de la Orden Mexicana de Nuestra Señora de Guadalupe, México, 1854.

Interesante Estudio sobre la Instrucción Láica Obligatoria, Puebla, 1889.

KASKA, SAMMLUNG DES BARONS, *Bibliotheca Mexicana*, Berlin, 1911.

LARRAINZAR, MANUEL, *Algunas Ideas sobre la Historia y Manera de Escribir La de México*, México, 1865.

Lea, Henry Charles, *The Inquisition in the Spanish Dependencies*, New York, 1908.

Lehrmann, Walter, *Methods and Results in Mexican Research*, Paris, 1909.

Lester, C[harles] Edwards, *The Mexican Republic. . . ,* New York, 1878.

M., *Bibliotheca Mexicana*, Paris, 1868.

McBride, George McCutchen, *The Land Systems of Mexico*, New York, 1923.

Moheno, Manrique, *Partidos Políticos . . . en la República Mexicana*, México, 1910(?).

Martínez, Victor José, *Sinopsis Histórica, Filosófica y Política de las Revoluciones Mexicanas*, México, 1874. A second edition published with notes, México, 1884.

Martínez Carillo, Rafael, *Apuntamientos sobre las Leyes Agrarias de México*, México. Prologue is dated 1923.

Mateos, José María, *Historia de la Masonería en México, 1806-1884*, México, 1884.

Mateos, Juan Antonio, *Historia Parlamentaria de los Congresos Mexicanos de 1821 y 1857*, 11 vols. in 5, México, 1877-1886.

Mena, Ramón and Rangel, Nicolás, *Monografías Mexicanas de Historia. . . ,* México, 1921.

Mendieta y Núnez, Lucio, *El Problema Agrario de México desde su Orígen hasta la Época Actual*, México, 1923.

Mexico and Central America, n.p., 1858.

Mexico and the Monroe Doctrine, n.p., 1865(?).

Molina Enríquez, Andrés, *La Reforma y Juárez*, México, 1906.

Navarro y Rodrigo, Carlos, *Vida de Agustín de Iturbide. . . .*, Madrid, 1919.

Noll, Arthur Howard, *From Empire to Republic*, Chicago, 1903.

Otero, Mariano, *Ensayo Sobre . . . la Cuestión Social y Política que se agita en la República Mexicana*, Mexico, 1842.

PALAVICINI, FÉLIX F., editor, *Historia del Congreso Constituyente de 1857*, México, 1916. An abridgment of the work of Francisco Zarco.

PARRA, PORFIRIO, *Estudio Histórico-Sociológico sobre La Reforma en México*, Guadalajara, 1906.

PENA Y REYES, ANTONIO DE LA, *La Diplomacia Mexicana*, México, 1923. In *Archivo Histórico Diplomático Mexicano*, Num., 1.

PÉREZ VERDÍA, LUÍS, *Compendio de la Historia de México*, Paris, 1911.

Personas que Han Tenido a su Cargo la Secretaría de Relaciones Exteriores desde 1821 hasta 1924, México, 1924. In *Archivo Histórico Diplomático Mexicano*, Num., 6.

PRIESTLEY, HERBERT I., *The Mexican Nation, A History*, New York, 1923.

————, *The Old University of Mexico*. In *University of California Chronicles*, vol. xxi, No. 4.

QUAIFE, M. M., editor, *Diary of James K. Polk*, 4 vols., Chicago, 1910.

RABASA, EMILIO, *La Organización Política de México. La Constitución y la Dictadura*, Madrid, 1917 (?).

RAMSEY, A. C., editor, *The Other Side: or Notes for the History of the War between Mexico and the United States . . .*, New York, 1850.

RÉDARES, J. M., *Estudios Históricos sobre . . . Masonería . . . [y] de la Influencia Moral de la Masonería*, México, 1870.

RIPPY, J. FRED, *The United States and Mexico*, New York, 1926.

RIVA PALACIO, VICENTE, editor, *México; a través de los Siglos . . .*, 5 vols., Barcelona, 1888-1889.

RIVA PALACIO, MANUEL PAYNO, JUAN A. MATEOS and R. M. DE LA TORRE, *El Libro Rojo, 1520-1867*, 2 vols., México, 1905-1906.

RIVERA, AGUSTÍN, *Anales Mexicanos; La Reforma y el Segundo Imperio . . .*, México, 1904.

Rives, G. L., *The United States and Mexico, 1821-1848*, 2 vols., New York, 1913.

Ross, Edward Alsworth, *The Social Revolution in Mexico*, New York and London, 1923.

Sierra, Justo, director literario, *México, su Evolución Social.* . . . 3 vols., México, 1900-1902.

Smith, Justin H., *The Annexation of Texas*, New York, 1919.

————, *The War with Mexico*, 2 vols., New York, 1919.

Sosa, Francisco, *Las Estatuas de Reforma*, México, 1900.

————, *Biografías de Mexicanos Distinguidos*, México, 1884.

————, *Notícias Biográficas de Don Ponciano Arriaga*, México, 1900.

Velarde, José and others, *Apuntes y Documentos para la Historia del Correo en México*, 1908.

Zamacois, Niceto de, *Historia de Méjico desde sus tiempos más remotos hasta nuetros días*, 23 vols., Barcelona, 1878-1888.

Zayas Enriquez, Rafael de, *Benito Juárez, su Vida—su Obra*, México, 1906.

Zedillo and Barros, *Alegato de Buena Prueba en el Recurso de Amparo Promovido con Motivo de la Adjudicación que la Capilla de la Preciosa Sangre . . . hizo el Ministro de Hacienda . . .*, México, 1869.

Zerecero, Anastasio, *Memorias para la Historia de las Revoluciones*, México, 1869.

APPENDIX

A. PERSONNEL OF THE PRESIDENCY*

Period of the First Federal Republic; 1824-1837.

Oct. 10, 1824-Apr. 1, 1829, Guadalupe Victoria.

Apr. 1, 1829-Dec. 18, 1829, Vicente Guerrero.

Dec. 18, 1829-Dec. 23, 1829, José María Bocanegro, ad interim.

Dec. 23, 1829-Dec. 31, 1829, Pedro Velez, Luís Quintana, Lucas Alamán, Provisional Government.

Dec. 31, 1829-Aug. 14, 1832, A. Bustamante.

Aug. 14, 1832-Dec. 24, 1832, Melchor Musquiz, ad interim.

Dec. 24, 1832-Apr. 1, 1833, M. Gómez Pedraza.

Apr. 1, 1833-May 16, 1833, Valentín Gómez Farías, acting.

May 16, 1833-June 3, 1833, A. López de Santa Anna.

June 3, 1833-June 18, 1833, V. Gómez Farías, acting.

June 18, 1833-July 5, 1833, A. López de Santa Anna.

July 5, 1833-Oct. 27, 1833, V. Gómez Farías, acting.

Oct. 27, 1833-Dec. 15, 1833, A. López de Santa Anna.

Dec. 16, 1833-Apr. 24, 1834, V. Gómez Farías, acting.

Apr. 24, 1834-Jan. 28, 1835, A. López de Santa Anna.

Jan. 28, 1835-Feb. 27, 1836, M. Barragán.

Feb. 27, 1836-Apr. 19, 1837, José Justo Corro.

Period of the Centralized Republic; 1837-1846.

Apr. 19, 1837-Mar. 18, 1839, A. Bustamante.

Mar. 18, 1839-July 10, 1839, A. López de Santa Anna.

July 10, 1839-July 17, 1839, N. Bravo.

July 17, 1839-Sept. 22, 1841, A. Bustamante.

Sept. 22, 1841-Oct. 10, 1841, J. Echeverria.

Oct. 10, 1841-Oct. 26, 1842, A. López de Santa Anna, dictator.

Oct. 26, 1842-Mar. 5, 1843, N. Bravo, substitute.

Mar. 5, 1843-Oct. 4, 1843, A. López de Santa Anna.

* The exact dates vary with the authorities, but those given above appear to be the most reliable.

Oct. 4, 1843-June 4, 1844, V. Canalizo.

June 4, 1844-Sept. 20, 1844, A. López de Santa Anna.

Sept. 20, 1844-Dec. 6, 1844, V. Canalizo.

Dec. 6, 1844-Dec. 30, 1845, José Joaquín de Herrera.

Jan. 4, 1846-July 28, 1846, M. Paredes y Arrillaga.

July 29, 1846-Aug. 4, 1846, N. Bravo.

Period of the Second Federal Republic; 1846-1858.

Aug. 5, 1846-Dec. 23, 1846, Mariano Salas.

Dec. 23, 1846-Mar. 21, 1847, V. Gómez Farías, acting.

Mar. 21, 1847-Apr. 2, 1847, A. López de Santa Anna.

Apr. 2, 1847-May 20, 1847, Pedro María Anaya.

May 20, 1847-Sept. 16, 1847, A. López de Santa Anna.

Sept. 20, 1847-Nov. 13, 1847, M. de la Peña y Peña.

Nov. 13, 1847-Jan. 8, 1848, Pedro María Anaya.

Jan. 8, 1848-June 3, 1848, M. de la Peña y Peña.

June 3, 1848-Jan. 15, 1851, J. de Herrera.

Jan. 15, 1851-Jan. 6, 1853 Mariano Arista.

Jan. 6, 1853-Feb. 7, 1853, Juan de Ceballos.

Feb. 7, 1853-Apr. 20, 1853, Manuel de Lombardini, dictator.

Apr. 20, 1853-Aug. 12, 1855, A. López de Santa Anna.

Aug. 15, 1855-Sept. 12, 1855, Martín Carrera.

Oct. 4, 1855-Dec. 11, 1855, Juan Álvarez.

Dec. 11, 1855-Jan. 14, 1858, Ignacio Comonfort.

B. CHURCH PROPERTY CONFISCATED BY THE GOVERNMENT

(The following information is taken from Zamacois, *Historia de Méjico,* tomo XV, p. 283, note, where it is quoted from an article of Don José Julian Tornel).

	Value Confiscated *pesos*
Royal order for expulsion of Jesuits	9,423,489.37
Law of "Consolidation"	10,505,594.70
Contributions of missions of Upper California to the troops	271,311.46
Similar contributions of the missions of the North (cash)	6,000.00
Item (17,000 oxen at 6 *pesos* per head)	102,000.00

Appropriated from the Pious Fund.................. 1,207,671.30
Further appropriations from the Pious
    Fund at rate of 146,000 *pesos*
    per year 2,920,000.00
Loss to the clergy through drafts of the
    government from 1836 to 1841.................. 1,400,000.00
Law of June 25, 1856..................................... 45,000,000.00

                                                        70,836,066.83
      Total as given by Zamacois........................ 70,836,005.00

INDEX

Alamán, Lucas, favors monarchy, 150; position in 1853, 220; death, 221.

Álvarez, Juan, relations with masons, 70, note, 237; summons to liberals, 105; accused of *sansculottism*, 105, 106, note; guerrilla chieftain, 137; concerning Texas, 140-141; in the south 155; attitude, 226; relations with Comonfort, 228, 238, 241 and note; opposes Carrera, 235; kept informed as to conditions, 235; calls *Junta Patriótica*, 235; chosen president, *ad interim*, 235; disagreement in cabinet, 237; retirement, 241.

Anaya, Pedro María, as president substitute, 193; as president, 196.

Angostura, Battle of, 191; causes of defeat of Santa Anna at, 192.

Arispe, Miguel Ramos, 52.

Arista, Mariano, as president, 218; character, 218; rebellion against, 219; resignation, 219.

Army, relations with Church, 4, 126; historic background of, 23; growth in power, 48; estimated size of, 49; reduction of, 73, 205, 248; allied with conservatives, 97; in election of 1835, 105; relations with Santa Anna, 129; cost of, 164, 173-174; method of raising, 164; power of, 179; joins Church against government,

240 and note; actual strength, 248; in Constitution of 1857, 304.

Atocha, "Colonel," relations with Santa Anna, 152, 193; relations wtih President Polk, 152; advice to United States, 152.

Austin, Stephen F., attitude to Church, 81, note.

Ayutla, Plan of, demands of, 228; congress provided for by, 266.

Barragán, M., relations with Gómez Farías, 103; to take charge of government, 105; death, 111, note.

Barragán, M. de la Peña y, attitude to Santa Anna, 191.

Beach, Moses Y., "helps" Scott 192; application for charter for a national bank, 192-193.

Berduzco, governor of Queretaro, 186.

Bill of rights, in Constitution of 1857, 283 ff.

Bishops, power of, 172; in Constitution of 1857, 309-310.

Bocanegra, J. M., in Council of Government, 133.

Boulbon, Raousset de, invasions of Mexico, 225-226.

Bourbons, difficulties of, 28.

Bravo, Nicolás, vice president, 55; as a mason, 57 and note; opposes Victoria, 58; temporary executive, 121; in convention, 131; calls "Assembly of Notables", 132; takes charge of government, 154; resigns in favor of Salas, 157.

DATE DUE